Peacekeeping and Peace Enforcement in Africa

Peacekeeping and Peace Enforcement in Africa

Methods of Conflict Prevention

ROBERT I. ROTBERG

ERICKA A. ALBAUGH

HAPPYTON BONYONGWE

CHRISTOPHER CLAPHAM

JEFFREY HERBST

STEVEN METZ

THE WORLD PEACE FOUNDATION
Cambridge, Massachusetts

BROOKINGS INSTITUTION PRESS
Washington, D.C.

Peacekeeping and Peace Enforcement in Africa may be ordered from:
BROOKINGS INSTITUTION PRESS
1775 Massachusetts Avenue, N.W.
Washington, D.C. 20036
Tel: 1-800/275-1447 or 202/797-6258
Fax: 202/797-6004
www.brookings.edu

DT
353
.P43
2000

Library of Congress Cataloging-in-Publication Data:

Peacekeeping and peace enforcement in Africa : methods of conflict prevention / Robert I. Rotberg, editor.
   p.   cm.
Includes bibliographical references and index.
ISBN 0-8157-7576-8 (alk. paper)
  1. Africa, Sub-Saharan--Politics and government—1960– 2. Civil war--Africa, Sub-Saharan—History—20th century. 3. Mediation, International—History—20th century. 4. Peacekeeping forces--Africa, Sub-Saharan. 5. Africa, Sub-Saharan—Armed Forces—Foreign countries. I. Rotberg, Robert I. II. Title.
  DT353 .P43 2000   00-010380
  327.1'7'0967--dc21   CIP

                    9 8 7 6 5 4 3 2 1

The paper used in this publication meets the minimum requirements of the American National Standard for Information Sciences—Permanence of Paper for Printed Library Materials. ANSI Z39.48-1984

                         Typeset in Times Roman

                 Composition by Oakland Street Publishing
                           Arlington, Virginia

                    Printed by R.R. Donnelley and Sons

Contents

Preface

Peacekeeping and Peace Enforcement in Africa: Methods of Conflict Prevention contains six tightly interwoven essays and a summary of extended consideration of preventing conflict in Africa through the efforts of United Nations peacekeeping detachments or African states organized for the containment or reduction of their own belligerencies.

—"Peacekeeping and the Effective Prevention of War" considers the four types of UN peacekeeping endeavors, particularly as they have applied and will in future relate to the hostilities of Africa.

—"African Peacekeepers and State Failure" examines the consequences of state failure for peace in Africa, especially the marginalization of African imbroglios in Western and UN eyes, and the likely hazards of relying on African states—even hegemons—to enforce the peace in Africa.

—"Peacekeeping and the Peacekept: Developing Mandates for Potential Intervenors" relates the many ways in which militant African insurgencies have and can twist well-intentioned interventions to their own advantage. This chapter analyzes the oft-false assumptions of peacekeeping, and how the mandates of such missions are not always well squared with realities on the ground.

—"African Peacekeeping and American Strategy" analyzes the United States' twenty-first-century view of African intrastate wars, and explains why the U.S. response to African crises will continue to be limited and difficult to mobilize. The chapter recommends a rethinking of U.S. responses to and support of African peacekeeping initiatives.

—"Employing African Forces in Peace Operations in Africa" shows how Africans can organize effective sub-regional responses to conflict prevention, and the obstacles to any successful home-grown approach.

—"African Responses to African Crises: Creating a Military Response" provides a rationale and a blueprint for a concerted African embrace of its own imbroglios, and the preventive efforts to match. That chapter also introduces the final chapter, "Preventing Conflict in Africa—Possibilities of Peace Enforcement," which contains an abbreviated summary of spirited discussions on these issues by African and Western political and military leaders.

These chapters were written in 1999 and 2000, and then re-written or revised in mid-2000. The final chapter summarizes discussions that occurred in 1999.

Rachel M. Gisselquist copyedited the book for the World Peace Foundation and contributed significantly to its coherence and analytical rigor. She was assisted by David Kearn and Deborah Weinberg. Julia Petrakis prepared the index. Each of the authors is indebted to numerous others, but the major debt of gratitude is to the Trustees of the World Peace Foundation.

CHAPTER ONE

Peacekeeping and the Effective Prevention of War

Robert I. Rotberg

THE CONCEPT OF keeping a peace, in Africa and elsewhere, is becoming less rather than more meaningful in the twenty-first century, both as theory and as practice. In common parlance, as well as that of the UN General Assembly and the U.S. Congress, soldiers organized or authorized by the UN become "peacekeepers" when they are sent to a (usually) developing nation to prevent interstate war, to reduce further hostilities between or among angry groups within a country, and generally to deter conflict. Their generic job is to keep the peace— to prevent people from killing other people—as situationally or otherwise defined in UN-speak by the Security Council or, rarely, by UN-member governments. Only infrequently, however, are peacekeeping missions provided with the mandate, the money, or the firepower actively to create a peace. Usually they are envisaged as passive providers of something designated as a peace. It is somehow assumed that the mere presence of "neutral" soldiers will separate warring parties, calm heated passions, and prevent renewed combat of the kind that brought about the need for the mission in the first place.

Peacekeepers can perform those roles (and more) but only when they are properly instructed or encouraged, or permitted to do so. The killing of Kenyan peacekeepers and the capture of hundreds of hapless Zambian peacekeepers by rebels in Sierra Leone in spring 2000; the injuries inflicted on U.S., French, and Polish peacekeepers in spring 2000 in the troubled cities of Kosovo; the dangers faced by Australian peacekeepers in East Timor in winter 2000; and the notorious killings of Pakistani and U.S. peacekeepers in Somalia in 1993 illustrate problems with both the metaphor and the paradigm of peacekeeping as an instrument of global war containment and hostility prevention. Such incidents, especially local attacks on peacekeeping detachments, discourage the UN, those countries that supply peace-keeping contingents, and those (usually other) nations that fund the world's attempt to deter conflict by interposition. As Metz reports in a later chapter of this book, "peacemaking in failed states [is] radically different than ... truce monitoring...."[1]

Those who cry out that peacekeeping has failed have a legitimate point. So, too, advocates of UN peacekeeping become discouraged when Sierra Leonean rebels kill and capture peacekeepers and the nominal rulers of the Democratic Republic of the Congo only very churlishly give the UN the freedom to try to strengthen a ragged cease-fire. When some of the most needy recipients of international interposition oppose it, why bother?

Somali warlords opposed peacekeeping missions and eventually forced them out. That was the goal of the Revolutionary United Front in Sierra Leone. Only where the two sides to a conflict equally want a separation can the peacekeepers perform their job effectively with a minimal mandate. In Cyprus, for example, a small UN peacekeeping force (UNFICYP) has presided over a peace (really a partition) since 1974, if not from 1964, because neither side has had much to gain from attacking the other. So the peacekeepers have provided a useful buffer.

Atwood believes that "each time UN forces are successfully challenged or over-whelmed by those who oppose a peace mandate, serious damage is done to the United Nations. Each time the forces of anarchy triumph over global governance, it is more difficult the next time...to prevent conflict or preserve peace."[2]

Where effective partition has not been accepted militarily or politically, or where local forces are not necessarily under the control of a central authority, UN and other peacekeepers need broadened mandates to keep the peace. Where they do not receive such mandates, or where they do, but lack the necessary firepower, then local forces, even ragtag rebels, as in Sierra Leone, or mutual revenge seekers, as in Kosovo, can wreak havoc with missions and with the very concept of preventing and reducing conflict by limited intervention.

The entire notion of peacekeeping as a unified and calibrated instrument is badly misconceived. In fact, the United Nations and the world powers have used peacekeeping as a catchall metaphor, and a deliberately chaste and limited one at that. Partly to mollify recipients and funders, partly to persuade itself of the limited and temporary quality of prospective engagements, and partly so as not to raise the specter of rapid reaction forces forgone, the UN has traditionally sent out peacekeepers to contain all manner of crises as they have presented themselves. Strategic planning has been subsumed by tactical demands. One size has fit all. The urgent has always driven out the important.

The first UN mission was UNSCOB—the UN Special Mission on the Balkans. From 1947 to 1952 it watched the Greek side of the borders of Greece. The second mission (UNTSO—the UN Truce Supervision Organization) was sent to supervise the truce in the Middle East. It still exists to monitor cease-fires, supervise armistice agreements, prevent isolated incidents from escalating, and assist other UN peacekeeping operations in the region. The third (UNMOGIP—the UN Military Observer Group in India and Pakistan), to Jammu and Kashmir, was dispatched in 1949 to supervise the cease-fire between India and Pakistan. Although that line has changed, and India has asked UNMOGIP to leave, it remains in place under and according to Security Council mandates. Although that small mission continues in place to this day, another (UNIPOM) was also sent to the same area in 1965–66.

From 1949 to 1988 there were an additional seven peacekeeping missions— two to the Sinai (UNEF I and II), two to Lebanon (UNOGIL) and (UNIFIL), to the Golan Heights (UNDOF), to the Yemen (UNYOM), to the original Congo (ONUC), to West Irian or Western New Guinea/West Papua (UNSF), and to Cyprus. Like the very first UN detachment, these initial thirteen missions were mandated mostly to observe, monitor, and report—all in a neutral, circumspect manner. Unlike the situations that subsequently ensued, most of these missions were dispatched to oversee a border, albeit a hotly contested one, between nations. The hostilities that followed, being within states, had no convenient borders. Partition or separation was harder to arrange and patrol. As Roberts concludes, "the achievements of UN peacekeeping" in the pre-1988 era were "modest [but] real: they included the effective freezing (although not the resolution) of certain conflicts; some reduction of the risk, or extent, of competitive interventions by neighboring or major powers, and the isolation of some local conflicts from the East-West struggle, so that the local conflicts did not exacerbate the Cold War."[3]

Since 1988, the number of missions has escalated as warfare within states has become our era's most pernicious threat to peace. There were four verification and observer missions to Angola during the 1990s. There were missions to the Central African Republic, Chad/Libya, the new Congo, Liberia, Mozambique, Namibia, two to Rwanda, two to Sierra Leone, one to Somalia, and one to the Western Sahara. In the Americas, UN missions went to Central America, the Dominican Republic, El Salvador, Guatemala, and four to Haiti. In Asia, they went to Afghanistan, two to Cambodia, one to East Timor, and one to Tajikistan. In Europe, the UN sent missions to Bosnia and Herzegovina, four to Croatia, and single ones to Georgia, Kosovo, Macedonia, and the former Yugoslavia. In the Middle East, missions went to Iran/Iraq and Kuwait.

There have thus been a total of forty peacekeeping missions from 1988 to mid-

2000, mostly in territories where the keeping of local peace on the ground has been much more problematic than in the earlier decades of the Cold War. Not only has the frequency, size, and cost of these missions increased since 1988; their complexity, their risk, and their difficulty has intensified exponentially. Tried and true UN expectations for the keeping of peace no longer applied after 1988, or applied mostly in the breach. The comparatively comfortable paradigm of the occasional observer mission no longer applied. The new challenges were, in the 1990s and beyond, much more along the lines of ONUC, 1960 to 1964, in the Congo, when the UN had to impose order and attempt to initiate an exercise in good governance.[4] But in the 1990s and since, the UN has never been confident of obtaining either its accustomed resource base or its accustomed rosters of well-trained and well-supplied peacekeepers.

Even so, the record of peacekeeping has not been so dismal as its recent failures would suggest. Indeed, if we understand peacekeeping as broad metaphor rather than a paradigm, we can see that peacekeeping includes tasks and missions that are both less and more than what casual newspaper readers (or Congressmen) understand peacekeeping to be. If the task of peacekeeping in troubled times can be understood for what it really is, and not for what it could be, it might be easier to design more successful missions and to fund them. Furthermore, if peacekeeping is appreciated to have been and to be more than sets of frustrated mercenary detachments trying to avoid bloodshed (as in Sierra Leone) and to be transformed in conception and in practice to be peace builders or peace enforcers, then there may be renewed utility for "peacekeeping" in today's troubled times.

Peacekeeping encompasses four functions. These distinctions are not conceptual niceties; they have strategic and practical utility for the UN, for funding nations, for the countries who contribute soldiers and policemen to the missions, and to a broad public that today has little understanding of the variety of tasks that the UN has performed and is being asked almost daily to perform. Peacekeeping can exist only where there is a peace to keep; but there is an even more fundamental need for peace enforcement and peace building, and for post-conflict transformation and reconstruction, than there is for classically conceived Chapter VI peace maintenance activities.

The four too-little appreciated categories of UN peace intervention in hostile environs are:

1. Expanded Monitoring

What is here termed "expanded monitoring" is stereotypical peacekeeping, or "holding the ring."[5] These missions, usually small in size but large in symbolic significance, arrive in the wake of a brokered cease-fire between (heretofore) large-scale combatants. The soldiers in the mission are expected to observe, report, and publicize violations of the agreed cease-fire. Their very presence is meant to have a deterrent effect, but they as individuals and as a collective mission are not expected physically to intervene to prevent the outbreak of renewed hostilities. Nor are they expected to disarm and demobilize the fighters. Indeed, the peacekeepers are themselves lightly armed and, depending on the precise nature of their instructions, forbidden to retaliate even in self-defense.

As has been seen most recently in Sierra Leone, and earlier in Lebanon and Somalia, these type I missions are wholly unsuitable to situations where there is no peace to keep—where a cease-fire is fragile and not in the interest of one or both of the contending parties. Where cease-fires have been imposed (by Nigerian soldiers in Sierra Leone) and not been accepted more or less voluntarily, where disarmament and demobilization of combatants are tasks for the future, where both sides are equally belligerent, or where a rebellious side is arguably stronger militarily than a constituted government, classical peacekeeping of the type I variety is bound to be too dangerous and prone to failure.

Impartiality—the hallmark of classical peacekeeping and the rationale for lightly arming expanded monitoring forces—is only suited to situations where peace is acceptable to both sets of indigenous fighters, or where one side (usually a government) has won a clear victory over the other. In June 2000 it appeared that the Ethiopian-Eritrean war had been won by Ethiopia. An expanded monitoring force could subsequently patrol the new or the old border and observe and report violations, if the stronger side agreed and if Eritrea, much weakened by the events of May and June 2000, were prepared to concede whatever strategic gains were sought by Ethiopia.

Numbers constitute another critical variable. Small, comparatively inexpensive peacekeeping detachments are appropriate only for those hostilities that have come to an effective or near-effective conclusion. Type I peacekeepers are appropriate, and need not be numerous or expensive, when both sides have exhausted themselves. But when combat has but paused, and many thousands of (usually) irregular and thus poorly disciplined soldiers are still seeking advantage (as in Sierra Leone), lightly armed, smallish detachments of UN mercenaries will not do. "The UN's Department of Peacekeeping Operations knew that the contingents in Sierra Leone were under-strength and poorly equipped," claims Ignatieff, yet UNDPO "failed to protest publicly" when the Security Council sent them anyway.[6]

Classical peacekeeping of the type I variety has been predicated on the assumption that the big powers of the Security Council would pay for comparatively inexpensive missions of (limited) duration and the supposedly more neutral, less powerful, and more needy nations of the UN system would supply peacekeepers for a substantial fee. These smaller, worthy countries—Fiji, Botswana, Bangladesh, etc.—would profit and contribute to global peace without any Cold War taints. But assumptions appropriate to the Cold War era no longer apply.

Jett argues, moreover, that the UN is always short of personnel for peacekeeping. First-rate armies are usually unwilling to put their soldiers at risk. Thus most peace-keeping detail is left to countries of the developing world. "The United Nations sends some of the worst soldiers in the world off to situations where it can only hope they are not called on to actually do anything."[7] Alas, too often, they are, or at least should be.

Another assumption intrinsic to type I peacekeeping is that a multinational force, with serious communications handicaps (as in Sierra Leone and Somalia), as well as command and control problems, can cope with the challenges of a type I mis-sion. That is certainly reasonable if hostilities are contained and expected to be rare. But a multinational force with a plethora of lines of authority and incom-patible communications systems performs poorly when there are serious chal-lenges in the field. Mixed and unmatched equipment makes a troubled mission more difficult. So does the complete lack of standardized doctrine, mutual train-ing, and political awareness.

These many defects are capable of being overlooked or overcome where the UN mission is accepted as legitimate and helpful by the contending parties. Like-wise, it is a major failure of the UN leadership, the Security Council, and both funders and troop suppliers, to assign type I peacekeeping mandates to situations where UN missions are imposed or are regarded as illegitimate by at least one side, and where cease-fires are at best fragile.[8] Such cases cry out for more robust responses to local and regional order. The UN sets itself up for failure when it cobbles together a type I force to cope with type II, III, or IV situations.

Structurally, the UN argues that it has no other choices since the world's super-power will not pay and will not readily assist UN peacekeeping efforts for fear of being dragged into the globe's many tough internal belligerencies. But it is a major mistake to suppose that type I monitoring, designed for an earlier and more straightforward era, can succeed in containing or resolving most of the disruptive internecine wars of the twenty-first century.

Atwood has a rational response to Congressional reluctance to support UN peacekeeping in today's much more dangerous era. "Each time a UN force is under-funded and unprepared, the chances are greater that American forces will be needed." He adds his voice to those who decry the decision of the United States to reduce its contributions to UN peacekeeping from 31.7 percent to 25 percent. Doing so, "is shortsighted in the extreme," he writes. It guarantees an inadequate answer, or recourse later to a fully American-backed or American-supplied force. The United States, he writes, should no longer "play the spoiler."[9]

II. Regime Change Assurance

UN peacekeeping has successfully contributed to the maintenance of global or regional peace where there have been distinct peaces to keep and realistic cease-fires to monitor. It has also performed its peacekeeping function to great local and international acclaim where retreating colonial powers (like South Africa in Namibia) or once locally dominant authoritarian regimes (like the Front for the Liberation of Mozambique—FRELIMO—government in Mozambique) asked for or accepted a UN mission to preside over a transfer of power from an *ancien régime* to a modern one—from autocracy to democracy.

UN Transition Assistance Group (UNTAG) and UN Operation in Mozambique (UNMOZ) are exemplars.[10] After laboriously brokered cessations of warfare, UN missions were the obvious choice to ensure the peaceful and successful transfer of power from the old to the new. Neither of those two missions (nor UNTAC [UN Transitional Authority in Cambodia]) could have succeeded if disarmament and demobilization agreements had not been intrinsic components of the end-of-war protocols and if the UN missions had not insisted over and over on the deal-breaking quality of those prior agreements.

In Namibia and Mozambique, exhaustion had set in and the sources of financial and diplomatic support for the less legitimate side had largely vanished. It was a condition of those cases, and also of the Cambodian one, that combat had served its purpose (if there had ever been a legitimate purpose) and that it was time to move on. So the UN could credibly insist upon the removal of the weapons of war and the withdrawal (much easier in Namibia) or dismantling of offensive armies.

As the name of the Namibian and Cambodian missions indicates, the role of the UN in these cases was to orchestrate and ensure a transition and, as in Cambodia, a meaningful election. There was momentum toward a new dispensation and the UN was essential to that transformation. Fortunately, in each case, the UN was able to mount large, politically led missions to oversee the complicated logistical and educational, not to mention military, aspects of the several transitions. In each case, too, the UN missions were led by experienced persons who had local knowledge and sufficient time to meld disparate national contingents into a cohesive force for change.

It is not that there were no setbacks and crises during each of these transitions. Rather, the significant point is that these missions: (a) were not regarded as illegitimate by one or more of the belligerents, and (b) each had sufficient numbers of troops and firepower to impose the will of its clear-minded leader. Most of all, their mandates were expansive. The heads of mission were given the authority and the tools with which to accomplish sets of ambitious goals. There was every presumption of good offices, but not of passive impartiality.

The leaders of these type II missions knew that they had local (sometimes honored in the breach), regional, and international backing for their tasks of replacing civil war with a democratic beginning. Their job was to ensure free and fair elections and thus to launch a new kind of government in countries where democracy and good governance were unknown.

The Namibian, Mozambican, and Cambodian missions are widely acknowledged to be models of accomplished success. It must be reiterated that they were never conceived as limited or neutral missions. They were more than monitoring exercises. They existed not in a moral or diplomatic vacuum but instead as a clear extension of an international solution to long-running threats to regional and global order.

III. Peace Enforcement and Intervention for Peace

The UN has lost lives and wasted funds—and failed—where it has attempted to play impartial peacekeeper when a more considered, tougher, and more vigorous exercise in peace enforcement was required. Or, to repeat, where there was no peace to keep or where cease-fires were more grudging and tactical than real, the UN has jeopardized its type I and type II reputations by not differentiating those kinds of scenarios, capable as they are of being addressed by monitors and transitional brokers, from more hostile type III situations (the Democratic Republic of the Congo, Sierra Leone, Somalia, Rwanda, Burundi, Sri Lanka, and so on).

Type III situations demand peace intervention or peace enforcement, as envisaged by the UN charter but now accomplished most often unilaterally (Tanzania in Uganda, 1979; Vietnam into Cambodia in 1978–79; India into Sri Lanka, a failure in 1987–90; ECOMOG and Nigeria into Liberia in 1990 and Sierra Leone in 1997; Angola into Congo-Brazzaville, 1997; South Africa into Lesotho, 1998; Senegal into Guinea-Bissau, 1998; and NATO into Kosovo, 1998).[11] The inability to disarm and demobilize Somalis and Sierra Leoneans is obvious and palpable. The gross failure to interpose in Rwanda in 1994 is now widely accepted.

Limited mandates will not work well in the Congo, nor will insufficient troops without common training, standardized command and control doctrines, or compatible armaments and communications. But the larger issue in Sierra Leone and the Congo, as in Somalia, Lebanon, and Kosovo (as contrasted to Namibia, Mozambique, and East Timor) is confusion of objective. The UN (and the Security Council) blunders when it tries to respond to calls for peace in type III zones of distress by creating and dispatching missions conceived along type I lines, and is handicapping them from the start (as in the Congo) by what they can and cannot do. Clapham's parsing of the contradictions and complications inherent in these dilemmas is very trenchant. For the UN, and thus for the peacekeepers, there is a strategic goal—the imposition of a new political order, and stability. For factions among the peacekept, however, the objective too often is tactical—the buying of time to regroup and to loot. Cease-fires negotiated outside zones of hostility need not hold, nor be expected to hold, once the combatants return to their forces on the ground.[12]

Where there is no real peace to keep (whatever the ad hoc modalities on the ground), peace enforcement is necessary. A rapid reaction force, supplied a fortiori in the Sierra Leonean case by Britain under a pretence, rescued the floundering, confusingly led, and badly deployed UN mission. The British paratroopers had firepower (which the peacekeepers lacked) and a sense of direction. Their clear-eyed commanders possessed a far-reaching, no-nonsense mandate.

The UN's legitimacy is not sufficient to convert warriors into compliant ex-combatants. Only when the UN or a regional organization (like ECOWAS) is empowered to intervene with lethal force can some semblance of order be restored to rebellious provinces. Otherwise, chaos will rule (as in Sierra Leone and Somalia), and the entire cause of generic peacekeeping will be undermined.

Prime Minister Tony Blair made the case for British action starkly and clearly: "I know there are those…who believe that we should do nothing beyond offer some words of sympathy and condemnation. But that would be to turn our back…on those poor, defenceless people in Sierra Leone, when we could do something to help them. It's one of the reasons why Britain counts in the world. Britain is seen to have values and be prepared to back them up. And Britain's strength in the world matters. It matters not just for what we can do for people but for our influence, for jobs, for investment. It is also in our national interest to do what we can to support the United Nations and to tackle instability in world affairs wherever we can."

Blair went on to say that Britain could not help in every crisis. But in Sierra Leone there was a historic responsibility. "Instability, even thousands of miles away, can lead…to fewer jobs back home, … more drugs … more refugees in the world."[13] Geoff Hoon, Britain's Minister of Defence, having secured Sierra Leone's main airport and helped to weaken the Revolutionary United Front (RUF), announced the replacement of the initial paratroop strike force by marines. "Britain will continue to stand by the people of Sierra Leone in their search for permanent peace," he told the House of Commons.[14]

Absent the rapid reaction force that the UN was urged in 1958 to create,[15] and given the stinginess of the United States in supporting the UN in general and the peacekeeping/peace intervention process in particular, it is critical to accept five propositions:

1. The UN cannot easily intervene militarily for peace to prevent intrastate or interstate conflicts. Nor can it do so rapidly, if at all.

2. The UN should not attempt to use insufficient force or pretend that a type I mission will suffice to deal with type III situations.

3. If the UN cannot act, regional or sub-regional organizations need to be encouraged and empowered to intervene militarily for peace in their own areas. Big power training and funding ought to be made available to prepare for and sustain such regional or sub-regional intervention capabilities.

4. Ideally, the Security Council should create a rapid reaction force for global peace capable of being dispatched quickly to interpose itself between combatants or, more realistically, to impose a peace on belligerents in an intrastate conflagration. The Secretary-General of the UN needs this force and expanded powers to use it in emergency crisis situations. (A World Peace Foundation study showed how funds could be generated from the UN itself to support expanded peacekeeping.)[16]

5. Type I responses to disorder presuppose good will, and thus in those cases the good offices of the UN are sufficient. But there are fewer and fewer type I cases in the twenty-first century's disordered world and less and less good will. Only type III responses fit such hard cases, and the UN should not try to label them peacekeeping exercises, or pretend that it can meet such dangerous challenges with the funds and the mandates now available to it.

The greater proportion of the world's civil wars are in Africa. So are the greater proportion of UN peacekeeping missions and non-UN interventions. More than twenty-two African countries have themselves contributed more than a hundred times to UN missions.[17] Given the record of the last decade, when intrastate conflict has been so prevalent, Africa is likely to remain the locus of instability and insurgency. Already, since 1990, at least 5 million persons, mostly civilians, have been killed in the wars of Africa. Two of those internal conflagrations, in Angola and the Sudan, are twenty-five and seventeen years old, respectively. In one, in Angola, UN peacekeeping has failed over and over (for many of the reasons enumerated above). The Somali implosion is a decade old, with no conclusive answer in sight.

For Africa, there is no easy UN-supplied remedy. Instead, there is a potential African response, with heavy emphasis on the adjective "potential." As chapters 6 and 7 make clear, African military and political leaders accept the obvious fact that Africans are best placed and best motivated to intervene for peace in conflicts on their own continent. These leaders also accept the notion that Africans can do so effectively and economically (witness Tanzania in Uganda and Nigeria in Liberia and Sierra Leone). But how? As Metz and other authors in this book suggest, "Africa needs a whole new mode of multinational activity that *makes* peace rather than keeps it, and *constructs* stable political, legal, and economic systems rather than reconstructs them."[18]

As discussed at much greater length by Brigadier Happyton Bonyongwe's chapter below— "Employing African Forces in Peace Operations in Africa"—as well as in chapters 6 and 7, Africans favor the creation of sub-regional crisis response forces capable of intervening to prevent, contain, or reduce intrastate conflict. Those forces would be pre-trained together according to common doctrines, with established communications, intelligence, and command and control prescriptions. Contributing countries within a sub-regional framework would designate companies or battalions to join the crisis response force and to train with it. There would be a standing headquarters, but no permanent standing force in place. With the designation of a crisis, the force commander would summon his troops from the contributing countries and go into action. Bonyongwe discusses each of these propositions, as well as the potential construction of a Southern African Development Community Peacekeeping Brigade, and how such an instrument of peace could function.

That last function—going into action—would depend crucially on the willingness of the Western powers to fund peace intervention missions, supply transport and communications capabilities, and provide the necessary training. At a series of meetings sponsored by the World Peace Foundation, representatives of the Western powers pledged their support in general.[19] If Africans could organize crisis response forces, the West would be generous and responsive. Already, the United States, Britain, France, Denmark, and Norway have individually and collectively funded and cooperated with a number of training initiatives and joint exercises. The U.S. African Crisis Response Initiative of the Department of State actively has pursued the goal of building African capacity for peacekeeping, if not peace enforcement.[20]

What is lacking is a consensus on several key issues: Who declares a crisis appropriate for intervention by a crisis response force? Who decides on the mandate for the intervention, including an exit strategy? To whom does the commander of the crisis response force report, and to whom is he or she accountable?[21] Military leaders are also skeptical about the existence of political will in Africa sufficient to sanction and motivate the creation of crisis response forces and to use them to limit intrastate conflict. As Clapham notes in his chapter below, "it is extremely difficult to develop effective mandates for intervention unless one state—and one leader—is prepared to take the initiative, commit the necessary resources, accept the inevitable costs, and put together a coalition...." The lead state, he continues, must be the major state in a sub-region.[22] Herbst, in a following chapter, believes flatly that "the emerging model of African intervention will depend on...[a]...regional hegemon deciding to intervene and then creating a coalition of other willing neighbors...."[23]

Whether hegemonic intervention is the only likely form of homemade intervention to reduce the frequency and lethality of African conflicts, on these and grounds of domestic weakness there is a very low probability that Africans can contain their own crises by pre-trained, pre-positioned sub-regionally organized joint action. Hegemons will continue to do the intervening where, when, and if it suits their own national interests. Where there are no clear-cut hegemonic imperatives, or where there is no or little consensus for hegemonic action, Africans will remain prey to intrastate irruptions of discontent, protest, and greed. Overall, given the current doldrums of peacekeeping (too narrowly conceived), self-interested hegemons and not the disinterested representatives of world order will determine whether or not most Africans during this century live in conditions conducive to peace and development.

IV. Peace Building and Reconstruction

As an extension of type III peacekeeping, the UN has at long last embarked explicitly on an experiment in post-conflict reconstruction as a logical concomitant of generic peacekeeping (really peace enforcement). In East Timor (UNTAET), the UN has for the first time in the long history of peacekeeping assumed responsibility for rebuilding a war-torn society. Its self-professed task, following the initiative of the Secretary-General and blessed by the Security Council, is no less than the creation of a stable, democratic, prosperous, internationally respectable new country, reconstructed out of the debris of Indonesian colonialism and wanton mayhem.

If this new post-colonial model of temporary tutelage or trusteeship, with appropriate international sanction, succeeds, it ought to provide a paradigm for UN oversight or control of the state reconfiguration process in Somalia, in Sierra Leone, in the Congo, and in future territories emerging (with UN assistance) from the throes of civil war or defeated colonialism. States that have collapsed can theoretically be resuscitated through the extension of transitional assistance to tutelage. East Timor is a special case, and so are the mainly African examples of state collapse or failure, but there is an increasing realization that the politically incorrect notion of revamping failed states is one of the key current tasks of the international system. Standard peacekeepers cannot do the job. Impartiality is not the key attitude or skill required.

In the twenty-first century, peace enforcement, followed by state rebuilding, will likely tax the will and the resources of the UN system. For example, Burma (Myanmar) may be a candidate for such transitional status (combining the best of types II and IV) at some time in the future. So might Kosovo, some of the states in the Caucasus region, West Papua, and countries in Central Asia—as well as the several African cases.

In previous centuries, states came and went. If they failed, another entity absorbed them. Now, states implode and few external actors want their territory. So the borders remain, and the collapse is entirely internal. Circumstances like these are all too common, especially in Africa. The East Timor model suggests that type IV cases will, if the UN succeeds there and continues to have the necessary political courage, become more and more typical. If a mechanism can be devised for the UN to recommit failed states into a trust status, this time to the UN itself, then peacekeeping will begin to develop fully into a process of reconstruction supervised by the UN or its designated sub-contractors (as in the League of Nations' mandatory system).

It is important for the UN to cease labeling these type IV situations generic peacekeeping. Taxonomically, that would be inaccurate, but the better reason is that the more transparent and open the UN can be about the varieties of modern peacekeeping, the easier it will be to rouse support for one or more of the other kinds of peacekeeping and peace building. Lumping them together obscures the different and significant functions each plays. Lumping them together tars the appropriate with the ill conceived and suggests incorrectly that one size fits all— that the problems of the world can all be dumped on the UN's doorstep and be solved or reacted to in similar, theoretically inexpensive ways. The nostrums of the Cold War era are no longer appropriate to the conflicts of this century. Nor can the template for Cyprus, say, fit the new Congo when the underlying antagonisms and situational dynamics are so very different.

Finances are crucial, too. No longer can penny-pinching panaceas succeed in accomplishing much, if anything, in a now much more anomic and violent world. With lethal small arms having become so cheap and so readily available, insurgencies almost anywhere can be fueled inexpensively and easily.[24] Just as avarice (as well as diamonds) has contributed mightily to the intractable character of the Angolan and Sierra Leonean civil wars and has influenced the continuing conflict in the Sudan, so mineral and other spoils will attract ethnic or other seekers of riches for decades to come. When Mobutu Sese Seko was faltering as Zaire's dictator, improving the lot of Congolese motivated many opponents. But so did his and the state's riches, which have continued to attract the attention of rebels, backers of rebels, supporters of the nominal government, and everyone in the region who seeks pieces of the action.

The intrastate wars of the modern world are not artifacts, despite those who prophesy the end of insurgency.[25] The UN will thus have as many calls on peacekeeping in coming decades as it has had in the last. Improving the UN's ability to respond to one crisis after another will therefore depend partially on satisfying its sources of funding, and primarily on developing an understanding within itself, and outside, of what peacekeeping really is—the types of peacekeeping—and what peacekeeping can and cannot accomplish under particular circumstances and in particular contexts, especially in Africa.

The UN has no business sending type I peacekeepers into type III situations. The dangers and the disarray of the world, now painfully obvious to the UN and everyone else after the debacle in Sierra Leone, must serve as an incentive not to abandon but to rethink and reorganize the UN's approach to the peace challenge.

Notes

1. Steven Metz, "African Peacekeeping and American Strategy," below, chapter 4.

2. J. Brian Atwood, "Atwood Targets Key Issues of Peacekeeping Reform," *The World Paper*, May/June 2000.

3. Adam Roberts, "The Crisis in UN Peacekeeping," in Chester Crocker and Fen Osler, *Managing Global Chaos: Sources of and Responses to International Conflict* (Washington, D.C., 1996), 299.

4. For the first Congo experience, see Thomas R. Mockaitis, *Peace Operations and Intrastate Conflict: The Sword or the Olive Branch?* (Westport, Conn., 1999), 11–42.

5. See Mockaitis, *Peace Operations*, 1.

6. Michael Ignatieff, "A Bungling UN Undermines Itself," *New York Times*, May 15, 2000.

7. Dennis C. Jett, "The UN's Failures Are Everyone's Fault," *New York Times,* May 22, 2000.

8. See Christopher Clapham, "Being Peacekept," in Oliver Furley and Roy May (eds.), *Peacekeeping in Africa* (Aldershot, U.K., 1998), 304.

9. Atwood, "Key Issues." For the U.S. doctrine, see Michael G. MacKinnon, *The Evolution of US Peacekeeping Policy under Clinton: A Fairweather Friend?* (London, 2000); Metz, "African Peacekeeping," below, chapter 4.

10. For a discussion of "success" in the domain of peacekeeping, see Lise Howard, "UN Multidimensional Peacekeeping in Civil Wars: The Causes of Success," unpublished MS, April 2000. For the two success stories, see Sam Barnes, "Peacekeeping in Mozambique," in Furley and May, *Peacekeeping*, 159–78, and Donna Pankhurst, "Namibia," ibid., 207–22. For the mixed case of Cambodia, see Michael W. Doyle, "War and Peace in Cambodia," in Barbara F. Walter and Jack Snyder (eds.), *Civil Wars, Insecurity, and Intervention* (New York, 1999), 181–210.

11. For Lesotho, see the extensive discussion by Prime Minister Pakalitha Mosisili, below, pages 176–86. On the general point, Clapham, "Peacekept," below, chapter 3.

12. Clapham, "Peacekept," below, chapter 3.

13. Tony Blair, broadcast, May 19, 2000 in www.BritainUSA.com.

14. Geoff Hoon, speech in House of Commons, May 23, 2000 in www.BritainUSA.com.

15. U. S. Secretary of State John Foster Dulles, backed by a Congressional vote, suggested that a UN rapid reaction force be created. See Brian Urquhart, "Cash-Starved UN Aiming Big Guns at Anxious Demand for Peacekeepers," *The World Paper* (May/June 2000); Urquhart, "For a UN Volunteer Military Force," *New York Review of Books* (June 10, 1993); Urquhart, *A Life in Peace and War* (New York, 1987), 137–38.

16. Leon Gordenker, *The UN Tangle: Policy Formation, Reform, and Reorganization*, WPF Report 12 (Cambridge, Mass., 1996).

17. Roy May and Gerry Cleaver, "African Peacekeeping: Still Dependent?" *International Peacekeeping*, IV (1997), 17.

18. Metz, "African Peacekeeping," below, chapter 4.

19. The meetings were held in 1997 at Harvard University, in 1998 in Malawi, and in 1999 in Tanzania. For the reports of the three meetings, see Jeffrey Herbst, *Securing Peace in Africa*, WPF Report 17 (Cambridge, Mass., 1998); Dana Francis, *Peacekeeping or Peace Enforcement? Conflict Intervention in Africa*, WPF Report 21 (Cambridge, Mass., 1998); Robert I. Rotberg and Ericka A. Albaugh, *Preventing Conflict in Africa: Possibilities of Peace Enforcement*, WPF Report 24 (Cambridge, Mass., 1999). On the roles of the West, and Africans, see also Herbst, "African Peacekeepers," below, chapter 2; Rotberg, "African Responses," below, chapter 6; Ericka A. Albaugh, "Preventing Conflict in Africa," below, chapter 6.

20. Herbst, *Securing Peace*, 28–31. Metz, "African Peacekeeping," below, chapter 4, also discusses ACRI's role in training the peacekeepers.

21. See Clapham, "Peacekept," below, chapter 3; Rotberg, "African Responses to African Crises," below, chapter 6.

22. Clapham, "Peacekept," below, chapter 3.

23. Herbst, "African Peacekeepers and State Failure," below, chapter 2.

24. Michael Klare and Robert I. Rotberg, *The Scourge of Small Arms*, WPF Report 23 (Cambridge, Mass., 1999).

25. Cf. Ted Robert Gurr, "Ethnic Warfare on the Wane," *Foreign Affairs*, LXXIX (2000), 52–64.

CHAPTER TWO

African Peacekeepers and State Failure

Jeffrey Herbst

THE MOST IMPORTANT development in peacekeeping in Africa in the 1990s was the evolving African consensus that the countries south of the Sahara had to take responsibility for most interventions in the future. The long-held African faith in the United Nations—fueled by the large African presence in the General Assembly—dissolved in the face of the outright failures in Somalia and Rwanda and the inability of the international body to act early and effectively in Liberia, Sierra Leone, and the Democratic Republic of the Congo (DRC). There has also been a gradual disillusionment with the Organization of African Unity (OAU) in light of its perennial inability to organize.

Instead, African political and military leaders now clearly indicate that the emerging model of African intervention will depend on one African country (perhaps the regional hegemon) deciding to intervene and then creating a coalition of other willing neighbors to complete the operation. International legitimacy will only be sought post facto, as many African leaders are no longer willing to wait for the seemingly endless debates in Addis Ababa and New York to reach closure. The interventions in Lesotho (led by South Africa), Liberia and Sierra Leone (both led by Nigeria), and Guinea-Bissau (led by Senegal) all followed this general model.

The new African assertiveness has been welcomed by the international community. In fact, the major U.S. African peacekeeping effort, the African Crisis Response Initiative (ACRI), is explicitly based on the premise that the United States should provide training to African troops who will do the actual peacekeeping.

Similarly, France, the Nordic countries, and the United Kingdom, among others, are all attempting to increase the African capacity to intervene in states that have failed, may soon experience catastrophic institutional collapse, or are a threat to their regions.

However, the assumptions behind the (now widely held) idea that "African solutions to African problems" are somehow more appropriate, more ethical, and more efficacious than other types of intervention have not, to date, been analyzed. This chapter evaluates the potential for Africans to intervene and examines who the likely intervenors will be and why they might chose to intervene. It concludes by arguing that the prospects for benign intervention—whereby the peacekeepers act in a manner that is not guided first and foremost by their own parochial national interests—are unlikely in Africa. Also, by subcontracting intervention to African states, the international community is essentially saying that conflicts in large countries such as Angola and the Sudan are hopeless. This admission is a stunning moral and ethical lapse at the beginning of the twenty-first century.

Why States Fail

The debate over who should do the peacekeeping in Africa has skipped past a critical question: why do African states fail in the first place? Unless there is a clear understanding of the structural causes of state failure in Africa, there cannot be a persuasive remedy to the problem of institutional collapse. If the more prominent African countries are now to step to the front and assume leadership on peacekeeping, the dynamics of state failure must be examined in order to see if the skills and resources these countries can bring to bear can actually solve the problems that drove them to intervene in the first place.

A leader who wants to exercise power in Africa has to confront a simple problem: the continent is sparsely settled. Africa had only six to eleven percent of the world's population in 1750, five to seven percent in 1900, and only eleven percent in 1997.[1] Relatively low population densities have meant automatically that it always has been more expensive for African states to exert control over a given number of people than for European and other densely settled areas. States have a particularly difficult time controlling the sparsely settled hinterlands where the population is dispersed atomistically over a large area.

During the precolonial period, political systems developed that took account of the difficulty of broadcasting power: it was not assumed that a state automatically controlled its hinterlands, as sovereignty was often shared with other political units. Boundaries were not artificial lines but porous zones that were not assumed to stop armies. States took a variety of different forms (e.g., city-states, empires, or nation-states) depending on the ability of leaders to project power over the landscape.

Europe only began to colonize Africa systematically in 1885. Eventually, the colonialists did rule formally over political capitals (overwhelmingly situated on the coasts to allow for easy communication and trade with Europe) and over specific economic assets (such as mines and plantations) in the interior. However, elsewhere in the vast African hinterlands, the European presence was often minimal. In 1939, the average British District Commissioner was responsible, with his staff of Africans, for an area roughly the size of Wales. Ruling over the roughly 43 million people in British tropical Africa in 1939 were a grand total of 1,223 administrators and 938 police. Similarly, there were 3,660 officials to govern 15 million Africans in French West Africa, 887 to govern 3,200,000 in French Equatorial Africa, and 2,384 to govern 9,400,000 in the Belgian Congo in 1938.[2]

The limits on how this "thin white line" could rule Africa were obvious. Joyce Cary, whose classic colonial novel *Mister Johnson* was published in 1939, describes well the muted ambition of the colonial officials: "No long views—the age for long views ended twenty years ago—and above all, not too much zeal."[3] At about the same time, Sally Herbert Frankel, in a critical economic treatise, was calling Africa "a continent of outposts."[4]

After 1939, in many ways the first high-water mark of European colonialism in Africa, the conquering powers were distracted by World War II and did little to extend their administrative networks. When the war ended, the natural progression of colonial rule might well have been to build from the center outward, so that eventually the entirety of each colony was physically controlled. This did not happen for several reasons. First, the colonialists still confronted the traditional African problem: the costs of extending rule in sparsely populated areas were exceptionally high, given limited benefits. Second, after 1945, the European powers were rebuilding and therefore hardly had the resources to make a major investment in Africa. Finally, although few understood it immediately after World War II, the tidal wave of African nationalism would soon crash over the continent, leaving in its wake dozens of independent countries by the mid-1960s.

The new African leaders who came to power forty-plus years ago faced the same daunting geography that their European predecessors had confronted and still possessed only incomplete administrative systems. However, with independence came the internationally accepted idea that the newly independent African states were the sovereign powers throughout the areas defined by their borders. Of course, the notion of sovereign control was, for many African countries, a legal fiction, as there was a significant gap between what many states actually controlled and their territory as defined by the boundaries inherited from the Europeans. However, it was relatively easy to maintain appearances in the 1960s and 1970s. The afterglow of the peaceful achievement of power in most countries lasted for years. Most African economies were growing, buoyed by global economic growth and relatively high prices for basic commodity exports that formed the basis of the formal economies of most African countries. The global strategic competition between the United States and Soviet Union also discouraged threats to the design of states in Africa or elsewhere. One of the implicit rules of the Cold War was that supporting efforts to change boundaries was not part of the game. In fact, the great powers usually intervened (as was the case with Zaire, Chad, and Ethiopia) to protect the integrity of existing states.

As a result of numerous changes, the actual nature of at least some African countries' sovereignty is now being exposed. The long economic crisis that many African countries have experienced since the late-1970s has caused a profound erosion of their governments' revenue bases. Even the most basic agents of the state (for example, agricultural extension agents, tax collectors, and census takers) are no longer to be found in many rural areas. Some states are increasingly unable to exercise physical control over their territories. The Economic Commission for Africa lamented that, because of the poor condition of many road systems, "whole areas are practically cut off from capital cities."[5] Low or negative per capita economic growth in some African countries will cause this sort of gradual dissolution to become even more common in the future.

The extremely limited revenue base of many African countries is also partially responsible for one of the most notable developments on the continent over the last thirty years: the change in the military balance between state and society. Whatever their other problems, African states at independence usually had control over the few weapons in their country. However, as states atrophy, their militaries also erode: readiness declines as there are no funds for training, equipment is no longer maintained, and many soldiers are not even paid. At the same time, those who wish to challenge a government have been able to arm, helped by the spillover of armaments from conflicts throughout the region and by the cheap price of weaponry after the Cold War. As a result, African militaries—which for decades faced no armed threat—are now sometimes suddenly confronted by internal rebellions where they are outgunned.

Finally, total aid to Africa is decreasing and, even more critically, donors are redirecting the remaining aid to countries that are achieving some success with their economic and political reforms. It is only natural that those countries that are failing spiral further downward. Somalia entered its particularly sharp downward trajectory in part because it could no longer play the United States off against the Soviet Union in order to receive more aid. It has been precisely those states (including Somalia, Ethiopia, Liberia, the Sudan, and former Zaire) that received large amounts of aid during the Cold War that have declined the most now that donors no longer reward them simply because of their putative strategic significance.

Now that so many of the domestic and international supports for African states have disappeared, it is inevitable that some states collapse. The contradiction of states with only incomplete control over their hinterlands but full claims to sovereignty was too fundamental to remain submerged for long. The turning point occurred when Yoweri Museveni took power in Uganda in early 1986. This was the first time that power had been seized in independent Africa by a leader who had gone back to the bush and formed his own army. It was a literal instance of the hinterland striking back. Previous military takeovers had originated in the national army and were essentially palace coups. Soon after, men in other countries who had a taste for power and a grievance around which to mobilize followers found that there was an underpoliced and incompletely controlled space in the rural areas where they could assemble a rebel force.

As a result, since 1986, inspired and sometimes supplied by Museveni (who has attempted to remake his East African neighborhood by force), armies created to compete against national forces in Rwanda, Zaire, Ethiopia, Sierra Leone, Congo-Brazzaville, and Chad have been able to take power by winning an outright military victory. Other countries (including Angola, Central African Republic, Guinea-Bissau, Liberia, and the Sudan) have experienced dramatic conflict that has resulted in mass destruction. The wars in Angola and the Sudan, each lasting decades, have been particularly devastating to the millions killed, maimed, or made refugees in each country as rebels in the hinterlands fight the capital in wars that no one can win.

In some countries, state failure has meant that no one has been able to take charge. In Somalia in January 1991, the Siad Barre government was overthrown but no other group was powerful enough to succeed it. There was a complete collapse of order. At various points in the torturous history of the Liberian civil war, the government's writ of authority did not extend beyond or even within the capital city of Monrovia. In such situations, populations have been subject to horrific abuses, as warlords and teenagers with machine guns terrorized and extorted the unarmed.

Since politics abhors a vacuum, the failure of states to control their own territories has also greatly increased the dangers of regional conflicts as countries move to protect their own vital interests. The war in the DRC has its origins in the breakdown of the old Zairian state. Uganda and Rwanda initiated the rebellion, which eventually resulted in Laurent Kabila overthrowing Mobutu Sese Seko in 1997 because both were under threat from militants who were part of the old Hutu government in Rwanda and who had found sanctuary in eastern Zaire after the Tutsi came to power in 1994. The rebellion was supposed simply to clean out the Hutu militants, but each time the rebellion confronted the Zairian army, Mobutu's soldiers ran because they were not willing to fight for a government that had not paid them. However, Kabila was unwilling or unable to provide the security guarantees that his erstwhile patrons demanded, and Kampala and Kigali therefore initiated a new rebellion in 1998. This rebellion almost succeeded in overthrowing Kabila, but Angola, Namibia, and Zimbabwe intervened to keep Kabila in power. The war bogged down quickly but it is obvious that no matter who eventually wins, no one will be in control of the vast territory of the DRC for many years to come.

Despite this seeming chaos, there is a pattern to state decay in Africa: large countries fail in a different manner than small countries. Due to the problems posed by low population density, small countries are more likely to retain control over their populations for longer periods of time than geographically large countries where the capital is far away from large segments of the population. This is not to argue that all will go well in small countries. As Liniger-Goumaz notes in his aptly titled book about Equatorial Guinea, *Small Is Not Always Beautiful*, even very small countries can have fantastically corrupt and incompetent regimes that impoverish their nations. Under Macias Nguema (1968–79) and Teodoro Obiang Nguema (1979–), Equatorial Guinea has become more impoverished, and one-third of the population has gone into exile.[6] Goumaz quotes one 1986 State Department description of Equatorial Guinea: "Professional and labor organizations are non-existent; the country is under absolute rule of the President."[7] Similarly, the State Department's 1997 annual human rights report noted an exceptional degree of governmental control even in the midst of decline: "Government authorization must be obtained for meetings of more than 10 persons in private homes for discussions that the regime considers political."[8] Similarly, the genocides in Burundi and Rwanda required high degrees of control over the entire territory.

In large countries, the problems that many states in Africa experience— populations that are atomistically dispersed across a rural hinterland, low and declining tax bases, security forces that are poorly equipped and ill trained, and the uncertain strength of national identity—become especially burdensome because capitals find that their writ of authority dissipates over the vast distances that their countries encompass. Young and Turner describe a very different type of decay for then Zaire compared to Equatorial Guinea: "During the phases of ascendancy and expansion, the state exuded an appearance of force and power. . . . This imagery was then exploded by the period of decay and crisis, in which the infirmities of the state again became conspicuous."[9] Even if it had wanted to, the state in Zaire could not have arranged the kind of genocide that Rwanda experienced in 1994: there was simply too much land in which people could escape the reach of the state. Due to the difficulties of geography, large states with widespread population distributions find that the liabilities of their size and shape are more readily apparent than those of small states, which continue to exercise authority over their more limited land masses even in times of decline.

In particular, wars in big countries with especially difficult geographies often take a different course than in countries where it is easier for the state to reach the hinterland and vice versa. It is particularly notable that in wars in small states, the capital itself becomes the battleground: Bissau, Brazzaville, Freetown, and Maseru were all destroyed in 1998 and 1999 because it was so easy for combatants to get to the center of power. In contrast, wars in larger states have the potential to end with a territorial division (as was the case with Ethiopia when Addis Ababa was saved in 1991 by granting Eritrea its independence) or simply to drag on because the capital cannot reach the rebels in the countryside and the rebels cannot march on the central state in, say, Angola or Sudan. The size and shape of African countries does not guarantee a particular outcome but does determine the contours that the conflict may follow.

African Solutions for African Problems

Within Africa, there had always been a desire to have Africans lead interventions. Despite the achievement of independence by most African countries in the early 1960s, foreign military intervention by the ex-colonial powers and others highlighted the fragility of the newly won political power and served to strengthen the historic memory of colonial domination. As General R. P. Mboma, Chief of Tanzania's People's Defence Force noted, "At the time of the Organization of African Unity's inception in 1963, the heads of African states were convinced that Africans had an '*inalienable right*' to control their own destiny."[10] Thus, *West Africa*, the major news weekly on the continent, called as early as 1964 for an "African Fire Brigade" that could serve as an interpositional force in international conflicts (for example, between Ethiopia and Somalia, Rwanda and Burundi, and Morocco and Algeria) and that could also address domestic upheavals in individual countries. *West Africa*'s motivation was the debacle in Tanganyika, where British troops had to intervene to quell a revolt by the East African country's restive army, a profound embarrassment given then President Julius Nyerere's clarion calls for an end to all foreign influence and his criticism of Western powers during the Cold War.[11] However, it was the catastrophe in the Congo, where outside intervention by the United Nations, Belgium (the former colonizer), and other powers, apparently motivated by Cold War concerns, ended in the death of Congolese Prime Minister Patrice Lumumba, that solidified the African view that foreign intervention, even under humanitarian guises, would always be questionable.

Still, in the long interval between Congo and Somalia, the notion of African solutions to African problems was more a platitude than a guide to everyday policy. The Africans had tremendous faith in the United Nations, not least because the General Assembly was one of the few institutions in which the countries south of the Sahara had power and influence. Membership in the General Assembly was also one of the most important icons of African sovereignty. To dismiss the role of the United Nations was to lessen, at least implicitly, the international salience of the guarantor of African sovereignty. Finally, in the 1960s through the 1980s, African countries were so devoted to the notion of all countries being sovereign that it was difficult, if not impossible, for them to take on interventions that were not of the traditional type backed by the General Assembly.

It was the failures of Somalia and Rwanda that reignited the view that reliance on the international community would be highly problematic. For many African countries, the fundamental challenge posed by Somalia was clear: would the United States, the last remaining superpower, allow Mohamed Farah Aideed and his few hundred fighters to chase it out of Mogadishu? When the question was answered in the affirmative, the implausibility of Western peacekeeping even in the new world order became self-evident. As William Nhara, coordinator of conflict prevention and research in the OAU's Division of Conflict Management, noted, "Regional organisations should realise that there is a need to take on the primary responsibility for their own problems, especially those relating to issues of peace, security and stability. This is necessary as Africa's external partners are increasingly less enthusiastic about sharing its problems."[12]

Western powers, especially the United States after Somalia, were also anxious to encourage the notion that conflict management could be subcontracted out to regional organizations. After several missteps, in early 1997, the United States unveiled the African Crisis Response Initiative (ACRI). The United States proposed to provide training to several African countries in order to develop a capacity for peacekeeping that might be mobilized at some future date. By mid-1997, Washington was able to obtain commitments from seven African countries (Ethiopia, Ghana, Malawi, Mali, Senegal, Tunisia, and Uganda) to allow eight battalions (Ethiopia agreed to provide two) to be trained. Under the program, about sixty trainers from U.S. Army Special Forces units headquartered at Fort Bragg are sent to each African country for sixty days to provide basic training in soldiering and some special skills relevant to peacekeeping (for example, an emphasis on refugees and some advice on how to deal with humanitarian organizations).[13] About $1 million worth of communications equipment is provided to each battalion. A total of $15 million was budgeted by the United States for the ACRI in fiscal 1997 and $20 million in fiscal 1998.[14]

American officials have gone to considerable lengths to state that they are not leading the African peacekeeping initiatives, especially after earlier diplomatic miscues when the United States seemed to suggest that it wanted to help create and help lead a force for intervention (the ill-fated African Crisis Response Force). As Marshall McCallie, then U.S. Ambassador in charge of the ACRI, noted, "Essentially, what we are doing and others are doing would be training units that would be able to respond to a crisis." Indeed, the American description of the ACRI seems to go out of its way to ask for leadership by others. McCallie's briefing is informative:

> What we are suggesting is not a force. What we are suggesting is a—almost a clearinghouse. It would be an association without membership. It would be an informal gathering of states that are interested in peacekeeping in Africa. And they would address what type of training would be useful, what type of joint exercises would be useful.[15]

The desire to leave peacekeeping to the Africans became even more heartfelt after the collapse of the UN peacekeeping effort in Angola in 1998. This operation, like that in Somalia, cost well over $1 billion, led to the deaths of dozens of peacekeepers, and left the country in ruins. African military and political leaders understand that they are essentially on their own.

Thus, because of a variety of historical, tactical, and political developments, "African solutions to African problems" has been embraced across the world as the operational code for future peacekeeping operations in Africa. No one believes that African countries alone can conduct formal peacekeeping operations, and there has been very serious work done on how African and Western forces might cooperate during internationally mandated operations and on what kind of training it is necessary to provide. However, it is clear that the emerging vision of peacekeeping foresees African soldiers as the backbone of any intervention force. Further, especially as disgust with UN operations increases, there is also a significant desire to "subcontract" the decisionmaking process to African countries, either the OAU or sub-regional groupings such as the Southern African Development Community (SADC). One of the stated contingencies ACRI-trained troops might respond to is an intervention authorized by a regional grouping of African states.

Prospects for Benign Intervention

A core assumption of the peacekeeping literature is that intervenors enter a country with the best of intentions. This assumption, seemingly problematic given the oft-repeated refrain in international relations that countries act according to their interests, came about because of the manner in which peacekeeping evolved after World War II. The classic type of peacekeeping with which the "blue helmets" of the United Nations were associated was the creation of an interpositional force between armies that have agreed to a cease-fire. These peacekeeping forces were mandated under Chapter VI of the United Nations charter, which required that the peacekeepers be neutral and prohibited them from using force unless attacked. The peacekeeping forces were usually composed of forces from countries that not only had no interest in the conflict but had no obvious interests in the area. Thus, a Ghanaian contingent has long had a significant presence in the United Nations peacekeeping force in the Golan Heights. The countries that supplied the peacekeepers were motivated by exceptionally high UN per diems, which made peacekeeping a profitable activity, by the prospect of their armies being equipped and trained by the UN, and by a commitment to internationalism, albeit at a very low price.

After the Cold War, when it seemed briefly that the remaining superpower would be intimately involved in peacekeeping operations, the assumption of the neutral intervenor could be retained. For instance, few could suggest an ulterior motivation for the U.S. intervention in Somalia: the United States had no traditional interests (strategic or economic) in Somalia and it seemed obvious that President George Bush was motivated largely by humanitarian concerns.

Are There Benign Hegemons in Africa?

Especially when intervention is left to the neighbors, as it increasingly is in Africa, the assumption of the benign and neutral intervenor must be examined carefully. Obviously, the most plausible scenario for benign peacekeeping would be for a very large country to lead an intervention in a much smaller country that is, at best, largely extraneous to its own concerns. This is now the emerging African view and one that coincides with the long-held precept in political science that for a collective good to be produced, one country may have to take on costs disproportionate to the benefits it expects to reap. The model intervention by a benign hegemon is the effort led by President Nelson Mandela, assisted by other Southern African leaders, in 1994 to prevent a royal coup by Lesotho's King Letsie III. South Africa so dominates Lesotho that it could not be said that it was largely motivated by its own interests. Further, the moral stature of Mandela and the fact that the intervention was designed to prevent a coup preempted any discussion that South Africa was anything other than a benign intervenor seeking to insure the status quo. However, there are few places in Africa where a similar scenario could be played out. Indeed, the disastrous 1998 intervention by South Africa in Lesotho demonstrates that good intentions by themselves are not enough. It is also obvious that no other leader has Mandela's moral stature and that the motives of countries when they intervene must at least be examined more closely.

Further, what is startling about the current regional situation in Africa is that, outside of southern Africa, where South Africa is the natural leader and is relatively stable by the standards of the neighborhood, all the big countries are in serious trouble, even by the standards of their regions, and cannot plausibly play the role of disinterested regional hegemon. This is not a coincidence but a natural development, given the evolution of sovereignty and the problems of control outlined above. Nigeria, by dint of its large population, dominates West Africa; however, its continual domestic political and economic problems long ago ended any discussion that it might be a neutral regional policeman. Nigeria has intervened in parts of the region, but, as discussed below, many of the domestic pathologies from which it suffers travel with its troops to foreign countries. In Central and East Africa, the DRC is the natural hegemon, but it has been dysfunctional as a country for so long that the capital, Kinshasa, cannot project power over its own territory, much less into other countries in a professional and unbiased manner. Ethiopia is the dominant country in the Horn of Africa but it is only very slowly recovering from the decades-long civil war that eventually led to the independence of Eritrea in 1993. The war between Ethiopia and Eritrea probably ended any possibility that Addis Ababa could act as a benign hegemon in the region.

Indeed, it is striking that Africa's largest countries, with the exception of South Africa, are more likely to be discussed as destinations for peacekeepers than as benign hegemons leading disinterested interventions. DRC has been the destination for a variety of intervenors for several years now, and both Nigeria and Ethiopia, given the centrifugal pressures they are experiencing, are routinely discussed as possible failed states. Indeed, far from size being correlated with power, as has traditionally been the case in the international relations literature, it appears that a significant size, within the African context, is a relatively good predictor of poor state performance. It is telling that of the African countries participating in the ACRI, only Ethiopia is among the largest African countries that would normally be thought of as a natural intervenor.

Buying Disinterested Intervenors

The other prospect for benign intervention would result if African countries were subsidized by the international community to intervene in areas where they would not normally have interests. If African intervenors did not have immediate interests and they were on the international payroll, benign intervention might be tenable. However, such benign intervention would have to be purchased by the international community, since it would have to be done by relatively small states (with small armies) that are far from a theater of operation. It seems unlikely that the international community will be willing to pay a high price to buy neutrality. For instance, the ACRI comes with no guaranteed funding except for the limited training it provides. It is hoped that funding to get the ACRI-trained troops to their targets and to sustain them will be provided by the international community on an ad hoc basis.

However, the failure of the international community to provide disinterested parties with funding has been a major problem for peacekeeping in Africa. Thus, Tanzania's participation in the intervention in Liberia—a good example of an intervention where they were no obvious national interests at stake—was persistently hampered by an inability to secure outside funding from the United States or the United Nations.[16] The non-Nigerian forces that originally constituted part of the Economic Community of West African States (ECOWAS) Monitoring Group (ECOMOG) force in Liberia (Ghana, Sierra Leone, Gambia, and Guinea) eventually departed, in part because they were not willing to pay the costs of an extended intervention even in a neighboring country. African countries, which became accustomed to having all expenses paid when participating in the old-style Chapter VI interventions sponsored by the United Nations, now clearly recognize that finance is a formidable barrier to intervening in conflicts where their immediate interests are not at stake. Nor are the impediments to disinterested intervention limited to African countries. When former UN Secretary-General Boutros Boutros-Ghali called upon sixty non-African states to form a standby force for Burundi, only one (Bangladesh) volunteered.[17]

Disinterested intervention is hampered also by logistics, especially when trying to intervene in a large country. The ability to move forces is crucial to peacekeeping. The official U.S. doctrine for peacekeepers notes simply, "Transportation by air, land, and sea, is the 'linchpin' of your operation. . . ."[18] Logistics is obviously especially important if the countries to intervene are chosen because they are not in the neighborhood and therefore presumably do not have an immediate agenda involving the domestic politics of the destination country. However, there is no chance of any African country or set of countries having the capability to intervene in another region in the foreseeable future. Even South Africa has only an extremely limited capability to project force, given that most of its forces during the apartheid period were developed to prevent border incursions. Without a strong and robust logistical capability, the ACRI or any other proposal will not be able to get around the central paradox of peacekeeping in Africa: those who are willing to intervene without an ulterior motive beyond humanitarian concerns do not have the capacity to project the necessary force.

As a result, benign peacekeeping is exceptionally difficult for most African nations. For instance, the 1998 intervention by Senegal into Guinea-Bissau to prevent chaos in that country after a profound split developed within that country's military turned out exceptionally poorly. Indeed, despite the fact that the Senegalese military has received significant assistance from both the United States and France, its forces, by themselves, were not able to dislodge rebel military units from their quickly built fortifications. This was an especially disappointing performance because the minimal goals of the ACRI and French training were for Senegalese to have at least the capacity to intervene in Bissau.

Thus, disinterested intervention in Africa, ironically, usually happens under the sponsorship of Western nations. Zimbabwe and Botswana both had units in Somalia during Restore Hope, perhaps as clear an example of disinterested intervention as is possible. Indeed, the United States and the UN had made it a high priority to attract African nations who would lend more legitimacy to the intervention. Similarly, the African units that have participated in peacekeeping operations in Angola and Mozambique did so under UN sponsorship and were therefore on the UN payroll.

Intervention with a Motive

Instead of benign intervention, what is clear from the very recent history of international relations in Africa is that many of the most dramatic and effective instances of intervention have been by parties with a profound motive in a particular type of intervention. The Rwandan/Ugandan intervention in former Zaire in 1997, which led to Laurent Kabila coming to power, was done specifically to eliminate the security threat posed to Kampala and, especially, to Kigali, by Hutu groups based in eastern Zaire. The effectiveness of this operation (the refugee camps were emptied, millions of Hutu were returned to Rwanda, and the armed Hutu groups lost some of their best sanctuaries and their lifeline to international assistance) stands in stark contrast to the endless dithering by non-

Western powers over intervention first in Rwanda in 1994 and then in Zaire in 1996 as the refugee crisis became dramatic. That Rwanda, small by almost any measure, was able to help establish, support, and, to some extent, direct a successful (on its own terms) intervention into its much bigger neighbor clearly demonstrates how peculiar the relationship between size and power has become in Africa and just how great the possibilities of intervention are for a country with strong motives.

Angola also demonstrated in 1997 that it was possible to change the course of a country dramatically when it sent a significant armed force to Congo-Brazzaville to overthrow the democratically elected government of Pascal Lissouba and replace him with former dictator Denis Sassou Nguesso. The Angolans had found Nguesso to be a more attractive leader as they sought to end their own civil war by cutting off outside support for the National Union for the Total Independence of Angola (UNITA).

Nigeria's interventions first in Liberia in 1990 and later in Sierra Leone in 1997 are more complicated cases. The initial movement into Liberia was motivated in part by humanitarian concerns, especially worries over the fate of Nigerians resident in Liberia. The Liberian intervention also attracted several African partners and the Nigerian forces in both Liberia and Sierra Leone were legitimated *post hoc* by the international community. However, the Nigerian interventions could hardly be considered disinterested. In addition to humanitarian concerns, then Nigerian President Ibrahim Babangida sent forces to Monrovia to help his ally and friend Samuel Doe stay in power. The Nigerian forces proved able to hold Monrovia but could not defeat the forces of Charles Taylor in the Liberian interior. Indeed, the pathologies of Nigeria's patron-client system soon transferred to Liberia, as some local commands in ECOMOG began to make significant money through mineral and logging concessions.[19] Despite many years of fighting, the Nigerian forces did not prevent the war from spilling over into Sierra Leone and, in the end, had to ratify the election of Taylor, even though they had fought for many years to keep him from coming to power.

In Sierra Leone, the 1997 coup against President Ahmad Tejan Kabbah was eventually reversed (the putative motivation for the Nigerian intervention), although the country suffered from several rounds of brutal conflict. Intervention in either Liberia or Sierra Leone would have been a complicated and difficult task for any country. However, the fact that Nigeria had significant interests in both cases and, at least in Liberia, developed a panoply of patronage opportunities, probably combined to make a benign and disinterested intervention unlikely to impossible.

Finally, intervention by African countries in their neighbors for non-humanitarian reasons may increase as a response to other interventions. Thus, when Uganda and Rwanda helped support a second uprising in eastern Zaire in 1998, this one to overthrow their former puppet Laurent Kabila, Angola, Namibia, and Zimbabwe sent troops to protect Kinshasa and to defeat the invaders. The motivations for Luanda, Windhoek, and Harare intervening, when all three were suffering from drastic economic conditions at home, is not clear, but their rhetoric suggested that they were extremely unhappy about Rwandan and Ugandan adventurism. It may be the case that Kabila had managed to extend his own web of commerce and patronage to these other countries. Whatever their motivation—and this particularly complicated episode may not be untangled for years—it is clear that no one could confuse Angola, Namibia, and Zimbabwe with disinterested peacekeepers modeled on the old Chapter VI operations.

Policy Implications

In the academic literature and in most policy discussions, there is a clear divide between peacekeeping and intervention. Such a dichotomy was possible because, in the classic instances of peacekeeping, forces sent to ratify the ends of conflict were clearly endorsed and supported by the international community. Intervention, on the other hand, was something that states did to further their own parochial interests. However, in Africa, there will probably be a much hazier boundary between intervention and peacekeeping. The international community no longer wants to ratify and support as many peacekeeping operations as before, especially in Africa, because the United States and the major European powers no longer want to pay the bill. At the same time, at least some African countries will argue that, from their national perspectives, there is no difference between peacekeeping and intervention in Africa. Rwanda and Uganda had clear peacekeeping concerns (given the over-the-border incursions by Hutu groups) when they sponsored the intervention in eastern Zaire, and Luanda also had, at least by its own lights, a need to cut off possible support from UNITA flowing from Congo-Brazzaville. Similarly, Angola, Namibia, and Zimbabwe have all argued that their 1998 intervention in the DRC was done to further the cause of international peace in the face of external aggression, an argument that also eventually convinced Mandela (who had initially opposed further internationalization of the conflict).

However, if peacekeeping and intervention are synonymous in Africa, it should be understood that most armed interventions will be designed to further the interests of the intervenors. It is unlikely that the interventions will be designed with a high priority assigned to respecting human rights, and the forces involved may not be trained according to the emerging norms for peacekeepers. Most importantly, the intervention may not be designed to promote peace in an unbiased manner but to help one or another party in the host country that is friendly with the intervenor. African militaries that intervene may also find that they develop new commercial interests in the host country—as happened with Nigeria in Liberia and with Zimbabwe in the DRC—that further divert them from the cause of peacekeeping and peacemaking in an unbiased manner. The facts that African intervenors only feel that it is necessary to seek international legitimacy after the fact, and that the international community has so abandoned any responsibility for African humanitarian problems that it feels comfortable with that charade, should further the prospects of interventions that are tied to the national interests of the lead countries.

Two stark policy implications emerge from this discussion. First, western countries must understand that they are playing with fire when they prepare African armies for peacekeeping, especially as that training always involves a significant combat element. After the trainers go home, the United States, and other western nations, lose whatever control they may have had over the units trained and the materiel provided. African countries therefore may be more tempted to intervene in the affairs of neighbors even if they still do not have the resources to be the benign intervenor farther afield. It may be, to take the worst case scenario, only a matter of time before the ACRI equipment provided to Ugandan troops is found in the hands of pro-Ugandan rebels operating in eastern DRC. Even for the ACRI countries, chosen explicitly because they were least likely to embarrass the United States, there is also the possibility that ACRI equipment could be used in internal operations against domestic opponents. This is especially likely in Senegal and Uganda, where there is significant armed internal opposition to Dakar and Kampala. African governments will use their armies to counter whatever security threats they perceive and will simply not leave equipment or units on the shelf because they received training from Western countries. Indeed, these may be the units and equipment that are called upon to go into the field first.

Second, the emerging consensus between Africans and Western policymakers concerning peacekeeping means that some of the worst state failures and wars in Africa—those that are occurring in big countries—simply will not be addressed. Even coalitions of small African states cannot intervene in the big countries that are failing. Thus, the world is simply abandoning Angola, the Sudan, the DRC, and other grave humanitarian disasters by letting the available Africans take the lead on peacekeeping. This rather stunning failure should not be allowed to go unnoticed even if some might celebrate it as the dawn of the new age of African solutions for African problems.

Conclusion

The ambition of "African solutions to African problems" is an admirable one. It signals the end of the West's patronizing attitude to Africa and is another indication that the dream of true political independence for the countries south of the Sahara is increasingly becoming a reality. If African wars were between states, and third parties simply needed to position themselves between armies that had already agreed to end hostilities, the prospect of Africans controlling peacekeeping operations would be unambiguously positive. However, the particular dynamics of state decay south of the Sahara suggest that African countries often cannot and will not act as benign intervenors. In small countries, African peacekeepers may act more as invaders than as peacekeepers and in large countries there may not be any African solution offered.

"African solutions to African problems" also means that the West increasingly will not be able to determine how intervention and peacekeeping are implemented. Currently, the United States and European countries appear to want the best of all worlds: let the Africans do the fighting but hope that the Africans will pay attention to Western sensibilities. In the brutal world of international relations, which parts of Africa are finally beginning to resemble, such hope is farfetched. The United States and the European countries will have to deal with African intervenors on African terms or realize that the West has become irrelevant.

Notes

1. Calculated from John D. Durand, "Historical Estimates of World Population: An Evaluation," *Population and Development Review*, III (1977), 259, and World Bank, *World Development Report 1998*, 191.

2. Anthony H. M. Kirk-Greene, "The Thin White Line: The Size of the British Colonial Service in Africa," *African Affairs*, LXXIX (1980), 26, and Robert Delavignette, *Freedom and Authority in French West Africa* (London, 1950), 18.

3. Joyce Cary, *Mister Johnson* (London, 1961, orig. pub. 1939), 209.

4. Sally Herbert Frankel, *Capital Investment in Africa: Its Course and Effects* (London, 1938), 30.

5. Economic Commission for Africa, *Survey of Economic and Social Conditions in Africa, 1991-2*, E/ECA/SERP/94/1 (Addis Ababa, 1994), 117.

6. Max Liniger-Goumaz, *Small Is Not Always Beautiful: The Story of Equatorial Guinea* (London, 1988).

7. Ibid., 168.

8. U.S. State Department, *Country Reports on Human Rights Practices for 1997*, found at: www.state.gov/www/global/human_rights/1997_hrp_report/eqguinea.html (2/10/00).

9. Crawford Young and Thomas Turner, *The Rise and Decline of the Zairian State* (Madison, 1985), 77.

10. R. P. Mboma, "The Role of Regional Bodies in Preventive Diplomacy and Peacekeeping," in Jakkie Cilliers and Greg Mills (eds.), *Peacekeeping in Africa II* (Johannesburg, 1996), 109.

11. "African Fire Brigade," *West Africa* (February 15, 1964), 169.

12. William Nhara, "The OAU and the Potential Role of Regional and Sub-Regional Organisations," in Cilliers and Mills, *Peacekeeping*, 100.

13. Training is done by U.S. Special Forces because they are the lead units on all foreign U.S. military training.

14. Marshall McCallie and David E. McCracken, "On-the-Record Briefing," July 28, 1997, found at www.state.gov/www/regions/africa/acri_briefing_970728.html; and Steven Metz, "African Crisis Response Initiative," testimony before the Subcommittee on Africa of the House International Relations Committee, 105th Cong., 1st sess., Oct. 8, 1997.

15. McCallie and McCracken,"Briefing."

16. Mboma, "Role," 116.

17. Herbert Howe, "Lessons of Liberia: ECOMOG and Regional Peacekeeping," *International Security,* XXI (1996/1997), 145.

18. Joint Warfighting Center, *Joint Task Force Commander's Handbook for Peace Operations* (Fort Monroe, Va., 1997), VI-5.

19. See, for instance, William Reno, *Warlord Politics and African States* (Boulder, Colo., 1998), 105.

CHAPTER THREE

Peacekeeping and the Peacekept: Developing Mandates for Potential Intervenors

Christopher Clapham

Legal and Political Mandates

The "mandate" is the essential base on which any peacekeeping or peace enforcement mission must depend. It is needed, first, to provide the mission with *legitimacy* as an activity properly undertaken on behalf of the international community and the people of the intervened-in state, rather than as the mere imposition of force by one state over another of a kind that would normally be characterized as power politics or even aggression. Second, it defines the *objectives* of the mission: military forces intervening in conflicts in other states must have a very clear idea of what they are expected, and what they are *not* expected, to do.

Looked at in this way, mandates are essentially legal documents, and considerable attention has therefore understandably been paid to ensuring that they meet the necessary international legal requirements. This means, first, that they must emanate from appropriate international institutions that have the right to take decisions over critical issues of state security, sovereignty, and the use of military force; and second, that they must define sufficiently clearly the "rules of engagement" under which forces are deployed. These tasks in themselves give rise to some extremely tricky problems. Though the legal status of mandates has classically been resolved by recognizing the United Nations Security Council as having a global responsibility for ensuring the proper use of force, in practice a number of important peace enforcement missions—the North Atlantic Treaty Organization (NATO) intervention in the former Yugoslavia, the Economic Community of West African States (ECOWAS) intervention in Liberia, the Southern African Development Community (SADC) intervention in Lesotho—have been undertaken directly by sub-regional organizations, with only subsequent, if any, reference to the United Nations. The right of international organizations to approve mandates for intervention in states that have not agreed to them is likewise unclear. Considerable uncertainty thus remains over who is entitled to mandate intervenors to do what.

The definition of the rules of engagement also raises major difficulties, not least because initial mandates are characteristically couched in terms that prove to be inadequate once the mission actually gets under way. Conflict situations frequently develop in ways that are not allowed for at the start, and indeed may reflect the injection into the previously existing situation of the peacekeeping force itself. Both for diplomatic and financial reasons, and because of a frequently over-optimistic assessment of the ease with which the intervening force may be expected to achieve its goals, initial mandates are frequently cast in minimal terms: a small force is expected to be able to achieve its objectives in a short period, with minimal direct use of coercion. "Mission creep" is an inherent and inevitable feature of intervention, and mandates must be kept under continuous review and adapted as circumstances change: the idea that in any arena of international politics, let alone in any form of military operation, it is possible to lay down precise blueprints in advance and follow them through to their conclusion is simply deluded. Many of the most striking examples of mission "failure" arise because the initial task of the intervening forces has been overtaken by events, and the mission is unable (for whatever reason) to cope with a new set of circumstances which it had not envisaged and for which it was not designed.

A classic and tragic example case is that of the UN Assistance Mission for Rwanda (UNAMIR) force in April 1994: Originally deployed with the apparently straightforward task of policing a political settlement reached by the various Rwandan groupings, it suddenly found itself in a situation in which that mission was completely redundant. It was then called on to pursue the totally different objective of securing the lives of the largest possible number of threatened members of the Rwandan population. Its failure to perform that task—under orders from New York and despite the impassioned pleas of the force commander on the ground—led to the deaths of hundreds of thousands of innocent people and to the discrediting of the UN as a viable source of security in the region.

As this case indicates, mandates for intervention should not be seen simply as legal documents. Underlying any effective legal mandate, there must also be a viable *political* mandate, which is required to ensure that any intervention is able to build and maintain the levels of political support without which it will have at best only very limited prospects of success. One very familiar example will make the point: In 1993, the UN Operation in Somalia (UNOSOM) II intervention force was fully mandated by the Security Council, under Chapter VIII of the UN Charter, to exercise powers unprecedented for external forces within a UN member state. It took only the killing of eighteen U.S. marines (who were not formally part of the UNOSOM force at all) in Mogadishu on 3 October 1993 for the political mandate for the operation within the United States to collapse, leading to an immediate loss of effectiveness for UNOSOM and to its rapid withdrawal. Legal mandates, in short, are not enough.

Political mandates can, in turn, be looked at from two perspectives. First, as in the example given above, there is the perspective of the *intervenors*, who seek to ensure the essential backing of their own domestic constituencies and the wider diplomatic community within which they have to operate. The second perspective has been almost entirely neglected. It concerns the legitimacy of intervention for the peoples of the intervened-in state: a successful intervention must have a political mandate, not merely among the peacekeepers, but among the *peacekept*. While the killing of the U.S. marines in Somalia may have destroyed UNOSOM's mandate in the United States, it was itself the result of UNOSOM's failure to secure an accepted mandate within Somalia and among Somalis. Most basically, the function of a peacemaking mission is to make peace, and that, in turn, requires the creation of a viable political settlement among the peoples and major political groupings of the state within which the intervention takes place. Unless this is achieved, the mission has failed; and the greatest danger facing inadequately thought-out interventions is that, rather than creating the basis for such a settlement, they may weaken or even destroy it.

The rest of this chapter concentrates on political rather than legal mandates and assesses the requirements for securing such mandates, first among the peacekeepers, and second among the peacekept. It concludes by summarizing some of the critical political criteria that potential intervenors should keep in mind.

Mandates for Peacekeepers

The Regional Setting

Intervention by a state in conflicts within another state is readily justified as an international obligation—in the way, for example, that President George Bush described the U.S. forces in Somalia as doing "God's work" or that President Robert

Mugabe has justified the role of Zimbabwean forces in the Democratic Republic of Congo (DRC) as upholding the Organization of African Unity's (OAU's) commitment to maintaining the sovereignty and territorial integrity of its member states. But though there are certainly occasions when just moral arguments may attract a great deal of sympathy, these are rarely enough (as the Somali case again shows) to secure an intervention the political mandate that it needs. Nor does the support of institutions such as the United Nations, however important it may be to provide a legal rationale, carry much clout in political terms. The UN is simply too distant, too global, and too subject to the dictates of the great powers to bring much support to an operation that does not already have the required backing among those most directly engaged in it. For this purpose, the two arenas that matter are the immediate *regional* setting and the *domestic* constituency within the intervening state itself.

The first is the most readily subject to general comparative analysis. Intervention is necessarily a projection of power. Given that conflicts within particular states—and especially African states, with their readily permeable borders—cannot be insulated from their wider regional setting, intervention must inevitably reflect and, in turn, affect regional power relations. It also raises very sensitive issues of sovereignty and influences the structure of domestic politics: even if, for example, intervention only takes place on the invitation of the government of the intervened-in state, the status of that government and how the intervention will affect both the internal balance of forces and the relationships between domestic political factions and their external allies remains problematic. To take two obvious African examples from 1998, the intervention requested by the newly elected government of Lesotho was a very different matter from that requested by the unelected government of the DRC.

There is, therefore, a need for regional political mechanisms to provide not just formal authorization but also continuing support for intervention among the group of states whose own security is most directly affected. Where effective sub-regional organizations exist, they provide the appropriate setting. In turn, the states within such organizations are required to develop regional security systems, or in other words, to agree among themselves on how their security is most endangered and how it should be maintained. This is by no means a simple task. Regional security systems involve agreement on *domestic* political structures and thus encroach on the sovereignty of individual states: if military intervention or the collapse of public order in one state is deemed to constitute a security threat to its neighbors, and thus to justify their intervention, rules for intervention must be agreed in advance between the states concerned. The Banjul Declaration by the ECOWAS countries provides the clearest example of such agreement. For another, regional security systems raise critical issues of sub-regional *leadership*: leadership is central to any effective security system and the very uneven distribution of capabilities among the states within a particular region often preordains certain states to take a leading role. At the same time, it is essential that this role should be accepted by other states within the region and limited by conventions that prevent it from degenerating into the mere imposition of domination by regional hegemons over their weaker neighbors.

Within Africa, it is possible to identify two sub-regions, West Africa and Southern Africa, within which such a regional security system is at least partially present. Each has a sub-regional organization (ECOWAS and SADC), a broadly accepted set of principles for common regional action, and a readily identifiable leader. There are some smaller groupings of states, such as those of East Africa, which have been able to work out cooperative relationships among themselves. In other parts of the continent, notably the Horn of Africa and Central Africa (including the DRC, despite its membership in SADC), there is no such organization, set of principles, or acceptable leader. In these circumstances, regional mandates for intervention are not available: where states intervene in the affairs of their neighbors, they do so simply as expressions of their own state interests and levels of power. Where, as in Somalia, there is widespread agreement that some form of intervention is needed, the intervention has to be authorized at the supra-regional level, and it carries all the dangers associated with operating in an unsettled regional, as well as domestic, environment.

The need for agreement on domestic political structures means, in effect, that all the states within the regional security system must be constituted in similar ways, such that they all recognize a comparable set of threats and broadly agree about the means by which these threats should be overcome. The first requirement is that they must accept a common basis for the territorial structure of the state itself: a Somali state that defined its legitimate territory in terms of the area inhabited by members of a single Somali nation was, for instance, simply incapable of forming a common security system with other states which defined themselves in terms of the territorial frontiers inherited from the late nineteenth century colonial partition. Any such definition creates its own strengths and weaknesses and, in turn, raises potential areas of contention that may inhibit the formation of regional security systems. Having almost universally accepted the colonial partition as the basis for state formation, for example, African states must also accept the way in which this partition often divides indigenous societies, leaving border zones in which people on either side of the frontier continue to have considerable affinities with one another and become involved in one another's security problems.

Regional states must also be broadly similar in their structures of domestic government. This has been most obvious in southern Africa, where any security system that encompassed both white-ruled and majority-ruled states was simply inconceivable: the "Constellation of Southern African States" promoted by the *apartheid* regime in South Africa, along with mechanisms such as the Nkomati Accord, through which that regime sought to impose its hegemony, could never create any viable basis for regional security because it could never rest on any agreed definition of what *kinds* of states could co-exist within the region. The creation of any regional security system had to await the advent of majority rule in South Africa. Even majority rule, however, does not guarantee any common basis for security: a state governed in accordance with its own precepts of the requirements of Islam, such as the Sudan in recent times, is inherently threatening to neighboring states with Muslim populations which do not define themselves in the same Islamic terms. In the Cold War era, socialist states backed by the USSR were at least potentially threatening to capitalist states backed by the United States, and vice versa.

By far the most effective basis for regional security collaboration in the present era is that governments throughout the region should be democratically elected through open multi-party systems and be recognized as legitimate and democratic by their neighbors. It is the spread of liberal democratic government throughout most of southern Africa, and not merely the end of white minority rule, that has made the development of a regional security system possible. It is important to recognize, however, that democracy, too, carries its own in-built tensions as a basis for regional security. It requires the democratic credentials of each state within the region to be accepted by its neighbors. And, in a continent in which electoral losers have often been reluctant to accept the legitimacy of their defeat, it requires incumbent governments to run elections in a way that is considered fair by their neighbors. These neighbors must then be prepared to turn a deaf ear to disgruntled opposition politicians who run with their tales of woe to the nearest state with the capacity to intervene. Both in Zambia and in Lesotho, to take two recent cases, leaders of opposition parties which had historically been aligned with the African National Congress (ANC) in South Africa have sought its help in overturning the results of elections at home. By the same token, if democracy is the basis for security, then regional intervention is implicitly legitimate as a means of displacing a clearly undemocratic government. Another essential requirement for building regional security is that democracy should not exacerbate divisions between neighbors. Although democratic governments generally maintain more peaceful relations with their neighbors than do autocratic regimes, in specific cases democracy may increase regional tensions, especially when population groups straddle borders and a group that is strongly placed within one state sympathizes with its fellows who are in opposition across the frontier. In eastern and central Europe, for example, ethnic conflicts which were suppressed beneath the heavy hand of Soviet autocracy have become far more salient since the end of the Cold War.

The most critical issue facing effective regional security systems is however that of leadership. It is extremely difficult to develop effective mandates for intervention unless one state—and one leader—is prepared to take the initiative, commit the necessary resources, accept the inevitable costs, and put together a coalition of like-minded states that are prepared to devote some of their own resources to the physical capacity of the operation and (often more important) its diplomatic acceptability. The lead state must, moreover, be the major state within the region, or—in a region where no single state is marked out by its size and capabilities— one whose role the other main regional states accept. The problem is that leadership is inseparable from power and, indeed, from hegemony: in accepting its right to lead, lesser states within the region concede the lead state's right to exercise power over themselves and, implicitly, to intervene in their own domestic affairs. On some occasions, power differentials may be such that the idea of leadership itself is scarcely appropriate: the U.S.-led intervention in Grenada in 1983 was carried out in collaboration with a group of eastern Caribbean states led by the Dominican prime minister Eugenia Charles, whose appearance at a press conference beside President Ronald Reagan aroused only bewilderment as to who on earth she was.

African states, for very understandable reasons, have been particularly sensitive to any threat to their sovereignty and reluctant to accept the leadership of regional powers by which that sovereignty might be eroded. This sensitivity underlies the commitment to the sovereign equality of all member states in the Charter of the OAU and the refusal of the OAU to establish any equivalent to the UN Security Council. Regional leadership in Africa is also readily eroded by the ability of smaller states to look for protection outside the region, notably to superpowers or former colonial powers, which may themselves seek to limit the pretensions of would-be regional leaders. Nigeria's capacity to exercise leadership within West Africa, for example, has been constantly inhibited by the ability of smaller states in the region, most of which are francophone, to seek protection from France. South Africa has been deeply skeptical of regional security schemes promoted by the United States.

Cracking the problem of regional leadership clearly calls for sensitive diplomacy, notably on the part of the would-be hegemonic state, and for close and friendly relations, especially at heads of state level. It also, and more critically, requires an agreed basis for security collaboration, which is accepted and secured by the regional leader, and in which the leader recognizes its obligation to act only in accordance with a consensus of the regional community as a whole. The recognition of the rights of smaller states must be built into this consensus. If democracy is to be the basis for regional security, then it is likewise essential for the regional leader to be unimpeachably democratic itself. The promotion of democracy in Liberia and Sierra Leone by an ECOWAS Monitoring Group (ECOMOG) force led by General Sani Abacha's Nigeria was always problematic. Though South Africa now incontestably meets the democracy criterion, its ability to develop effective regional leadership is still significantly impeded by the traumatic impact of the *apartheid* era on instability in Southern Africa, as well as by problems of securing acceptance of its leadership credentials in states such as Angola and Zimbabwe.

At least in West and Southern Africa, however, these problems are not insuperable, and recent developments have done a great deal to encourage the hope that they can be overcome. In Northeast and Central Africa, on the other hand, there are structural (rather than merely practical) problems that make the development of effective regional security systems extremely difficult to envisage. In each region, there are bitter legacies of conflict that—as the recent Ethio-Eritrean and Congo wars all too clearly indicate—are very hard to overcome. In the Horn, neighboring states have been constructed in such different ways that their conceptions of security are inherently at odds. In Central Africa, the only potential regional leader, Congo, is itself so weak and divided that it creates opportunities for intervention within itself, rather than serving as a base from which to promote stability elsewhere.

The Domestic Political Setting

It is much more difficult to suggest general answers to the problem of how to secure a mandate for intervention within the *domestic* politics of potentially intervening states. Different states, and their peoples, have different conceptions of their external rights or obligations. In Western Europe, for example, both France and the United Kingdom retain a post-imperial vision of their places in the world that is entirely lacking in Germany or Italy. They are correspondingly much readier to intervene in regional crises like those in the former Yugoslavia. In Africa, Nigerian élites have long shared a sense of the country's "leadership role" in West Africa, and indeed the continent as a whole, whereas the post-*apartheid* South African government has been altogether more inhibited. Different countries are accordingly more or less willing to accept the costs of intervention: one of the most striking features of the post–Cold War era has been the reluctance of public opinion in the sole potential global hegemonic state, the United States, to accept the death of even a single American soldier as an appropriate price to be paid for that hegemony.

Two broad though paradoxical conclusions can, however, be drawn from the greatly increased level of democracy in Africa since the end of the Cold War. On the one hand, the development of effective political mandates for regional peace-keeping requires states to be able to maintain support for intervention among their own populations. As already noted, democracy provides by far the most satisfactory basis for the creation of regional security systems, not least because it helps to ensure a correspondence between international security and security at the level of the ordinary citizen. If and as African states become increasingly democratic, they should become increasingly secure, externally as well as internally. On the other hand, domestic electorates place domestic (and especially economic) concerns at the head of their policy agendas and are characteristically extremely reluctant to support external military activities. In very many ways, this is no bad thing. Democratic states are far less likely than autocratic ones to engage in external aggression, and their populations are generally deeply aware of the close relationship between the external use of military force and domestic repression—a relationship made very clear in Zimbabwe in 1999 by the torture by the military authorities of two journalists who had written critically about the internal implications of Zimbabwe's intervention in the DRC. The same inhibitions, however, equally apply to engagement in peacekeeping missions; especially when human and financial costs escalate, voters find it difficult to see why their countries should be engaged in humanitarian activities beyond their borders. The advent of democracy in both South Africa and Nigeria has, on the one hand, reduced the threat that each state poses to its neighbors, but has, on the other, reduced their willingness to help maintain regional security. These are two sides of the same coin. Democracy thus does impose on would-be intervening states an obligation to educate their citizens as to the importance of regional security for their own welfare.

Mandates for the Peacekept

The welfare of the peoples of the intervened-in state, and of the immediate region whose own security is affected by conflict—the peacekept, in other words—provides the ultimate justification for any intervention.[1] That the intervention should secure the backing of these people is central to the moral, as well as the political, mandate of the operation. At the same time, such a mission is extraordinarily difficult and may well often be impossible to achieve in its entirety, since the existence of very serious differences among the peacekept necessarily forms the precondition for intervention in the first place. Equally, the interests of the peacekept are often almost entirely ignored in the formation of the peacekeeping force itself. While the participation of the different peacekeeping countries, and the rules of engagement under which these will operate, are the subject of active diplomacy among the would-be peacekeepers, it is readily assumed (as in Somalia) that the peacekept will necessarily welcome and benefit from the operation, and they may not be consulted at all. With this in mind, we must look at the interface between peacekeepers and peacekept and relate this interface to the conditions under which peacekeeping operations are most likely to succeed and to the problems which they must avert if they are not to fail.

First, while outsiders may view conflicts as "irrational" and meaninglessly destructive, the conflicting parties, in their own estimation, are likely to be fighting for good reason. Outsiders characteristically have difficulty in distinguishing Tutsi from Hutu, Mano from Krahn, or Abgal from Habr Gidir, and find it difficult to understand why such divisions should fuel and channel (even if they do not directly "cause") the conflicts which they have come to settle. For insiders, these divisions matter. In any case serious enough to call for external peacekeeping, moreover, the conflict almost invariably will have been taking place for a considerable period and will have destroyed lives, property, and domestic political institutions; exacerbated distrust; and intensified the divisions along which they have been socially structured.

Second, domestic combatants can rarely be expected to share the broad value orientations of the intervening forces. Even the commitment to peace itself cannot be taken for granted, and what "peace" means to the combatants may be very different from what it means to the peacekeepers. For peacekeepers, the commitment to "peace" itself is inherently *procedural*, since it presupposes that conflicts can be resolved by means from which violence is excluded; from this premise follows a belief in negotiation and compromise, validated by reference to the democratic rights of the majority and the universal human rights of minorities as the means through which disputes should be resolved.

For combatants, on the other hand, *substantive* questions take precedence over procedural ones: they are basically concerned about who wins, not about the means by which victory is secured. A lack of any deep commitment to peaceful conflict resolution, among at least a substantial element of the conflicting forces, is presupposed by the fact that conflict is taking place at all. Nor can it be assumed that combatants will share the values which, to many of the peacekeepers, form part of an elementary conception of "humanity." The Rwandan genocide provides the most traumatic example of deliberate behavior on the part of combatants which for most of the would-be peacekeepers fell way beyond any conceivable idea of human action. The actions of Somali warlords, or the casual butchery of civilian populations in Liberia, provide further examples of the gulf in expected standards of action between peacekeepers and peacekept. In some cases, this gulf creates deep antipathy for the peacekept among the peacekeepers and helps to account for (though not to justify) human rights abuses by the peacekeepers which would otherwise be difficult to understand.[2]

This lack of commitment to "humanitarian" values and concern for substantive rather than procedural issues is often especially marked among the leaders of conflicting parties, who are at the same time the people with whom the peacekeepers have to deal. Leaders such as Mohamed Farah Aideed in Somalia, Charles Taylor in Liberia, and Jonas Savimbi in Angola have readily been condemned for their lack of humanity and for their selfishness and unscrupulousness in undermining peacekeeping proposals and reneging on commitments that they had promised to honor. But condemnation is no substitute for explanation: as political entrepreneurs who are fighting for very high stakes and who have placed their own lives (along with those of many other people) in the balance, such leaders can be expected to fight by every means at their disposal.

Third, the peacekeeping operation itself is necessarily viewed in a very different light from the two sides. Peacekeepers necessarily view themselves as bringing *solutions* to the conflicts that they are concerned to resolve. That is why they are there. These solutions, of course, vary widely according to the nature of the conflict itself and the level of agreement that has been reached by the internal parties; in some cases, as in Zimbabwe in 1979–1980, Namibia in 1989, and Mozambique in 1993–1994, the peacekeepers saw themselves as helping to assure the proper implementation of a settlement which had already been broadly agreed; in others, as in Liberia in 1990 and Somalia in 1992, they intervened in an attempt to impose a solution on parties who had not been able to achieve one themselves. Regardless of these variations, peacekeepers differ from participants, who perceive peacekeepers as contributing *resources*, which may be captured and used by one or more of the internal parties to the conflict in order to improve their own position within the conflict itself.

Peacekeepers may affect internal power relations even in cases where their role is technical and restricted. In Namibia, for example, the UN Transition Assistance Group (UNTAG) force was in some degree "captured" by the South African administration of the territory and used to ensure that at least some of its residual objectives (notably, preventing the South West African People's Organisation [SWAPO] from gaining a critical two-thirds majority in the elections) were achieved.[3] The more distant the prospects of a settlement and the more fluid the internal military situation, the greater are the opportunities offered to conflicting parties to manipulate the peacekeepers in such a way as to strengthen their own position vis-à-vis their internal rivals. The troubles of UNOSOM in Somalia and

ECOMOG in Liberia, as well as the strained relations between UNAMIR II and the newly installed Rwandan Patriotic Front (RPF) regime in Rwanda, all arose from the way in which peacekeeping forces were absorbed into the very conflicts that they had expected to resolve.

Nor are the resources that peacekeepers have to offer only political ones. In some cases, and Somalia provides the extreme example, peacekeepers bring financial resources which can be captured or expropriated in one way or another by the parties to the conflict and used in order to sustain the conflict itself.[4] Given that Somalia is an extremely poor country, offering a very limited economic base from which to maintain a long-lasting and highly destructive form of warfare, it can plausibly be argued that the peacekeepers, with the massive amounts of money and aid that they brought with them, helped to keep the conflict going at a level that would scarcely have been possible had the competing factions had to rely on the resources available on the spot. The provision of relief aid to Rwandan refugee camps in Zaire after July 1994, controlled as these were by the elements in the former Rwandan government who had been responsible for the genocide, is a further example of how external resources can be diverted in such a way as to foment conflict rather than resolve it.

Finally, peacekeepers tend to think in the short term, whereas combatants necessarily have to think in the long term. Peacekeeping is an "operation" that is bounded in time. There is no permanent role for peacekeeping forces in the domestic politics of the states in which they intervene: their mission is to come in, sort things out, and then leave. Almost invariably, they badly underestimate the length of time for which they will have to stay. The Unified Task Force (UNITAF) dispatched by Bush, which stormed ashore at Mogadishu in December 1992, initially expected to leave in time for the inauguration of President Clinton in the following month. But regardless of how long they have to stay, the end-point for peacekeepers is the moment when they can pull out, preferably leaving behind them some form of internal settlement that enables them to present the operation as a success. But the end-point for the peacekeepers is often no more than the starting point for the peacekept. They are—unless exterminated or driven out—permanent actors on the local political stage. Their prime concern is to position themselves as advantageously as possible for the moment when they are left to resume their domestic rivalries without external interference. What matters is whether the peacekeepers have left behind a domestic government capable of seeing off any challenges to its position, or whether their departure is no more than the signal for internal combatants to resume their rivalries unencumbered by external forces.

The effect of all of these considerations is to give the peacekept enormous leverage over the peacekeepers in the constant struggles for bargaining advantage that characterize the peculiar politics of peacekeeping operations. Peacekeepers readily assume their own "superiority" in approaching the situations that confront them. Characteristically drawn from the sophisticated armies of industrial states, with their high levels of discipline, training, equipment, and technological expertise, peacekeepers view themselves as coming in from the outside in order to help sort out the problems of underdeveloped states whose people have been unable to resolve those problems without external aid. In practice, the boot is almost invariably on the other foot. Domestic combatants have a clearer and longer-term view of what they are trying to achieve; they are uncluttered (or uninhibited) by the value systems within which the peacekeepers are operating; they are often very well aware of the domestic and international constraints on the behavior of the peacekeepers, while suffering from few such constraints themselves; and they have a far better grasp of the local political scene. Peacekeeping operations are therefore often most appropriately analyzed, not from the perspective of the peacekeepers, but from the perspective of local combatants using peacekeepers within the framework of their own internal conflicts.

Peacekeeping operations in Africa provide a highly varied range of situations within which to explore the relationships between internal political factions and those who come to keep the peace between them, and correspondingly make it possible to sketch out broad typologies of the way in which these relationships may work. These cases fall into three main categories. First, exemplified by Zimbabwe in 1980 and Namibia in 1989, are those that may be characterized as "pacted transitions." There is an internal political (and not merely constitutional) settlement that is broadly accepted by the major actors and that the external peacekeeping forces are brought in to guarantee. Second, there are "provisional settlements," which have been negotiated, usually under strong external pressure, by the internal combatants, but do not incorporate any broadly accepted political formula. In these cases, which include Angola, Mozambique, and Rwanda, the role of the external peacekeeping forces that are brought in to help manage the settlement is very much more uncertain. In the third category, that of "direct interventions," the peacekeeping forces intervene in ongoing conflicts in which no settlement has been agreed, and their relationship with the combatants carries a very high potential for conflict. Liberia and Somalia are the clearest examples of this type.

Pacted Transitions

In Zimbabwe and Namibia, as later in South Africa, the outlines of a settlement were clear from the moment that the white minority regime recognized that it could not continue to govern without the domestic and external legitimacy provided by internationally accepted majority rule. One side of this settlement was that open and internationally supervised elections would take place on a universal franchise, the winners of which—necessarily the African nationalist movement, which won most votes—would take over the government. The other side was that the minority could use the constitutional negotiations in order to entrench residual rights, which would likewise need to be internationally guaranteed. This settlement, moreover, could be expected to hold politically. The white minority would accept the advent of majority rule because they recognized their inability to resist it and because acceptance was preferable to continuing war as a means of maintaining their own long-term interests in the management of the state and the economy. The incoming majority could likewise be expected to accept the pact because they relied on the minority to supply essential services in the management of the state and the economy, which they needed but could not provide themselves. In short, they wanted to inherit an effective state and a working economy, and they needed the whites to help run it.

In these circumstances, the role of the peacekeepers was relatively straightforward because they could—short of thorough mismanagement on their own part—rely on the acquiescence and even the support of the most powerful groups among the peacekept. They were always liable to be manipulated, more or less knowingly or willingly, by one or both of the major internal parties to the settlement. But the underlying pact on which the settlement was based was robust enough for inevitable (and sometimes justified) charges of favoritism not to upset it. The anti-Zimbabwe African National Union (ZANU) bias shown by the British force in Zimbabwe, and the anti-SWAPO bias shown by the UN force in Namibia, did not prevent either of these parties from taking power. The problems in these cases arose from the predicament of those who were abandoned in the process of reaching an agreement acceptable to the holders of state and economic power on the one hand, and majority votes on the other: the [Abel] Muzorewa faction and the Zimbabwe African People's Union (ZAPU) in Zimbabwe, and the Democratic Turnhalle Alliance (DTA) in Namibia. These, however, were not problems for the peacekeepers but could be left for resolution once they had been withdrawn.

Provisional Settlements

The position is very different in the case of provisional settlements. In these cases, even though the internal combatants had been placed under sufficient external pressure to induce them to accept a negotiated solution, it did not have built into it any broadly accepted underlying pact. The key prize—control over the state—remained unallocated and was due to be determined by a subsequent election in the case of Angola and Mozambique and by an extraordinarily complex and unworkable power-sharing agreement (to be followed at some future date by a new constitution and elections to be held under it) in the case of Rwanda. In Rwanda, in particular, the two major actors—the Mouvement républicain national pour le développement et la démocratie (MRNDD) government and the RPF insurgent movement—were deeply irreconcilable, while it could not be assumed in either Angola or Mozambique that the incumbent Popular Movement for the Liberation of Angola (MPLA) and the Front for the Liberation of Mozambique (FRELIMO) governments, or the UNITA and Mozambique National Resistance (RENAMO) insurgencies would willingly accept electoral victories by their opponents. Even though the Mozambican settlement proved to be remarkably successful, "many more people died in Angola and Rwanda *after* peace agreements failed than during the years of war that preceded them," indicating that misconceived peace settlements can result in damage far greater than would have occurred had no attempt at conflict resolution been made at all.[5]

In such cases, peacekeepers are placed in a critical and invidious intermediary position. Rather than simply monitoring the implementation of a settlement that has in its essentials been agreed between the major internal parties, they are required to enforce a settlement which—signatures on a piece of paper notwithstanding—has never really been agreed. Combatants frequently agree, in principle, to peace proposals that they have no intention of implementing or to settlements that they will accept only if they emerge as the winners. Though they sometimes simply miscalculate their prospects of success, apparent acquiescence is often a useful bargaining strategy, designed to improve their access to external diplomatic, military, and financial resources and to place the onus for continuing conflict on their opponents. The relationship between peacekept and peacekeepers under these circumstances depends in part on the leverage that the peacekeepers are able to exert on the internal factions and, in part, on the resources available to the factions themselves and the factions' capacities to manipulate the peacekeepers to their own advantage. The first of these has understandably gained the greater attention, especially from those concerned to account for the failure of peacekeeping operations from the viewpoint of the peacekeepers. Both in Angola and in Rwanda, this failure led to appalling suffering and loss of life, and the need for peacekeepers to learn the appropriate lessons was therefore acute and deeply felt. In each case, the small size and tardy deployment of the peacekeeping force could be blamed, along with the precipitate withdrawal of the UNAMIR force at precisely the moment when it could have saved the lives of a great many people from slaughter.

At the same time, the differences between Angola and Rwanda on the one hand,

and the successful implementation of the peace process in Mozambique on the other, lay far more with the peacekept than with the peacekeepers. The factions responsible for breakdown—the MRNDD government and its supporters in Rwanda and the UNITA insurgent movement in Angola—in each case disposed of substantial political and military resources and had little, if anything, to gain from the implementation of a settlement from which they could only be the losers. In Angola, it had been an article of faith with Savimbi, ever since the precipitate Portuguese withdrawal in 1975, that had there been an election at the time of independence, he and his FNLA allies would have won it. It was in the belief that this was still true that he agreed to take part in the 1992 elections. With the loss of the election, readily rationalized as due to electoral fraud, he could immediately fall back on the army that he had not demobilized (and which it is extremely unlikely that he would ever voluntarily have demobilized) and on the financial resources provided especially by his control over many of the country's diamond fields. Had the vote gone the other way, the acquiescence of the MPLA government would have been every bit as problematic.

In Rwanda, it was the incumbent government—and notably the diehard Hutu supremacists within it—which stood to lose from the settlement and which had the capacity to nullify it. The peculiar circumstances under which the Arusha accords had been negotiated had given an exceptional degree of leverage both to the RPF and to the minority parties within the governing coalition in Kigali, which the MRNDD was obliged to accept under international pressure.[6] The Habyarimana regime and its allies, who had entrenched themselves deeply in power over a period of twenty years, were reduced, under the transitional arrangement agreed at Arusha, to a mere five members of a twenty-one member council of ministers, within which a two-thirds majority was necessary for any measure to be passed. Given that their would-be partners under the Arusha settlement were people to whom they were virulently (and, as it transpired, genocidally) hostile, that they controlled the national army, the regional administration, and the *interahamwe* death squads which they were then training, and that they had (so they felt, at least) an unconditional assurance of French support, their incentive to abide by the Arusha settlement was non-existent. In Rwanda, certainly, an actively deployed peacekeeping force could have saved a great many people from the appalling fate that befell them; but there, as in Angola, the formally agreed settlement could only plausibly have been implemented had this force been large, well-armed, and prepared to take a combatant role that lay well beyond the normal bounds of "peacekeeping" by multinational forces.[7]

The Mozambican story was different, not because of any major differences in the peacekeeping operation, but because of the very different situation of the peacekept, both the FRELIMO government and the RENAMO opposition. Mozambique had no equivalent to the oil and diamonds that gave the Angolan factions their autonomy. Both government and insurgents were deeply dependent on Western aid, which could be used to lever each of them to the negotiating table and to ensure that they would broadly abide by the outcome. RENAMO, in particular, had lost the autonomy that it had gained from its relationship with the *apartheid* regime in South Africa, and it lacked independent resources. Consistent external pressure, coupled with the "side payments" in terms of development aid and a role in local government, were enough to keep it in line.

Direct Interventions

The most critical problems, however, have arisen in those cases, as in Liberia and Somalia, in which peacekeepers have directly intervened in on-going conflicts, without even the very limited security afforded by a provisional settlement—an activity often referred to as "peacemaking," rather than "peacekeeping." In both Liberia and Somalia, the assumption that since the peacekeepers were more powerful than any of the local factions in terms of their numbers, weaponry, and organization, this strength would be enough to enable them to impose a solution to the conflict, turned out to be completely misconceived.

For a start, any claim by the peacekeepers to be neutral, as between the different contending parties to the conflict in which they intervened, rapidly became unsustainable. This claim, for a start, was not always made in good faith. In Liberia, especially, the ECOMOG states sided first with Samuel Doe and then with Amos Sawyer's Interim Government of National Unity (IGNU) against Charles Taylor's National Patriotic Front of Liberia (NPFL). In Somalia, however, the United States had no evident reason to support any of the numerous warlords against any of the others, and its claim to neutrality *in intention* may be accepted. In practice, it made no difference. Intervening forces become involved in the conflicts in which they have intervened and, in the process, come to favor some parties more than others, entirely regardless of what their initial intentions may have been. Neutrality proved as impossible to maintain in Somalia, where the U.S. forces were barely aware of the identity of the different factions before they moved in, as in Liberia.

The central problem is that the arrival of the intervening force in itself affects the balance of power between the different internal factions. By interposing itself between the combatants, or by taking control of places or resources that they had hoped to gain for themselves, the intervening force necessarily disadvantages some factions and, in the process, advantages others. Those who gain from its presence welcome it, whereas those who lose treat it with suspicion. Normally, the intervention freezes the military situation and thus prevents whichever faction is currently on the offensive from pressing home its military advantage. It thus helps the faction which is in the weakest military position, which therefore looks to the intervening force to protect it against its rival. In Liberia, the strongest faction at the time of ECOMOG's arrival in August 1990 was Taylor's NPFL, which then controlled most of the country and was about to launch an attack on Monrovia; from its viewpoint, ECOMOG cheated it of victory. In Somalia, Aideed's was the stronger of the two main factions fighting for control of Mogadishu and viewed UNITAF in much the same way as Taylor did ECOMOG. His weaker rival, Ali Mahdi Mohamed, had every reason to see UNITAF as relieving cavalry.

It is, in any event, very hard for an intervening force, suddenly thrust into an unfamiliar and dangerous environment, to avoid regarding those who help and support it as its friends and those who oppose it (and very possibly shoot at it) as its enemies. Even if it does not choose sides itself, sides are effectively chosen for it by the combatants. Once the force is on the ground, incidents almost inevitably occur that serve to confirm the preconceptions of the local contestants. In Somalia in February 1993, for example, an anti-Aideed faction managed to seize part of the town of Kismayo by a *coup de main*, catching the UNITAF peacekeepers by surprise. When Aideed's ally Omar Jess tried a similar trick a few days later, the peacekeepers were on their guard and managed to foil it. From Aideed's point of view, it was hard to avoid the conclusion that UNITAF had sided with his opponents—but if this particular event had not occurred to create that impression, almost certainly some other incident would have had the same effect.

But the intervening force is not merely compelled to take sides: almost inevitably, it finds itself lining up against the strongest of the domestic factions. This, in turn, not only exacerbates its military position but impedes any attempt to negotiate a political settlement and achieve its own withdrawal. Its presence becomes essential to the weaker groups which have become its clients and an affront to the stronger groups whose support is needed in order to achieve any lasting settlement. An understandable reluctance to abandon its allies to retaliation by its opponents only drags it deeper into the mire.

In both Liberia and Somalia, the manipulation of peacekeepers by peacekept is likewise illustrated by the numerous and invariably unsuccessful attempts to negotiate a settlement. A mere roll-call of failed mediations, named after the places where they took place, conveys a sense of their futility: the Freetown, Banjul I, Bamako, Banjul II, Virginia, Yamoussoukro I, Yamoussoukro II, Yamoussoukro III, Yamoussoukro IV, Geneva, Cotonou, Akosombo, and Accra agreements on Liberia; the Djibouti I, Djibouti II, Addis Ababa I, Addis Ababa II, Addis Ababa III and Nairobi agreements on Somalia. There is no point in going into the details. An attempt to establish a political structure that all of the indigenous parties can be induced to accept is virtually built into the peacekeeping enterprise. The peacekeepers cannot simply impose a settlement themselves, after the manner of a conquering army of occupation; nor can they blatantly side with one of the combatants and help it to impose a settlement on the others. It is therefore a necessary part of the operation that all—or virtually all—of the contending parties should agree. This in turn gives any major party a veto power over a settlement.

At the same time, however, the fact that the peacekeepers have arrived in order to impose a settlement, at a period when the contestants are not yet ready to agree on a settlement among themselves, means that the local factions are unlikely to have any real commitment to any agreement that is reached. For the peacekeepers, the settlement has a strategic goal: it is intended to put in place a new political order, which will ensure stability and enable them to withdraw. For the peacekept, it is no more than a tactical device, intended to buy time while they regroup for further conflict. Combatants may be induced to accept a settlement when one is negotiated in some outside location simply because they do not want to lose external support by appearing to reject it. Their acceptance does not carry any assurance that they will actually abide by the settlement once they return to their forces on the ground.

The process of negotiation in itself tends to strengthen the position of the leaders of the various armed groups or warlords, since these are the people who have to take part in it. The patient creation of a civilian political structure is much too costly, in terms of both the time required and the need to disarm the military factions, to be a practicable option for the peacekeeping force. During the first months of the UNOSOM I operation in 1992, before the UNITAF intervention, UN special envoy Mohamed Sahnoun tried to follow a strategy of building up links with clan elders in order slowly to undermine the position of warlords like Aideed or his rival in Mogadishu, Ali Mahdi; Sahnoun was later to describe this strategy as trying to pluck a bird's feathers one by one, until it could no longer fly. Whether or not this strategy could have succeeded, Sahnoun was given no opportunity to pursue it by a UN leadership in New York, which demanded faster results and eventually pushed him to resign. Subsequent UN representatives took the *realpolitik* approach—that it was necessary to do a deal with the people who had the power, the leaders of the military factions. In the process, they helped to give these leaders a level of external legitimacy that they might not otherwise have possessed and to enable them equally to reinforce their domestic control.

In Liberia, it worked rather differently, but the eventual result was much the same. After Doe's death in September 1990, ECOMOG sought to establish a regime in Monrovia with which it could do business and held a meeting of Liberian notables in the Gambia in order to select an interim president. Their choice of Sawyer, a man universally respected for his courage and integrity under both the Doe and the preceding William Tolbert administrations, could scarcely have been faulted. Established under ECOMOG protection in Monrovia, deprived of the opportunity to build up a political following in the rest of the country, which was controlled by Taylor, and obliged to work with the military factions which had sided with ECOMOG (and which notably included the unsavory remnants of Doe's brutal army), Sawyer nonetheless became little more than the prisoner of ECOMOG. He was eventually happy to give up the presidency and retire to private life.

Another way in which the external attempt to negotiate a political settlement easily becomes self-defeating is through the proliferation of factions. The peacekeeping force both protects factions against being suppressed and absorbed by more powerful groups and, by holding negotiations in which faction leaders bargain under the aegis of ECOMOG or UNOSOM for positions in a newly established government of national unity, encourages each and every would-be leader to establish his own faction in order to protect his negotiating position. Sometimes this proliferation of factions is encouraged by the intervention force, in order to divide and weaken existing groups; ECOMOG has plausibly been accused of establishing and arming factions in Liberia so as to undermine the NPFL. Sometimes factions divide because subordinates within them try to displace the leader or secede with their supporters to set up new factions on their own; the NPFL divided when the representatives whom Taylor had appointed to the newly established transitional government in 1994 rejected his leadership. In Liberia, factions that had not been represented at the meeting which established the transitional government, such as the Lofa Defence Force, demanded a place in it. Factions that had been involved in the negotiations (such as the Armed Forces of Liberia) reinvented themselves under a different name (the Liberia Peace Council), in order to avoid adherence to the cease-fire conditions to which they had agreed.

Neither in Liberia nor in Somalia did any of the participating factions feel any obligation to abide by the conditions that they had accepted under pressure from external peacemakers. These were not "real" negotiations or "real" conditions, since the discussions in Addis Ababa and Akosombo bore no discernible relationship to developments in Mogadishu or Monrovia. The saddest commentary on the process was provided by the UN special envoy for Liberia, a decent but entirely ineffectual Jamaican diplomat named Trevor Gordon-Somers, who, after one of the Liberian faction leaders had instantly reneged on a commitment to disarmament, complained that he had assumed that the negotiations had been conducted in good faith. He should have known better. It was only once Taylor and the Abacha government in Nigeria came to appreciate the futility of fighting against one another—at enormous cost to Liberians—that it became possible to broker a settlement in which the dominant regional state allied with the dominant internal faction to produce at least the possibility of restoring peace, a deal which was then validated by the July 1997 elections. In Somalia, any viable working arrangement had to await the complete withdrawal of the peacekeepers.

Conclusion

Though the development of robust political mandates among the peacekeepers is certainly an essential requirement for successful peacekeeping operations, success, in practice, has depended still more on the ability of the intervening force to develop a viable mandate among the peacekept. Only where a peace settlement or "pact" had already been broadly agreed between the major combatants could the peacekeepers play the role, in helping to ensure that the terms of the pact were honored on both sides, that conventional peacekeeping has assumed. On occasion, and notably in Mozambique, the bargaining position of the internal parties was sufficiently weak, and the leverage exercised by the peacekeepers was sufficiently great, for peacekeepers to be able to play a critical role in helping to resolve a very damaging conflict. Elsewhere, peacekeepers have all too often been dragged into conflicts that they could not resolve and all too often unwittingly helped to exacerbate. So, what are the lessons that potential intervenors should learn about maintaining their mandates among local populations? There are three negative lessons and some more positive suggestions to guide intervenors in what is always the very difficult task of peacemaking.

The first lesson is that, in an intervention, impartiality is a delusion. Intervention necessarily favors some local groups and leaders and disadvantages others. Even though intervention forces may find it essential to maintain at least an appearance of neutrality and to avoid needlessly offending local actors whose support or acquiescence may be important, they must recognize that their role is deeply political and plan accordingly. In particular, they need to ensure that their inevitable political engagement results from their own priorities and that they do not get forced into an unwanted political position through the manipulations of local factions.

A second lesson concerns the dangers of unworkable paper settlements. Often, there is enormous pressure on peacemakers to get the rival local factions to sign up to some kind of agreement, usually negotiated at a neutral venue outside the country, that has no plausible prospect of success and then is denounced and ignored as soon as the faction leaders return to their own country. Settlements can only be expected to work when they rest on a viable distribution of power among the domestic groupings involved.

A third danger is that of assuming that the responsible conduct of parties to a dispute, or their respect for human rights, provides any guide to their political support. When they are consulted, African electorates in conflict zones generally demonstrate an eminently rational assessment of the options open to them, which is often completely at variance from the expectations of outside observers. There can be no doubt, for example, that RENAMO in Mozambique was guilty of the most appalling atrocities. Yet in the 1994 elections, RENAMO received substantial support in the very areas where those atrocities had been committed. Taylor received 75 percent of the votes in the Liberian elections of 1997, despite (or indeed because of) the fact that he was largely responsible for the war which had brought untold misery to virtually all Liberians.[8] External mediators and peacekeepers readily assume that those domestic political actors who collaborate most reasonably with them will be likewise favored by the local electorate, but this is often far from being the case.

What more positive suggestions can then be made to guide peacemakers in their extremely difficult task of maintaining a local mandate for their mission and encouraging the eventual achievement of a viable political settlement? It must be emphasized that this task is indeed a difficult one—major political difficulties in the country made the intervention necessary in the first place—and that success is never assured. However, some basic principles can be identified.

First, it is critical to identify the essential bases for a settlement, which must in turn rest on the major sources of *power* within the country, and to act in such a way that these sources of power are incorporated into the settlement that the peacemakers are attempting to achieve, rather than alienated from it. These sources of power, in turn, break down into a number of elements, which may or may not be readily combined with one another. The first of these is demographic: no settlement that excludes the largest and most strategically placed population groups in the country is likely to succeed. A second is economic: most African states depend on very limited economic resources, which are often located in geographically restricted areas, and it is essential to ensure that these resources (and those who control them) are incorporated into the settlement. A third consists of the human resources that are needed to run a government, which may extend also to its military resources: though the peacemaking force may be able to influence the distribution of power, for example by neutralizing a particularly troublesome faction, it will be able to do so only to a limited extent.

The second major requirement is to identify a viable political leadership.

African states depend on leadership to a very high degree, and it is futile to expect any settlement to work unless someone is visibly in charge. Power-sharing constitutions readily appeal to those who are nurtured in the liberal political cultures of the Western world and gain a superficial plausibility from the way in which they can be used to help satisfy the competing demands of rival political leaders and factions, but they are unlikely to work out in practice. Some individuals, equally, have the capacity to exercise this leadership, whereas others do not, and a hardheaded assessment of the potential candidates is essential.

Third, once these basic requirements have been satisfied, it is important to identify plausible political coalitions through which potentially disappointed groups and individuals can be given an incentive to help support the political settlement, rather than undermine it. The restoration of peace to badly disrupted communities requires a commitment to reconciling all those who can be brought into the political process, without endangering that process itself. The policy of national reconciliation implemented by Museveni after 1986 provides an obvious example. On some occasions, it may even be necessary to buy off potentially obstructive faction leaders whose first concern is for their own personal welfare.

Finally, however, it must be recognized that this process of reconciliation is unlikely to be extendable to every group within a country. One of the most tragic consequences of protracted civil wars is that they bring to prominence groups and individuals who acquire a vested interest in continued conflict and have every reason to undermine whatever settlement may be reached. Some "spoilers" may simply be irreconcilable or indeed (understandably, given the traumas that such conflicts induce) psychologically disturbed. While every effort should be made to reduce their numbers to a minimum, for example, through rehabilitation programs for former combatants or by trying to split away the associates of a particularly obdurate faction leader, there is likely to come a point at which the settlement needs to be enforced, and the intervenors must be responsible for enforcing it.

These principles are easily enunciated. Implementing them, given the varying structures of different African states and amid the confusion and uncertainty of civil conflicts, is very difficult. It may not always even be possible.

Notes

1. This section draws on Christopher Clapham, "Being Peacekept," in Oliver Furley and Roy May (eds.), *Peacekeeping in Africa* (Aldershot, 1998), 303–19.

2. Human rights abuses by Belgian, Canadian, and Italian forces in Somalia attracted particular notice.

3. See Donna Pankhurst, "Namibia," in Furley and May, *Peacekeeping*, 207–22.

4. See Andrew S. Natsios, "Humanitarian Relief Intervention in Somalia: The Economics of Chaos," in Walter Clarke and Jeffrey Herbst (eds.), *Learning from Somalia: The Lessons of Armed Humanitarian Intervention* (Boulder, 1997), 77–95.

5. Stephen J. Stedman and Donald Rothchild, "Peace Operations: From Short-Term to Long-Term Commitment," *International Peacekeeping*, III (1996), 18.

6. I have examined the problems of the Rwanda settlement in Clapham, "Rwanda: The Perils of Peace-Making," *Journal of Peace Research*, XXXV (1998), 193–210. See also Gerard Prunier, *The Rwanda Crisis 1959–1994: History of a Genocide* (London, 1995), especially chapters 4 and 5; and Helen M. Hintjens, "Explaining the 1994 Genocide in Rwanda," *Journal of Modern African Studies,* XXXVII (1999), 241–86.

7. See Alan J. Kuperman, "Rwanda in Retrospect," *Foreign Affairs,* 79 (2000), 94–118.

8. See Charles Harris, "From 'Warlord' to 'Democratic' President: How Charles Taylor Won the 1997 Liberian Elections," *Journal of Modern African Studies*, XXXVII (1999), 431–55.

CHAPTER FOUR

African Peacekeeping and American Strategy

Steven Metz

THE AMERICAN PUBLIC and its elected leaders know little about Africa. Based on what they do know, hear, and see, Americans do not perceive either great strategic opportunities in Africa or significant risks if the region were totally left to its own devices: in Peter Schraeder's words, Africa has long formed a "backwater" for American policymakers.[1] Shaped by media sensationalism, the dominant image of Africa among Americans is very much that of a confusing "heart of darkness," a Hobbesian morass of constant war, famine, and violence. Better the United States should stay away, most think. Americans are torn between the urge to help Africa and the fear that doing so will become a waste of money and blood. Against this backdrop, American policymakers have searched for ways to play a role in Africa but with minimal costs or risks. Multinational peacekeeping is one way. Hence, the incentives for American involvement in African peacekeeping are great.

It is a daunting task. Africa is the region of the world most in need of effective structures and procedures for multinational peacekeeping. Internal violence, often with international dimensions, is common. And, because neither African states nor the militias, rebels, and insurgents who confront them have the military means to attain decisive military victory, conflicts often drag on, destroying fragile infra-

The opinions expressed here are solely those of the author and do not represent the official positions of the U.S. Department of Defense, Department of the Army, or the U.S. Army War College.

structure and leading to humanitarian disasters and refugee crises. Once such a conflict does occur, other African states, even when they would like to intervene, seldom have the resources to deploy and sustain military forces over great distances, or to create the sort of integrated command structure that a multinational peacekeeping operation needs. As a result, outsiders, whether individual states or international organizations, play a vital role in African conflicts.

If African states were able to develop the ability to deploy, sustain, and control effective multinational peacekeeping forces, many of the region's conflicts could be contained, ensuring the stability that is so essential for long-term progress. Africa needs an effective regional peacekeeping capability. But Africans will need help for some time. While the United States has rhetorical commitment to provide such help, it has not been translated into sustained effort on a scale to make a difference. This result is not surprising: U.S. involvement in African peacekeeping is a recent phenomenon. Only with the end of the Cold War did U.S. policymakers begin to take multinational peacekeeping seriously. Americans still have not yet decided precisely what role the U.S. should play, or how much effort and money should be devoted to it. Progress has been made in recent years as the United States first began to help augment Africa's peacekeeping abilities, but much more remains to be done. Put simply, American involvement in African peacekeeping is very much an undeveloped work.

Anatomy of African Conflicts

Africa needs effective multinational peacekeeping because of the security environment there. Internal wars are common, debilitating, and sometimes intractable. At their root is the weakness of African states. This weakness has many dimensions. For instance, the support base of African leaders is often intense but narrow, leaving many individuals, groups, and organizations as potential opponents. Africa's political practices have not stressed a broad inclusion in political decisionmaking, but rather the construction of narrow power bases built primarily on patron-client webs. Since the state is such a powerful actor in the economy, leaders are in a position to distribute not only political favors to followers, but economic ones as well. A supporter has a much more tangible stake in the preservation of his patron's political power than would a supporter of a particular leader in the West (where the link is as much shared perspectives and values as tangible rewards).

Further, because African regimes control many of the resources that do exist in the state—whether capital, political office, concessions, contracts, or something similar—they are held accountable by the public for a wide range of social and political problems. Stable political systems are those in which *either* the state satisfies a substantial proportion of the public (or at least the segment that can challenge it), or the discontented public blames something other than the government (like fate or external forces) for its misery. Most African states fall in between: their regimes are held accountable but do not have the resources to ameliorate discontent.

The complexity of most African societies also contributes to the frequency of internal war. While ethnic, religious, regional, and clan rifts have always existed, colonialism exacerbated them through patterns of group favoritism and "divide and conquer" policies designed to facilitate the process of administering a large population with a small number of colonial officials. While social divisions do not automatically condemn Africa to protracted violence, the type of rapid social and economic change underway on the continent often politicizes social rifts. Social and economic change breaks down old systems of order and control, setting off struggles to establish new ones. Under such conditions leaders may manipulate social rifts to mobilize support. Once unleashed, primal hatred can prove impossible to control as it rushes beyond the bounds of rational constraints. Just as Alabama Governor George Wallace did not intend to incite church bombings and Slobodan Milosevic may not have intended to cause the horrific massacres in Srebrenica and elsewhere by stoking ethnic enmity, they did precisely that. Today Africa sees a similar pattern as attempts to re-draw the matrix of political power tap deep discontent.

Africa's rapid population growth, when combined with decades of economic stagnation or regression, has dramatically increased the pool of the discontented. Sub-Saharan Africa as a whole, for instance, currently has an annual population growth rate of 2.8 percent, which means a doubling of populations every twenty-five years.[2] Even though there has been a substantial economic upturn in Africa during the past ten years, it remains extremely fragile and easily reversed by bad harvests, natural disasters like the floods that struck Mozambique in 2000, and downturns in the global market for primary products.[3] The World Bank estimates that it will take long-term growth of 8-9 percent per annum to make significant progress in reducing Africa's poverty, one of the foundations of discontent.[4] But, growth has already begun to slow in sub-Saharan Africa. According to the World Bank, it dropped from 4.7 percent in 1996 to around 2.3 percent in 1999.[5] The World Bank expects a 3.6 percent growth rate from 2002 to 2008, but this will barely keep up with population growth, suggesting little if any long-term progress in reversing the continent's poverty.

The fact that Africa is awash in arms facilitates armed violence. Although it is impossible accurately to gauge the number of small arms in circulation, the number is enormous. For example, Mozambique may have imported as many as 6 million small arms during its civil war, while in South Africa there are 4.1 million licensed firearms in civilian hands and somewhere between 400,000 and 8 million illegal ones.[6] Africa also has the heaviest concentration of landmines in the world, with over 30 million.[7] The situation is so serious that the United Nations Security Council passed a resolution expressing "grave concern at the destabilizing effect of illicit arms flows, in particular of small arms, to and in Africa and at their excessive accumulation and circulation, which threaten national, regional and international security and have serious consequences for development and for the humanitarian situation in the continent."[8]

When armed opposition does emerge, the weakness of African states hinders their attempts to seal or safeguard national borders, allowing people, supplies, and arms to pass easily from neighboring states. Contagion effects are common. Most African military forces are small, most having less than 50,000 men, with only a small percentage of them available for deployment abroad.[9] Enlisted personnel are very poorly paid (if paid at all). Even officers in some African armies must engage in outside business to attain a reasonable lifestyle. Since governments offer no social security nets in Africa, many states use the military as a jobs program, taking the uneducated, illiterate, and sickly into the service. Few African states have successfully built a national consensus on the nature of the security threat they face and thus have difficulty ensuring that the size of their military reflects their defense budget and national security objectives, and institutionalizing plans for the long-term development of greater skills and capabilities in their armed forces. Troop strength often reflects historical circumstances rather than present dangers.

African militaries are seldom able to acquire modern equipment or undergo realistic, large-unit training. According to the Kampala *Monitor*, "In most African armies, indiscipline, economic problems and laxity in management have relegated training to the back seat. It is not unusual to find entire brigades who have not fired a rifle since their basic training."[10] African militaries have particular problems with the maintenance of complex equipment; strategic mobility; advanced command, control, and intelligence; air power; and naval power. Often the major equipment that African militaries do acquire is inappropriate and expensive. Recently, for instance, Uganda sought T-55 main battle tanks, while Zimbabwe bought six Hind attack helicopters from Russia and was seeking additional MiG fighter jets.[11] Sometimes African militaries do not have people qualified to operate and maintain the equipment that they do possess. Because of these problems, few African states other than South Africa and, perhaps, Nigeria, Ghana, Ethiopia, Angola, and Zimbabwe are capable of power projection or sustained, intense military operations, despite the wealth of experience and leadership talent among the continent's armed forces.[12]

Theoretically, at least, African states might compensate for their individual weaknesses by constructing effective multinational mechanisms for conflict prevention, response, and resolution. The Organization of African Unity (OAU) has the greatest potential to play this role, but remains ineffective. The OAU was founded in 1963, in part, to protect fragile, new sovereignties. Its charter did not envision intervention in the sort of internal struggles that characterize Africa today.

The OAU is hamstrung by a structure that allocates nearly all power to summits of the member nations' heads of state. Personal and ideological animosities among these heads of state create problems (and nearly tore the OAU apart in the 1980s).[13] The OAU's first attempt at peacekeeping in Chad in the early 1980s was widely viewed in Africa as an embarrassing failure.[14] The OAU did provide observers following the negotiated settlement of disputes, such as Rwanda (1992–93) and Burundi (1993–96), but remains reluctant to undertake peace enforcement, particularly in intrastate conflicts.[15] Absent fundamental structural change, the OAU is unable to organize peace enforcement operations or stop armed conflict between member states.[16] In part, this is deliberate: African leaders suspect that if the OAU became more active in peacekeeping, the UN would become less so, thus paving the way for the disengagement from African security of the rest of the world community.[17]

Recently, sub-regional international organizations have begun to fill the void left by the ineffectiveness of the OAU. Such institutions have been a feature of Africa's political landscape for decades. Most began as mechanisms for economic cooperation. Recently, the trend has been toward the expansion of economic sub-regional organizations into the security realm. The Southern African Development Community (SADC), for instance, created a formal organ for defense, politics, and security in 1996.[18] In September 1998, it was used to justify an intervention into Lesotho by troops from South Africa and Botswana (at the invitation of Prime Minister Pakalitha Mosisili).[19] The Economic Community of West African States (ECOWAS) entered the security arena with the dispatch of multinational peacekeepers to Liberia in 1990. In 1999, it moved even further into the security field by establishing a Mediation and Security Council, a multinational stand-by force, and several Zonal Observation bureaus.[20] Like SADC, ECOWAS is built around a major regional power—Nigeria in this case.[21] ECOWAS has been seen by some other African nations as simply a cover for the spread of Nigerian influence.[22] Today there are signs that the East African Community (EAC) may follow SADC and ECOWAS by moving from a purely economic organization to one that at least encourages security cooperation among its members.

But efforts to create regional or sub-regional structures for conflict prevention, response, and resolution face a major obstacle: within the past ten years, many African leaders have offered support of one kind or another to insurgents, separatists, or rebels in neighboring states, usually as a form of indirect or proxy aggression. Often this support grows from some sort of personal animosity toward the ruler of a neighboring state. The target of the proxy violence then returns the favor by supporting violence in the initial instigator and the process spirals on. As a result, insurgents, separatists, and rebels seldom have difficulty finding patrons to supply arms or sanctuary, whether politically motivated (e.g., the Front Line States against apartheid), or inspired more by greed (e.g., Burkinabe President Blaise Campaore, who is thought to have provided supplies in exchange for diamonds to the Revolutionary United Front [RUF] in Sierra Leone, the Union for the Total Independence of Angola [UNITA], and the Liberian government of Charles Taylor).[23]

In combination, the weakness of African states, the practice of proxy or indirect aggression, and Africa's geography with its many remote and isolated areas, pave the way for protracted, parasitic wars. These wars begin as a way of attaining political inclusion (or separation if inclusion is impossible or unsatisfactory). But they drag on because the incentives for the combatants to continue outweigh the disincentives, whether some reward for peace or the risk of death or injury. Neither incentives nor sanctions are adequate in Africa. In most cases, the population as a whole is the victim of the struggle and seldom provides enthusiastic support for either the government or its enemies, since both use parasitic methods, abusing and drawing resources from the people rather than promoting their interests. Fragile systems for the production and distribution of food, health care, and education invariably collapse, leaving refugees dependent on aid from other states or nongovernmental organizations. Only a handful of these parasitic wars result in decisive military victory for one side. Many fester, eventually ending as a result of simply exhaustion by one side or the other rather than deliberate conflict resolution. This, then, is the environment in which African peacekeeping takes place.

Americans and Africa

The overwhelming majority of Americans have little knowledge of or interest in Africa. Few personally know an African or have a friend who has lived or traveled on the continent. American perceptions of the continent are half-formed, nebulous, and largely negative. The popular image is one of a region dominated by violence, starving refugees, endemic wars, brutal dictatorships, and crushing poverty.[24] Even the transcendental figure of former South African President Nelson Mandela and the end of apartheid in South Africa did not permanently change this perception. Most American political leaders, whether elected or appointed, hold views on Africa that are only slightly more sophisticated. In part, this lack of sophistication is an outgrowth of tradition, since American ties to Africa have always been limited. In contrast to Latin America, East Asia, or Western Europe, the United States never developed extensive trade with Africa (other than the import of petroleum and minerals). The only Americans with firsthand knowledge tend to be missionaries, Peace Corps volunteers, and specialized diplomats, scholars, and journalists. This is a miniscule constituency.

American involvement in African security has been equally limited. Until the late 1970s, Washington deferred for the most part to the former colonial powers with regard to the keeping of regional security. Following the collapse of the Portuguese empire in Africa and the emergence of pro-Soviet regimes in Angola, Mozambique, and Ethiopia, American concern with Africa did experience an upward spike. But the region was seen purely as a stage for competition with the Soviets rather than a realm of intrinsic concern. American engagement consisted of assistance funneled to allies such as the governments of Somalia and Zaire, or to insurgent movements, particularly Jonas Savimbi's UNITA. When the U.S. military was involved in Africa, the numbers were small. Very few American servicemen have ever been stationed in Africa or even been sent there for a short-term, temporary duty assignment. When the U.S. military was used in Africa, it was to conduct non-combatant evacuations during conflicts, limited duration training, or limited duration support to multinational peace operations like the Congo crisis of the early 1960s or the Rwandan relief effort of the early 1990s.[25] With very few Americans having shed blood in Africa, the emotional ties linking that continent to the United States are weak.

The low priority that Africa holds in U.S. foreign policy also reflects the fact that the region's cultural links to the United States are via African Americans who traditionally have limited political influence; what influence they do have tends to be focused on domestic issues concerning racial equality and economic opportunity. For a time, it appeared that this focus might change as the anti-apartheid struggle inspired Americans of African descent and others to pay closer attention to the continent. By the 1980s, a diverse and effective anti-apartheid movement had taken shape, composed of African Americans, students, church groups, organized labor, and human rights advocates.[26] But the enthusiasm of the anti-apartheid movement did not lead to sustained American engagement on the continent.

This is not surprising. Historically, it has been easiest to mobilize Americans for foreign policy crusades against a clear aggressor or evil force. When both sides in a conflict appear equally flawed—as in Vietnam or the Balkans—mobilizing and sustaining support for American engagement is difficult. The anti-apartheid struggle could be cast as a crusade against evil. Most other African conflicts cannot. When American policymakers chose to intervene in ambiguous conflicts where there is not a clear aggressor or evil force, they find that they must do so through low-level, indirect effort, often taking the form of support to proxies. This is precisely what the Reagan administration did in Central America. But while there were enough hard-line anti-communists in the United States during the 1980s to sustain such low-level, indirect engagement in El Salvador and Nicaragua, there is no equivalent group espousing involvement in Africa's conflicts, whether in Angola, the Congo, the Sudan, Liberia, or elsewhere.

Today, American Africanists find little other than humanitarian concern to serve as a foundation for public mobilization. Tangible American interests remain limited. By volume, about 14 percent of U.S. crude oil imports come from Africa (compared to 18 percent from the Middle East).[27] American exports to sub-Saharan Africa account for less than 1 percent of U.S. totals.[28] By any measure, Africa is substantially less important to the U.S. economy than Europe, Latin America, or the Pacific Rim. In security terms, American policymakers have made the point that serious threats originate from Africa, including state-sponsored terrorism, narcotics trafficking, weapons proliferation, international crime, environmental damage, and pandemic disease.[29] Nigerian organized crime groups are heavily involved in the global heroin trade, and South Africa, Ghana, and Côte d'Ivoire are becoming important transshipment points for drugs.[30] Even these threats, however, are seen as less pressing than equivalent problems in southeastern Europe or Latin America. Unlike these regions, Africa is geographically distant from the United States and from areas like Western Europe, the Pacific Rim, or the Middle East where the United States has substantial economic or political concerns. None of Africa's security threats inspire support for large-scale, sustained American engagement.

Against this backdrop, U.S. policy in Africa intermingles bits of geostrategic thinking with humanitarian and cultural considerations. The handful of Americans who care about Africa contend that low-level involvement is a wise investment of strategic resources since it can help prevent the region's problems from expanding or spreading and set the stage for a time when Africans themselves can manage their region's security. At the same time, suffering in the region touches the humanitarian streak of the American public. Polls show that most Americans support giving more attention to Africa, and an overwhelming majority favors giving aid to needy countries, including those in Africa.[31] To some Africans, this humanitarianism seems insincere—even a smokescreen designed to camouflage

Machiavellian designs—but many Americans do express heartfelt concern over crises in Africa and are often willing to take some actions to ameliorate them.

Polling data suggest that the American public—in contrast to the perception of elected leaders and commentators—is in favor of contributing to African peace-keeping operations.[32] This suggests that if American leaders were truly dedicated to greater involvement in African peacekeeping, they could mobilize public support. But the public does not favor U.S. *leadership* of African initiatives. This affects elite attitudes: elected officials, policymakers, and most of the public who actively express positions on foreign policy agree that U.S. engagement in Africa should be limited. Hence, Africanists in the United States must struggle against apathy and outright opposition. The outcome is usually a compromise that satisfies no one as the U.S. seeks to do *something* to help the region but only in a very hesitant and indirect way. This is not likely to change.

Barring some fundamental shift in the global situation, the United States will support initiatives by others in Africa. Washington will not undertake expensive, large-scale, or bloody forays into Africa. American concern will continue to undergo ups and downs. These facts point toward multinational peacekeeping as the most logical tool of U.S. security policy in Africa.

Peacekeeping and American Strategy

Despite the apparent logic of stressing multinational peacekeeping in Africa, Washington's enthusiasm for this endeavor is as muted and ambiguous as its enthusiasm for more general engagement in Africa. This is understandable given the recent history of multinational peacekeeping and the wider contours of American national security strategy. Modern multinational peacekeeping grew from the confluence of three trends in statecraft: a growing sense of interconnectedness and shared humanity, a paternalistic approach to security, and an immense increase in the danger that regional conflicts might spread and escalate.

States have long used intervention and military force to promote their security interests and protect particular ethnic or religious groups. Humanitarian intervention—the use of force to protect noncombatants or innocents from the effects of war in the absence of direct national interests—is a more recent phenomenon.[33] It has arisen, in part, from the growing sense of shared humanity that, despite frequent and violent breaches, has characterized the twentieth century as the ideas of the European Enlightenment—liberal democracy, constitutionalism, and formal systems for the protection of human rights—became ascendant. Technology amplified the trend; the transportation and information revolutions allow many people to travel abroad to develop a rudimentary understanding of other cultures. The notion of shared humanity and brotherhood is also linked to the developing world's emergence in the late twentieth century. African nations, in particular, with their humanistic cultural traditions, popularized the concept of a non-racial brotherhood of man.

Great power paternalism was a second component of the march toward multinational peacekeeping. The ideas of the Reformation, the Enlightenment, and ascendant Liberalism led the European powers to seek a moral justification for empire and for warfare. The results were the concepts of just war and, in the case of colonialism, *noblesse oblige,* or "white man's burden"—the idea that the "civilized" powers, while they had a right to impose their control on what were deemed "less civilized" parts of the world, also had a responsibility to bring "civilization" and stability.

The industrialization and, eventually, the nuclearization of war augmented the need for multinational peacekeeping. Nuclearization made war potentially apocalyptic. For the great powers that shaped global statecraft, the events leading up to World War I showed that conflict between small states in what otherwise would be an insignificant part of the world had the potential to draw in competing great powers and ignite a major or world war. After World War II, nuclear weapons amplified this danger a thousandfold. It was in the interests of all to prevent or contain small wars lest they expand and escalate.

After World War II, decolonization, by increasing the number of small, sovereign states, increased the chances of internal war. Similarly, the Cold War increased the chances that internal wars would expand and escalate. The sense of shared humanity and paternalism created a perceived imperative for outside powers to prevent, end, or control internal wars. The problem was that the only historic mechanism for doing this was direct great power intervention. But, the two powers with the ability to intervene effectively—the United States and the Soviet Union—had no tradition of doing so outside of their geographically contiguous regions (the United States in Central America, Mexico, and the Caribbean; the Soviet Union in the Caucasus, Central Asia, and Eastern Europe). As the two superpowers gradually began using developing world conflict as a proxy struggle against each other, they lost legitimacy as peacemakers or honest brokers. The states with a tradition of intervention, particularly Britain and France, found that their publics no longer had the will for it (in the case of Britain) or that colonial wars demanded full national attention (in the case of France). Moreover, Britain and France carried the taint of imperialism and thus were seldom welcomed by regional parties locked in conflict.

Stalemate in the UN Security Council initially prevented it from stepping into this vacuum. But no other organization could do better. Leaders such as Secretary-

General Dag Hammarskjöld and Canadian Secretary of State for External Affairs (and later Prime Minister) Lester Pearson—both winners of the Nobel Peace Prize—sought ways for the United Nations to contribute to peace and stability in the face of superpower conflict. The form of peacekeeping that emerged from this search used military forces from small and medium powers to observe, patrol, act as buffers, keep order, and negotiate in situations where one or both parties to a conflict invited the intervention. This form of peacekeeping was useful but limited since it could only take place in those rare conflicts that either did not have Cold War overtones or where one or both superpowers were willing to allow it. UN peacekeeping forces were in places like Cyprus, Congo, Lebanon, Yemen, Suez, and the India-Pakistan border, but not in hotspots like Southeast Asia, Central America, or Southern Africa. With the exception of the UN operations in Korea and Congo— both of which occurred under peculiar circumstances—UN peacekeeping was what would later be called "Chapter VI" activities undertaken with the consent of the belligerents rather than the more intrusive "Chapter VII" peace enforcement and peacemaking operations. There was also no technique for UN intervention in a conflict where no legitimate government existed to extend the invitation.

The end of the Cold War brought both good news and bad news for multinational peacekeeping. On the positive side, it ended the automatic gridlock in the Security Council and opened the way for UN involvement in conflicts that it would have avoided in the past. For instance, between 1989 and 1993, the UN Security Council established nine peacekeeping operations in Africa.[34] Some of these, such as the United Nations Observer Mission in Mozambique (UNOMOZ) and the United Nations Transition Assistance Group (UNTAG) in Namibia were among the organization's most successful.[35] The end of the Cold War also sparked increased American interest in multinational peacekeeping. The U.S. military no longer had to focus on countering the Warsaw Pact and was thus freed for other missions.[36] As the victor of the Cold War, the United States felt responsible for the maintenance of world order. There is an old warning that says, "be careful what you wish for since you may get it." For the United States, it certainly applied to the end of the Cold War. The victory that had been sought for so long brought many challenges.

In 1992, the Bush administration chose Somalia as a place to begin establishing the rules and patterns that it hoped would define the post–Cold War world order. Somalia was thus one of the first of what would be known as "failed states," with a humanitarian disaster giving every sign of becoming worse. Following a collapse of the government in that country, widespread violence involving warlord armies and clan militias had complicated efforts to relieve a famine.[37] Like President Bush, UN Secretary-General Boutros Boutros-Ghali was seized with the idea that the end of the Cold War offered the opportunity for rewriting the norms of global conflict with room for a dramatic increase in the role of the United Nations. "In the course of the past few years the immense ideological barrier that for decades gave rise to distrust and hostility," Boutros-Ghali wrote, "and the terrible tools of destruction that were their inseparable companions has collapsed. Even as the issues between States north and south grow more acute, and call for attention at the highest levels of government, the improvement in relations between States east and west affords new possibilities, some already realized, to meet successfully threats to common security."[38]

With both the Secretary-General and the United States anxious to use Somalia as a testbed for a new, post–Cold War style of assertive peacekeeping or peacemaking, the UN Security Council passed a resolution in April 1992 authorizing multinational force.[39] From April 1992 to April 1993, the United States joined a wide coalition in the UN Operation in Somalia I (UNOSOM I) and Unified Task Force (UNITAF), which sought to reconcile warring Somali factions and provide security for famine relief activities.[40] In May 1993, UNITAF was replaced by the UN Operations in Somalia II (UNOSOM II), which attempted to take a more active role in nation-building and the disarmament of Somali factions, particularly in the capital city of Mogadishu.[41] In 1993 a series of bloody attacks on UN forces undercut support for the operation both within the United States and in the world community. In 1994 UN forces withdrew. Clearly, peacemaking in failed states was radically different than the truce monitoring and other activities that the United Nations had undertaken since the 1940s. Somalia showed just how complex and difficult it was.

For the United States, a battle in Mogadishu in October 1993 that led to the deaths of eighteen American soldiers and hundreds of Somalis was particularly traumatic.[42] This battle and the subsequent withdrawal of UN forces and American diplomatic personnel were portrayed as disasters by the American media, and accepted as such by many American political leaders. Despite the fact—as former Assistant Secretary of State Chester Crocker points out—that the multinational intervention in Somalia was actually successful outside of Mogadishu both in terms of averting humanitarian disaster and improving political conditions, American political leaders both inside the Clinton administration and elsewhere drew the conclusion that African conflicts were morasses and potential traps.[43]

The limited economic or historic ties that bind the United States to Africa, in combination with the extensive global commitments of the U.S. military, make public support for involvement in African peacekeeping inherently fragile. Somalia was an experiment. If it had gone well, the United States might have moved toward more extensive and more direct engagement in Africa. As it was, the Somalia experience—or, more accurately, the perception that the Somalia intervention was a disaster, since media coverage of the violence in Mogadishu drowned out coverage of the positive results of relief efforts in the countryside—eroded support for a leading role for the United States in Africa. Unfortunately, Somalia was seen as a model for all African conflicts. This perception was evident in the Clinton administration's unwillingness to intervene in Rwanda during a genocidal rampage by Hutu militias in 1994 and in Washington's footdragging and outright opposition to a multinational force intended to stave off a humanitarian disaster in Zaire during the 1996–97 war that led to overthrow of Mobutu Sese Seko.[44]

Reeling from the Somalia experience, the Clinton administration undertook a broad reassessment of its entire approach to peacekeeping and peace enforcement. Its conclusions reflected a shift in the administration's thinking from "assertive multilateralism" with U.S. leadership to a more limited and indirect role in peacekeeping.[45] It also led the administration to search for the long-elusive "African solutions to African problems."[46] On May 3, 1994, President William Clinton signed Presidential Decision Directive (PDD) 25, which outlined the new policy on peacekeeping and peace enforcement.[47] This document stressed that war fighting remained the primary mission of the American military, but that, under certain conditions, multilateral peacekeeping or peace enforcement under the aegis of the United Nations can serve U.S. national interests.[48] To do so, PDD 25 stressed, UN peace operations need substantial improvement and reform. It outlined a number of these, including greater selectivity in choosing where to intervene, involving regional organizations where appropriate, reducing costs (specifically, decreasing the U.S. assessment for UN peacekeeping operations from 31.7 percent to 25 percent), expanding the UN Department of Peacekeeping operations to include a Plans Division and an Information and Research Division, establishing a professional Peace Operations Training Program, and reforming the process by which the UN manages the financial aspects of peacekeeping operations.

Two other aspects of PDD 25 were important. One concerned command and control of U.S. forces involved in UN peacekeeping. PDD 25 stated that the president would never relinquish *command* authority over U.S. forces but would consider placing U.S. forces under the operational *control* of a competent UN leader for specific UN operations authorized by the Security Council.[49] PDD 25 also stressed that peace operations should be well defined and linked to a concrete political solution. They should provide a finite window of opportunity for combatants to resolve their differences and failed societies to begin to reconstitute themselves, rather than imposing peace on belligerents with no interest in stopping the fight.[50] When considering whether to support a proposed new UN peacekeeping operation, the Clinton administration stated that it would consider whether involvement advanced U.S. interests, whether there was an international community of interest capable of dealing with the problem, and whether there was a clear threat to or breach of international peace and security.

The Clinton policy on peacekeeping and peace support that coalesced after PDD 25 was one in which extensive, direct American involvement was a last resort. This policy reflected U.S. public opinion. A 1999 assessment by the Chicago Council on Foreign Relations, for instance, showed that 57 percent of the American public felt that the United States should take part in UN peacekeeping (and only 20 percent felt the United States should *not* participate), but 72 percent felt that the United States should only respond to international crises in conjunction with allies and coalition partners.[51] Even so, other American political leaders were less enthusiastic. The most important was Senator Jesse Helms (R-NC), chairman of the powerful Foreign Relations Committee. In a January 2000 address, Helms accused the United Nations of a "lack of gratitude" toward the United States and seeking to encroach on American sovereignty.[52] The U.S. military, while certainly not as vociferous as Helms, was also less enthusiastic about UN peacekeeping than many administration officials, largely because of fear that protracted involvement in peacekeeping would erode the military's ability to retain its prowess at warfighting—its primary mission.[53]

Following PDD 25, the United States used its military in multinational peacekeeping only when others proved incapable of dealing with the problem *and* when tangible national interests were at stake. From the administration's perspective, these conditions applied in Bosnia, since failure to act there had the potential to damage the morale or integrity of NATO, but did not hold in Zaire/the Democratic Republic of the Congo. And, as the 1999 operation in Kosovo showed, when U.S. military force was used, the preference was for indirect or stand-off operations, with American ground forces used only when the situation was calmed to the point that there was minimal risk of casualties. This approach does not bode well for American involvement in African peacekeeping.

The Clinton Approach to Africa

Because of the fragility of public and congressional support for engagement in Africa, the Clinton approach has been to avoid or preempt conflicts by helping friendly African states chip away at the root causes of violence. "Our immediate objective," according to the Clinton national security strategy, "is to increase the number of capable states in Africa; that is, nations that are able to define the challenges they face, manage their resources to effectively address those challenges, and build stability and peace within their borders and their sub-regions."[54]

Part of this approach has been to promote prosperity by helping African states integrate into the global economy and undertake market-oriented economic reforms.[55] The core program has been the President's Partnership for Economic Growth and Opportunity in Africa. It combines technical assistance to help liberalize trade and investment, an anti-corruption initiative, programs to extinguish bilateral concessional debt, and the organization of a U.S.-Africa Economic Cooperation Forum.[56] It calls for the Overseas Private Investment Corporation to dedicate $750 million to encourage private sector investment in Africa.[57] The Clinton administration lobbied for passage of the Trade and Development Act of 2000, which includes the Africa Growth and Opportunity Act. At the signing ceremony, President Clinton stated, "This bill ... promotes the kinds of economic reform that will make sub-Saharan nations, in the long run, better allies, better trade partners and stronger nations."[58]

The Clinton strategy considered the expansion and consolidation of democracy in Africa as important for minimizing the chances of conflict and violence. But while placing a high premium on democracy and human rights, the Clinton administration also, in the words of Assistant Secretary of State Susan E. Rice, stayed "actively engaged even in flawed, imperfect democracies."[59] The key question was how hard to push the truly recalcitrant governments. In general, the Clinton administration eschewed sanctions or isolation in all but the most egregious cases, such as the Sudan, and Nigeria under its military dictatorship. Most of the time, the administration remained willing to cooperate with less-than-perfect democracies on other issues such as countering narcotrafficking and on peacekeeping.

The Clinton defense policy in Africa has had two key components: shifting from patron-client relationships to more equitable partnerships; and augmenting the capabilities of African armed forces through military-to-military ties stressing education and training. The centerpiece was the African Crisis Response Initiative (ACRI).[60] ACRI is a scaled-down version of a more ambitious program called the African Crisis Response Force, proposed in late 1996, which sought to create an African military organization that could respond to complex emergencies with only limited outside help. For a variety of reasons, this program met with a less than overwhelming reception when announced by Secretary of State Warren Christopher. Despite the rebuff, the Clinton administration continued to pursue the idea of an organic peacekeeping capability in Africa, eventually settling on ACRI, through which U.S. Army Special Forces provided training and limited nonlethal equipment to African militaries.[61] ACRI training emphasizes commonality of communications, basic soldiering skills, and specific military activities required in peacekeeping with the ultimate objective of helping African military units meet UN standards in peacekeeping and humanitarian relief practices. By 1999, units from Senegal, Ghana, Uganda, Malawi, Mali, and Benin had received ACRI training.[62] ACRI-trained units had participated in peacekeeping in Sierra Leone, Guinea-Bissau, and the Central African Republic.[63] Perhaps more importantly, some of Africa's major powers were leaning toward participation. By 2000 President Daniel Arap Moi of Kenya had committed his nation to engagement in the ACRI process and American officials had begun to encourage Nigerian involvement.[64]

During its initial phase, ACRI was often criticized for its "one size fits all" approach. The training dealt solely with basic soldiering skills and peacekeeping activities. While this focus was appropriate for some African militaries, others such as Kenya's, South Africa's, and Ghana's were advanced to the point that they did not need such rudimentary training. By 1999 ACRI had begun to mature and expand.[65] Efforts were underway to tighten the connections between ACRI and the exercise programs run by the regional U.S. military unified commands and to augment coordination with the training offered by European states, particularly the United Kingdom, France, and Belgium.[66] In addition, ACRI is developing programs to offer training in higher command and control rather than simply battalion-level training and improving cooperation with Africa's major sub-regional organizations, SADC, ECOWAS, and the EAC.

By 1998 the Clinton administration recognized that some sort of program was needed that would help African officials develop better methods of civil military relations, defense budgeting, and national security strategy formulation. It developed the African Center for Security Studies (ACSS). ACSS was a component in a constellation of schools created by the U.S. Department of Defense to ease the transition to democracy.[67] According to the White House, "The goal is for ACSS to be a source of academic, yet practical instruction in promoting the skills necessary to make effective national security decisions in democratic governments, and engage African leaders in a substantive dialogue about defense policy planning in democracies."[68] But, unlike the other components of the Department of Defense constellation of schools, ACSS was not given a permanent location. The architects of ACSS thought it better to run the school as a series of seminars for a trial period, then assess its effectiveness and the degree of support for the program within the Department of Defense and Congress. The first ACSS course was held in Dakar, Senegal, in November 1999; the second in Gaborone, Botswana, in June 2000.[69]

In addition to ACRI and ACSS, the U.S. military has undertaken a wide range of other engagement activities in Africa.[70] These include:

—Combined exercises such as Military Medical Exercises in Africa (MED-FLAG) and the FLINTLOCK regional program, a Joint Chiefs of Staff-sponsored exercise designed to promote regional cooperation.[71]

—Combined training, including Joint Combined Exchange Training (JCET) exercises in which U.S. Special Forces train with host nation forces.

—Military contacts, including flag officer visits, maritime engagement programs such as port calls, civil affairs democracy seminars, civil-military relations mobile training teams, chaplain programs, assistance to the OAU Crises Management Exercise, and steps to enhance interoperability with potential coalition partners, including the United Kingdom and France.

—Security assistance programs, including foreign military financing (FMF); foreign military sales (FMS); foreign military sales–training (FMS-T); direct commercial sales (DCS); International Military Education and Training (IMET), which sends officers and noncommissioned officers from thirty-one African countries to American military schools; expanded IMET, which provides training for other sorts of security officials; and the excess defense articles (EDA) program.

—Humanitarian assistance programs, including the Humanitarian Assistance Program–Excess Property (HAP-EP); Humanitarian Civil Assistance Program (HCA) in which U.S. military units on overseas training and operational deployments conduct humanitarian projects such as well drilling and school construction; Humanitarian Assistance Program (HA), which provides funding for humanitarian projects; and demining activities.

The IMET program is one of the most important components of U.S. military engagement in Africa. By bringing senior or up-and-coming African officers to American staff and war colleges, the program helps to create a web of personal friendships (which can be useful in multinational peacekeeping), as well as to familiarize the African officers with American methods of military planning and training.

In general, the Clinton security strategy in Africa has sought an indirect and limited American role. The administration has thus stressed working with African partners, even flawed ones like Presidents Robert Mugabe, Moi, and Yoweri Museveni, and institutions like the Nigerian military. The risk of this approach is that an individual or institution defined as an American partner will turn unpalatably repressive and taint the entire "partnership" strategy.

The Dual Dilemmas

In the spring of 2000 a deployment of a UN peacekeeping force to Sierra Leone quickly disintegrated into a fiasco, with peacekeepers captured or killed and their weapons stolen. Only the timely entry of British forces stabilized the crisis. While the United States did offer some limited transportation support, its main effort was to encourage Nigeria to rescue the United Nations peacekeepers. The specter of Somalia still paralyzes American policy in Africa. Unfortunately, this paralysis is not likely to change, at least in the short term. American support for engagement in Africa and for UN peacekeeping will remain muted.

Because of President Clinton's personal worldview and his core support base, his administration is likely to represent a high-water mark in American attention to Africa. The United States may develop stronger ties with a handful of African states that continue democratization and economic reform, but there is little chance of a U.S. "Marshall Plan"-type initiative for Africa. Africa will remain what military strategists call an "economy-of-force theater" where the U.S. seeks to encourage stability and prosperity but at minimum cost and risk.

Africa's real security dilemma is far larger than the lack of American attention. It is clear that traditional forms of multinational peacekeeping, which were effective when there was a peace to be kept and there were economic and political systems that had functioned at one time, do not apply. Such an approach might have some utility for Africa's rare inter-national wars, such as that involving Ethiopia and Eritrea, but not for protracted internal wars such as those in the Congo, Sierra Leone, Liberia, the Sudan, and Angola. To make a difference in these places, Africa needs a whole new mode of multinational activity that *makes* peace rather than keeps it, and *constructs* stable political, legal, and economic systems rather than *re*constructs them.

Call this enlarged function *peacebuilding,* since it would include not only stopping armed conflict (as in "peacemaking"), but also the long-term development of political, legal, and economic systems and institutions that can forestall future outbreaks of armed conflict. It would require—as George Ayittey recommended for Sierra Leone—the creation of UN trusteeships or protectorates in failed states.[72] This outcome is certainly not desirable, but seems to be the only alternative to allowing Africa's internal wars to fester. It also represents an immense task.

Movement toward a peacebuilding capability must proceed on three parallel tracks. The first is continued political, economic, and policy reform by African states. If African leaders do not abandon proxy violence and indirect aggression and do not progress toward more inclusive (and hence less violence-prone) political systems, peacebuilding cannot take place. Under such conditions, the U.S. role in Africa should be limited to basic relief during humanitarian disasters or campaigns of genocide. In conjunction with European and other allies, the United States should develop methods rapidly to create and make stable humanitarian sanctuaries where nongovernmental organizations and private voluntary organizations can provide basic care, but that is all.

The second track would be a continuation of programs to help augment the conflict prevention, response, and resolution capabilities of African states. The world community should not "abandon" the continent as many African leaders fear, but Africans should clearly bear the primary responsibility for the security of their region. Ongoing U.S. efforts to help Africans augment their peacekeeping capabilities should continue. To do this, the United States should develop programs to solidify ties with Africa's sub-regional organizations. As these organizations mature, the United States should consider developing or expanding security relationships with them, focusing on the provision of education, advice, and assistance. When African forces do engage in multinational peacekeeping, the United States should provide the assets they are short of, particularly logistics support, transportation, and intelligence. And, when the United States does make a commitment—whether a direct pledge to the OAU or sub-regional organization, or through programs such as ACRI and ACSS—it should be for the long term. Africans become justifiably frustrated at annual vacillations in American assistance. Better a modest amount that remains consistent than steep peaks and valleys driven by the tides of Washington's politics. At the same time, the United States should continue its ongoing programs to coordinate peacekeeping support with its European allies.

The U.S. military should continue to stress professional military education in Africa. Nothing can bring larger rewards for a smaller investment. The money that the United States spends on African professional military education helps African states improve civil-military relations and build more effective security forces, but it also establishes working relationships between Americans and Africans that are invaluable during coalition operations. The prime complaint that most Africans have about American professional military education is its limited availability. There are simply too few slots at the American staff and war colleges for Africans.[73] Admittedly, there are good reasons for this dearth: the United States has many friends and allies around the world and only so many seats in its military schools, but if the efforts in Africa were focused on a handful of true partners and provided regularly, the impact of professional military education would be augmented. In addition, the United States should follow the example of Great Britain and France and supply an instructor to some of the African war and staff colleges. South Africa, Ghana, Tanzania, and Kenya might be candidates.

ACRI and ACSS are useful means of shaping the African security environment, but both need refinement and expansion. ACRI, for instance, should expand training to include support to civilian officials during natural disasters and pandemic disease outbreaks, as well as for peacekeeping. It should then focus increasingly on augmenting the ability of Africans to plan, command, and control both humanitarian relief and peacekeeping operations. No African country currently has the capacity to deploy a headquarters for a multi-brigade operation in any but the most peaceful environments.[74] Developing such capability could begin with a regular series of wargames, staff exercises, and simulations involving a range of African participants (both military and civilian) as well as Americans and Europeans. American facilities such as the Army's Battle Command Training Program, simulation programs run by private corporations, and the Army's Center for Strategic Leadership at Carlisle Barracks could provide the appropriate venue. Regular staff talks and conferences involving Africans, Europeans, and Americans could pave the way. African countries generally lack the funds to support such conferences, so their external partners should be willing to pick up the tab.

ACSS should undergo an equal evolution. American policymakers should think of it as the first college in a future African "democratic university" in which African states, Europeans, and the United States operate schools for law enforcement, economics, and political organization, in addition to defense planning and management. The U.S. Department of Defense and Congress must sustain support for ACSS and consider expanding it so that African states can build the expertise that they need in the defense arena. To push the process even further, the United States should run regular seminars for African defense scholars and civilian defense officials. Publication of a journal dealing with African security affairs would be helpful. The United States should consider including African civilians as students in its war colleges. At a more fundamental level, the United States must make a long-term commitment to ACSS. The Clinton administration did not give it a strong institutional sponsor.

The United States should actively support African-led and designed programs to improve regional cooperation in peacekeeping even if it has little control over them. A key form of support could be funding for transporting the "players" from African countries to exercise sites. The next step would be to begin augmenting the capacity of African militaries to provide their own logistics, mobility, and intelligence support. They could develop the capacity to plan, lead, and control even more complex peacekeeping operations within five years if given appropriate assistance. It will be at least ten years before most African militaries could deploy and sustain peacekeeping forces for extended periods of time far beyond their national borders without assistance.

The United States should actively pursue the greater involvement of Army National Guard units in shaping the African security environment. Army Special Forces were precisely the right units to provide the first phase of ACRI training, but it is time for a shift. Involving Army National Guard units would be particularly beneficial because they are experienced at supporting civilian authorities during disasters and crises—specifically the skills African militaries need. The National Guard State Sponsorship Program, through which the Army National Guard of a specific state develops a partnership with the military of a state from the former Soviet Union, should be extrapolated to Africa. Such a program would not only help expand the constituency for Africa within the United States, but would also help African nations better understand the advantages of a military that includes a strong reserve component. In fact, American strategy in Africa should actively encourage nations there to consider moving toward a military with a small professional cadre and a larger reserve component, both as a means of stretching defense budgets and improving civil-military relations.

The third track in the movement toward effective peacebuilding in Africa should be provision of some sort of "bridge" to tide the continent over until African states develop their own capacity. It would require a willingness on the part of the United States and its European allies to provide a rapid and effective response to humanitarian disasters in Africa. This is long past due. The Sierra Leonean tragedy, in combination with that of Kosovo, shows that rather than seeing American ground forces as a last resort used either when a conflict reaches horrific proportions or when most of the danger has passed, U.S. policymakers should use them as peacekeeping shock troops, entering first, disorienting those who are using violence and quickly establishing basic security, then rapidly handing control of a mission to coalition forces and withdrawing, leaving long-term peacebuilding to the multinational coalition. The U.S. military can and should be the "point of the spear" when humanitarian disaster or genocide looms. Eventually, Africans themselves may be able to provide the sort of shock troops that can deploy quickly and restore order. Until then, the United States and its European allies should accept the role.

Peacekeeping or peacebuilding in Africa's internal wars is difficult and expensive. But, if the United States continues to shy away from rapid and serious responses to these wars, they will often disintegrate into disaster, leading to innocent deaths and making ultimate resolution of conflicts more difficult. There is a chance, at least, that the American public and its elected leaders will become numb to Africa's suffering and simply grow to accept the misery. The United States must play a more influential role in leading the world community toward effective peacebuilding.

Notes

1. Peter J. Schraeder, *United States Foreign Policy Toward Africa: Incrementalism, Crisis and Change* (Cambridge, U.K., 1994), 3.

2. James E. Rosen and Shanti R. Conly, *Africa's Population Challenge: Accelerating Progress in Reproductive Health* (Washington, D.C., 1998), located at www.populationaction.org/programs/afpop/afpop_index.htm, 6/7/00. See also the data from the Population Information Network—Africa, located at www.un.org/Depts/eca/divis/fssd/popin/startframe.htm, 6/5/00.

3. See United Nations Economic and Social Policy Division, Economic Commission for Africa, *Economic Report on Africa 1998*, located at www.un.org/Depts/eca/divis/espd/toc.htm, 6/5/00.

4. *Africa: Macroeconomic Overview*, Fact Sheet released by the U.S. Department of State Bureau of African Affairs, March 27, 1998

5. World Bank, *Global Economic Prospects and the Developing Countries 2000*, Appendix I, Regional Economic Prospects, Sub-Saharan Africa, located at www.worldbank.org/prospects/gep2000/appx1/safrica.htm, 6/7/00.

6. Virginia Gamba and Sarah Meek, introduction to Virginia Gamba (ed.), *Society Under Siege: Licit Responses to Illicit Arms* (Halfway House, South Africa, 1998), 3–4. See also Michael Klare and Robert I. Rotberg, *The Scourge of Small Arms*, WPF Report 23 (Cambridge, Mass., 1999); Sarah Meek (ed.), *Controlling Small Arms Proliferation and Reversing Cultures of Violence in Africa and the Indian Ocean* (Halfway House, South Africa, 1998); Tandeka Nkiwane, Martinho Chachiua, and Sarah Meek, *Weapons Flows in Zimbabwe, Mozambique and Swaziland* (Halfway House, South Africa, 1999).

7. Message from Salim Ahmed Salim, Secretary-General of the Organization of African Unity to the First Continental Conference of African Experts on Landmines, Kempton Park, South Africa, May 19–21, 1997, reprinted in Jakkie Cilliers (ed.), *Toward a Landmine-free Africa: The OAU and the Legacy of Anti-personnel Mines* (Halfway House, South Africa, 1997), 7.

8. United Nations Security Council Resolution 1209, November 19, 1998, United Nations document S/1998/1091.

9. Roy May and Gerry Cleaver, "African Peacekeeping: Still Dependent?" *International Peacekeeping*, IV (1997), 8.

10. "African Armies Can't Stand Fire," *The Monitor* (Kampala), September 1, 1999.

11. "Museveni Begins Probe Into Tank Purchase," *The New Vision* (Kampala), January 2, 1999, reprinted in the Foreign Broadcast Information Service (FBIS) report, January 2, 1999; "Zimbabwe: Official Denies Extra Funds Sought for DRC War," South African Press Agency, Johannesburg, May 20, 1999, reprinted in the FBIS report, May 20, 1999.

12. South Africa, Nigeria, and Ghana have small commercial airlines and oceangoing fleets that could be used for military lift. Nigeria has employed commercial shipping to transport its military forces into and out of Liberia during the course of its ECOMOG involvement.

13. See Azzedine Layachi, "The OAU and Western Sahara: A Case Study," in Yassin El-Ayouty (ed.), *The Organization of African Unity after Thirty Years* (Westport, Conn., 1994), 27–39.

14. 'Funmi Olonisakin, "African 'Homemade' Peacekeeping Initiatives," *Armed Forces and Society*, XXIII (1997), 350–56; May and Cleaver, "African Peacekeeping," 12–13; Dean Pittman, "The OAU and Chad," in Yassin El-Ayouty and I. William Zartman (eds.), *The OAU After Twenty Years* (New York, 1984), 297–325.

15. James O. C. Jonah, "The OAU: Peace Keeping and Conflict Resolution," in El-Ayouty (ed.), *The Organization of African Unity*, 9–12; I. William Zartman, "African Regional Security and Changing Patterns of Relations," in Edmond J. Keller and Donald Rothchild (eds.), *Africa in the New International Order: Rethinking State Sovereignty and Regional Security* (Boulder, Colo., 1996), 53–55.

16. The Cairo Declaration of 1993 committed the OAU to enhance its conflict resolution and management capability. The United States has provided modest support for this initiative. It remains to be seen whether it will succeed. For analysis of the OAU's weakness at this task and suggestions for reform,

see Sam G. Amoo, "The Role of the OAU: Past, Present, and Future," in David R. Smock (ed.), *Making War and Waging Peace: Foreign Intervention in Africa* (Washington, D.C., 1993), 239–61.

17. Cedric de Coning, "The Role of the OAU in Conflict Management in Africa," in Mark Malan (ed.), *Conflict Management, Peacekeeping and Peace-Building: Lessons for Africa from a Seminar Past* (Halfway House, South Africa), 22.

18. See Jakkie Cilliers, "The SADC Organ for Defence, Politics, and Security," Institute for Defence Policy Papers, 10 (October 1996); Mark Malan, *SADC and Sub-Regional Security: Unde Venis et Quo Vadis* (Halfway House, South Africa, 1998).

19. "Lesotho Foreign Minister Defends Request for SADC Aid," broadcast on Johannesburg SAPA, September 22, 1998, reprinted in the FBIS report, September 22, 1998. See also Ericka A. Albaugh, "Preventing Conflict in Africa," chapter 7 of this book.

20. "Yearender Views Africa in the 21st Century," *Xinhua* (Beijing), December 22, 1999, reprinted in the FBIS report, December 21, 1999.

21. Such a configuration does not imply an inherent weakness of the organizations. After all, NATO also includes one militarily preeminent state and a number of secondary ones. In fact, these types of coalitions may be more capable of decisive action than one composed exclusively of peers.

22. Olonisakin, "African 'Homemade' Peacekeeping Initiatives," 356–65. See also Eboe Hutchful, "The ECOMOG Experience With Peacekeeping in West Africa," in Mark Malan (ed.), *Whither Peacekeeping in Africa?* (Halfway House, South Africa, 1999), 61–85; Michelle Pitts, "Sub-Regional Solutions for African Conflict: The ECOMOG Experiment," *The Journal of Conflict Studies*, IXX (1999), 49–68.

23. Douglas Farah, "Rebels Get Arms Through Burkina Faso, Sources Say," *Washington Post*, May 6, 2000.

24. Michael Clough, *Free at Last? U.S. Policy toward Africa and the End of the Cold War* (New York, 1992), 20–25.

25. See Dan Henk, *Uncharted Paths, Uncertain Vision: U.S. Military Involvements in Sub-Saharan Africa in the Wake of the Cold War* (Colorado Springs, 1998).

26. See Steven Metz, "The Antiapartheid Movement and the Populist Instinct in American Politics," *Political Science Quarterly*, CI (1986), 379-395.

27. Susan E. Rice, "U.S. Interests in Africa: Today's Perspective," address at the Columbia University Institute of International and Public Affairs, October 20, 1998, located at www.state.gov/www/regions/africa/rice_981020.html, 6/5/00.

28. Susan E. Rice, "United States Interests in Africa: Post–Cold War, Post-Apartheid," the 1999 Bram Fischer Memorial Lecture, Rhodes House, Oxford, England, May 13, 1999, located at www.state.gov/www/policy_remarks/1999/990513_rice_oxford.html, 6/5/00.

29. The White House, *A National Security Strategy for a New Century* (Washington, D.C., October 1998), 54–55.

30. Rice, "United States Interests in Africa."

31. "Africa Summit Plan Likely to Elicit Sympathetic But Guarded Response from US Public," an assessment of existing polling data by the University of Maryland Program on International Policy Attitudes, February 29, 2000, located at www.pipa.org/OnlineReports/Africa/analysis.html, 6/5/00.

32. Ibid.

33. See Simon Duke, "The State and Human Rights: Humanitarian Intervention Versus Sovereignty," in Fariborz L. Mokhtari (ed.), *Peacemaking, Peacekeeping and Coalition Warfare: The Future Role of the United Nations* (Washington, D.C., 1994), 149–73; Comfort Ero and Suzanne Long, "Humanitarian Intervention: A New Role for the United Nations," *International Peacekeeping*, II (1995), 140–56; Stephen J. Solarz and Michael E. O'Hanlon, "Humanitarian Intervention: When Is Force Justified?" *Washington Quarterly*, XX (1997), 3–14; Sean D. Murphy, *Humanitarian Intervention: The United Nations in an Evolving World Order* (Philadelphia, 1996); Tonny Brems Knudsen, "Humanitarian Intervention Revisited: Post–Cold War Responses to Classical Problems," *International Peacekeeping*, III (1996), 146–65.

34. Margaret Carey, "Peacekeeping in Africa: Recent Evolution and Prospects," in Oliver Furley and Roy May (eds.), *Peacekeeping in Africa* (Aldershot, 1998), 13–27.

35. See Donna Pankhurst, "Namibia," and Sam Barnes, "Peacekeeping in Mozambique," in Furley and May (eds.), *Peacekeeping in Africa*, 207–22 and 159–77.

36. As one illustration of the shift, in the years just before the end of the Cold War, the curriculum at the U.S. Army Command and General Staff College (which is an accurate indicator of the Army's focus) dedicated only one day to multinational peacekeeping. By the beginning of the twenty-first century, it was an important (but not dominant) item in the curriculum of military staff and war colleges, and the Army had established a Peacekeeping Institute to serve as a focal point for training, analysis, education, and doctrine development. (See the U.S. Army Peacekeeping Institute's home page at http://carlisle-www.army.mil/usacsl/divisions/pki/pki.htm).

37. See Walter S. Clarke, *Somalia: Background For Operation Restore Hope* (Carlisle Barracks, Penn., 1992).

38. Boutros Boutros-Ghali, *An Agenda for Peace: Preventive Diplomacy, Peacemaking and Peace-Keeping*, Report of the Secretary-General pursuant to the statement adopted by the Summit Meeting of the Security Council on 31 January 1992 (June 17, 1992), located at www.un.org/Docs/SG/agpeace.html, 6/5/00.

39. Security Council Resolution 751 (1992), April 24, 1992.

40. See Boutros Boutros-Ghali, *The United Nations and Somalia, 1992–1996* (New York, 1996).

41. See Peter Woodward, "Somalia," in Furley and May (eds.), *Peacekeeping in Africa*, 143–58.

42. For a narrative of the battle, see Mark Bowden, *Black Hawk Down: A Story of Modern War* (New York, 1999).

43. Chester A. Crocker, "The Lessons of Somalia: Not Everything Went Wrong," *Foreign Affairs*, LXXIV (1995), 2–8.

44. On Rwanda, see Steven Metz, *Disaster and Intervention in Sub-Saharan Africa: Learning From Rwanda* (Carlisle Barracks, Penn., 1994); Gerard Prunier, *The Rwanda Crisis: A History of Genocide* (New York, 1995); Patrick J. O'Halloran, *Humanitarian Intervention and the Question of Genocide in Rwanda* (London, 1995); Howard Adelman and Astri Suhrke (eds.), *The Path of Genocide: The Rwanda Crisis From Uganda to Zaire* (New Brunswick, N.J., 1999). See also Barbara Crossette, "Plans for Zaire Relief Mission Bog Down Over Details," *New York Times*, November 15, 1996; the comments of Department of State spokesman Nicholas Burns in the U.S. Department of State Daily Press Briefing, November 8, 1996; Thomas W. Lippman and Dana Priest, "Pentagon Wants Cease-Fire Pledge in Zaire," *Washington Post*, November 15, 1996.

45. William H. Lewis, "'Assertive Multilateralism': Rhetoric vs. Reality," in William H. Lewis (ed.), *Peacekeeping: The Way Ahead?* (Washington, D.C., 1993), 13-28.

46. Michael G. MacKinnon, "Rivals or Partners? Bureaucratic Politics and the Evolution of US Peacekeeping Policy," *International Peacekeeping*, VI (1999), 38.

47. See Nina M. Serafino, *Peacekeeping: Issues of U.S. Military Involvement*, Congressional Research Service Issue Brief 94-040, December 3, 1996. See also Michael G. MacKinnon, *The Evolution of U.S. Peacekeeping under Clinton: A Fair-weather Friend* (London, 2000).

48. *Clinton Administration Policy on Reforming Mulilateral Peace Operations (PDD 25)*, U.S. Department of State Bureau of International Organizational Affairs, February 22, 1996, 2-3. This is an unclassified summary of PDD 25.

49. The distinction between operational *command* and operational *control* is important for the U.S. military. Operational control "normally provides full authority to organize commands and forces and to employ those forces as the commander in operational control considers necessary to accomplish assigned missions. Operational control does not, in and of itself, include authoritative direction for logistics or matters of administration, discipline, internal organization, or unit training." Command authority does include administration, discipline, internal organization, and unit training. Source: Joint Publication 1-02, *DOD Dictionary of Military and Associated Terms*, 24 January 2000.

50. Edmund J. Hull, "UN Peacekeeping Operations: Worthwhile Investments in Peace," *U.S. Foreign Policy Agenda*, III (1998), 6.

51. John E. Rielly (ed.), *American Public Opinion and U.S. Foreign Policy 1999* (Chicago, 1999), 25.

52. Colum Lynch, "Helms's View Is Not U.S.'s, Albright Tells U.N.," *Washington Post*, January 25, 2000.

53. By the end of the 1990s, the perception was widespread that the U.S. commitment in the Balkans was in part responsible for discontent and difficulty in retaining personnel, particularly in the Army.

54. The White House, *A National Security Strategy for a New Century* (Washington, D.C., December 1999), 45.

55. Susan E. Rice, "U.S. Economic Policy Toward Africa," address before the Harvard University Business School, Africa Business Conference, Boston, Mass., January 30, 1999, located at www.state.gov/www/regions/africa/990130_rice.html, 6/5/00.

56. Susan E. Rice, "U.S.-Africa Relations," Remarks at the Agostinho Neto University School of Architecture, Luanda, Angola, October 29, 1998, located at www.state.gov/www/regions/africa/rice_981029.html, 6/5/00; and Madeleine K. Albright, "U.S. Policy Toward Africa," address on U.S. Policy toward Africa at George Mason University, Fairfax, Va., March 19, 1998, reprinted at http://secretary.state.gov/www/statements/1998/980319.html, 6/5/00. See also "President's Partnership for Economic Growth and Opportunity and African Growth and Opportunity Act," fact sheet released by the U.S. State Department Bureau of African Affairs, March 27, 1998; "U.S. Assistance and Debt Relief in Sub-Saharan Africa," fact sheet released by the U.S. State Department Bureau of African Affairs, March 27, 1998; Theodros Dagne, "Africa: Trade and Development Initiatives by the Clinton Administration and Congress," Congressional Research Service Report 98-92, March 2, 1998.

57. Susan E. Rice, Assistant Secretary of State for African Affairs, comments at the U.S.-Africa Energy Ministers Conference, Tucson, December 14, 1999, located at www.state.gov/www/policy_remarks/1999/991214_rice_energy.html, 6/5/00.

58. "Remarks by the President at Bill Signing of Trade and Development Act of 2000," Office of the White House Press Secretary, May 18, 2000.

59. Susan E. Rice, "Democracy in Africa," statement before the Subcommittee on Africa of the Senate Foreign Relations Committee, March 12, 1998, located at www.state.gov/www/regions/africa/rice_980312.html, 6/5/00.

60. For background and analysis, see Dan Henk and Steven Metz, *The United States and the Transformation of African Security: The African Crisis Response Initiative and Beyond* (Carlisle Barracks, Penn., 1997).

61. By 1999, some of the training responsibilities were being handled by contractors, particularly Military Professional Resources International (MPRI) rather than U.S. Army Special Forces.

62. See the ACRI web site at www.eucom.mil/programs/acri/index.htm.

63. Comments of Ambassador Aubrey Hooks quoted in Jim Fisher-Thompson, "Secretary of State Albright Highlights U.S. Africa Initiative," *USIS Washington File*, October 18, 1999, located at www.eucom.mil/programs/acri/usis/99oct18.htm, 6/5/00.

64. Author's discussions with Hooks and Scott Fisher of the ACRI Office of the U.S. Department of State, November 1999 and January 2000; Fisher-Thompson, "Pickering Says U.S. Wanted To Work With Nigerian Military," *USIS Washington File*, November 8, 1999, located at www.eucom.mil/africa/nigeria/usis/99nov08.htm, 6/5/00; "U.S. Urges Nigeria to Join Africa Crisis Response Program," *The Guardian* (Lagos), December 20, 1999, reprinted in the FBIS report, December 20, 1999.

65. This section is based on the author's conversations with members of the Joint Staff, Office of the Secretary of Defense, and the ACRI office at the U.S. Department of State.

66. On European efforts, see Eric G. Berman and Katie E. Sams, *Constructive Disengagement: Western Efforts to Develop African Peacekeeping* (Halfway House, South Africa, 1999), 13–22.

67. The first of these was the George C. Marshall Center for Security Studies which was created for military officers and civilian defense officials from former Warsaw Pact nations. See www.marshallcenter.org.

68. White House Fact Sheet on the African Center for Security Studies, April 3, 1998.

69. See Susan Ellis, "African Center for Strategic Studies Begin November 1 in Dakar," *USIS Washington File*, October 22, 1999, located at www.eucom.mil/programs/acri/usis/99oct22.htm, 6/5/00; Cindy Elmore, "DOD Africa Center Session Puts Spotlight On Stability," *European Stars and Stripes*, November 23, 1999, 4.

70. See *Peacetime African Engagement Activities*, Stuttgart: HQ USEUCOM, Middle East/Africa Division, n.d.

71. For an outstanding analysis of MEDFLAGS, see C. William Fox, *Military Medical Operation in Sub-Saharan Africa: The DoD "Point of the Spear" for a New Century* (Carlisle Barracks, Penn., 1997).

72. George B.N. Ayittey, "Sierra Leone Solution: Make It a U.N. Colony," *Wall Street Journal*, May 31, 2000.

73. For instance, at the U.S. Army War College, there are usually two students per year from all of sub-Saharan Africa.

74. William D. Bajusz and Kevin P. O'Prey, "An All-African Peace Force: An Immediate Option or Long-Term Goal for the Region?" *Strategic Forum*, LXXXVI (1996), 4.

CHAPTER FIVE

Employing African Forces in Peace Operations in Africa

Happyton M. Bonyongwe

THE AFRICAN PEACE and security situation remains a major concern for the international community. Many planners see the African continent as the principal ground for the conduct of peace support operations in the future. Indeed, initiatives to address Africa's perceived security challenge abound.[1] Past, present, and projected conflicts on the continent give credence to such security concerns. While one UN peace mission was deployed on the continent prior to 1989, seventeen have been deployed since 1989, suggesting a significant increase in the number of conflicts in which the deployment of peace support forces in Africa has been necessary.[2]

The primary responsibility to maintain international peace and security lies with the UN. Its role encourages the involvement of the developed world and major powers in peace operations in Africa. It discourages an approach whereby only Africans shed their blood on their continent, with the developed world assisting financially and "in spirit" only, an approach that would not augur well for the future of a species inhabiting the same planet.

Nevertheless, the role of African regional organizations in peace operations is important. As described in Chapter VIII of the UN Charter, it is a vital component of UN operations, particularly in the transition to the final involvement of UN forces. Further, experience with UN peace operations, particularly in Africa, indicates the UN's inability to execute successfully its responsibilities in this area and the need for new initiatives. Indeed, UN Secretary-General Kofi Annan's "Renewing the United Nations: A Programme for Reform" noted that "[t]he

United Nations does not have, at this point in its history, the institutional capacity to conduct military enforcement measures under Chapter VII [of the UN Charter] ... The Organisation still lacks the capacity to implement rapidly and effectively decisions of the Security Council calling for the dispatch of peacekeeping operations in crisis situations."[3]

Finally, there is a growing desire among Africans to solve their own problems. In his opening address to the Second Meeting of the Chiefs of Defence Staff of Member States of the OAU Central Organ, OAU Secretary-General Salim Ahmed Salim stated:

> OAU Member States can no longer afford to stand aloof and expect the International Community to care more for our problems than we do, or indeed to find solutions to those problems which in many instances, have been of our own making. The simple truth that we must confront today, is that the world does not owe us a living and we must remain in the forefront of efforts to act and act speedily, to prevent conflicts from getting out of control.[4]

New African initiatives, such as the OAU's Mechanism for Conflict Prevention, Management and Resolution, attempt to address the ravages of intrastate and interstate conflicts and to create a new path forward in the absence of effective external intervention.

Given this scenario, the role that African military forces will play in the conduct of peace support operations becomes of paramount importance for our future on the continent. This chapter examines the feasibility of employing African forces in peace support operations in Africa and then discusses the specifics of how these forces could be composed, summoned, and commanded.

Defining the Mission of "Peace Operations"

"Peace operations" are commonly understood to refer to "peace*keeping* operations," a term that can be misleading since it is used in two senses—a more restricted definition and a wider definition.[5] In this chapter, peacekeeping operations shall be defined under the more restricted definition to be deployments with the consent of all the parties concerned to monitor cease-fires or truces. They include diplomatic efforts to negotiate or advance a comprehensive peace. By this definition, peacekeeping is an operation relying for its success on the principles of consent, impartiality, and minimum use of force. Forces are lightly armed and use force only in self-defense or as a last resort. This is classical or traditional peacekeeping.

Since the end of the Cold War, some observers have sought to define peacekeeping more broadly, with a mandate to comprise anything from demilitarization—

including cease-fire monitoring and disarmament—to reintegration of combatants, humanitarian assistance, and election monitoring. Under such broader definitions, many recent multinational interventions for peace that have no relationship with traditional blue-helmet operations are termed "peacekeeping operations." In this wider context, deployments may involve UN military and/or police and, frequently, civilians as well. Such peace operations are better termed "multidimensional peacekeeping," "wider peacekeeping," or "Third Generation peacekeeping," and are not included under the definition of "peacekeeping" as used in this chapter.

For purposes of clarity, peacekeeping also should be distinguished from "peacemaking" and "peace enforcement," two other forms of peace operations. Peacemaking, as described in Chapter VI of the UN Charter, includes "negotiation, enquiry, mediation, conciliation, arbitration, judicial settlement, resort to regional agencies or arrangements, or other peaceful means of their own choice" to resolve disputes between hostile parties.[6] Peace enforcement, as described in Chapter VII of the UN Charter, includes action to *enforce* a peace, not necessarily with the consent of the parties, and may include armed intervention and combat or the threat of such action.[7]

While the role of military forces in peacemaking is limited and confined to military security assistance and military-to-military contacts, it is more pronounced in peacekeeping and peace enforcement. The greatest challenge is in peace *enforcement,* as military forces charged with this mission must be heavily armed and equipped in order to enforce a peace. Clearly, within peacekeeping as well, the more complex and wider the operations become, the more difficult they are for military forces to execute. It is essential that the capacity of future African forces be developed and forged in such a manner that they are able to conduct all types of peace operations successfully, from simpler Chapter VI peacemaking to more demanding Chapter VII peace enforcement.

Existing Models for Peacekeeping and Peace Enforcement by Regional Organizations

The following models for peacekeeping by regional organizations suggest possibilities for African peacekeeping and peace enforcement arrangements, under UN auspices or otherwise:

UN Standby Arrangements System (UNSAS)

The inception of the UN Standby Arrangements System was a result of recommendations by a study group in 1993. The system establishes standby forces able to be deployed, in whole or in part, anywhere in the world, at the Secretary-General's request for UN duties as mandated by the Security Council. Member states are required to contribute specified resources within an agreed response time. As of 2000, there were eighty-eight member states in the system, sixty-five of which had provided lists of their capabilities. Thirty-two had formalized their contributions by signing a Memorandum of Understanding that must be signed for forces or other resources to be deployed. UNSAS had 147,500 troops that could be made available to the UN.[8]

Declared response time by member states varies from less than thirty to more than ninety days, with about 40 percent of standby assets having a response time of thirty days or less. Under this system, a contribution agreement was to be signed between the UN and each contributing state, in principle, before the deployment of resources to the mission area. To widen the base, the Secretary-General has encouraged member states to form partnerships between states that need equipment and those willing to provide it. African countries are free to be part of this system. However, very few African countries have signed on.[9]

Multinational Standby Forces High-Readiness Brigade (SHIRBRIG)

The UN realized the importance of having the capability for rapid deployment of peacekeeping forces to avoid the time lapse between the decision of the Security Council to mandate an operation and the actual deployment of troops in the mission area. In December 1996, on Danish initiative, Austria, Canada, Denmark, the Netherlands, Norway, Poland, and Sweden signed a letter of intent to establish such a brigade. As a follow-up to this letter of intent, in August 1997 a small multinational military planning staff was established in Denmark, consisting of a few officers from each of the participating countries. The planning staff was charged with developing common training standards and procedures to be used in the national training of the forces, which, as in the UNSAS model, remain under the command of their home countries until summoned. Core functions of the brigade will be duplicated so that the brigade would be available for operations even if one country decides not to participate in a particular mission. The response time of SHIRBRIG is to be fifteen to thirty days and deployment time shall not exceed six months. In March 2000 SHIRBRIG had ten member and two observer countries. It had 5,000 troops ready for deployment at the Secretary-General's request.[10]

Rapidly Deployable Mission Headquarters (RDMHQ)

Experience has shown that when the Security Council authorizes the establishment of a new peacekeeping operation, it takes time for the mission to be staffed by suitable personnel, thereby reducing its operational efficiency during the crucial initial deployment and operational phase. To overcome this drawback, a group of countries introduced the concept of the RDMHQ in 1995. The concept envisaged

—a core of eight personnel (six military, one police, and one humanitarian) permanently based at UN Headquarters, New York,

—a second tier of twenty-nine personnel selected and earmarked from existing HQ staff who will join the RDMHQ when deployed, and

—a third tier of twenty-four personnel nominated by member states on standby in their home countries.

The RDMHQ is still in the planning stage, largely due to budgetary constraints.

Baltic Battalion (BALTBAT)

The three Baltic States of Estonia, Latvia, and Lithuania have cooperated to organize and train a joint battalion that is now fully operational for peacekeeping missions. Each nation provides a company while the battalion headquarters staff and Latvian Company are garrisoned in Adazi, Latvia. Training and provision of equipment was sponsored by the Nordic countries, the United Kingdom, France and the United States. Companies remain stationed in their home countries but assemble for training. Command rotates every three years.

African forces can easily adopt and adapt similar arrangements. BALTBAT, in particular, shows that a number of small countries, which may not be able to field a force of battalion strength alone, could cooperate and create a regional battalion that could be part of a larger multinational peacekeeping force.

Regional and Sub-regional Peace Operations in Africa

As the main regional organization in Africa, the OAU has an important part to play in peace support operations on the continent. It already has carried out a few peacekeeping operations. In 1963 it undertook a mission to observe peace between Algeria and Morocco. In 1981 it sponsored an observer mission to Chad. Between 1991 and 1993 it maintained a Neutral Military Observer Group (NMOG) in Rwanda. In 1993 it deployed the OAU Mission in Burundi (OMIB). In 1997 it had a small Military Observer Mission in the Comoros.[11] The OAU's determination to move forward was clearly spelled out by the establishment of the Mechanism for Conflict Prevention, Management and Resolution of June 30, 1993.

While the position of the OAU in Africa is important, however, it is the subregions that are emerging as the principal actors in recent peace initiatives and operations on the continent. Currently, each of the main sub-regions hosts at least one sub-regional organization:

—Inter-Governmental Authority on Development (IGAD) in the Horn of Africa
—Maghreb Union (UMA) in the north
—Southern African Development Community (SADC)
—Economic Community of Central African States (ECCAS)
—Economic Community of West African States (ECOWAS).

Due to cultural affinity and common social and historical configuration, people in a region or sub-region normally have more intimate knowledge of the evolution and political sensitivities of the conflict in question. Hence, African battalions may play a more effective role in peace support operations on the continent. Based on all accounts, the ten-day French-inspired Exercise Guidimaka carried out by West African battalions in 1998 was a great success.

Perhaps the most notable model of success for the role of sub-regional organizations in peace operations is the seven-year intervention in Liberia by the ECOWAS Monitoring Group (ECOMOG), notwithstanding the problems, political or otherwise, associated with the intervention. In this case, Nigeria absorbed most of the initial costs for the operation, which was later supported by the UN. There has also been a mini-ECOMOG mission in Sierra Leone, where the UN again joined by sending observers to supervise the disarming of former combatants.

The formation of the SADC Organ on Politics, Defence and Security and its associated subcommittees (for example, the Interstate Defence and Security Committee [ISDSC]), demonstrates a southern Africa poised to play an important role in enhancing peace and stability in the sub-region and, perhaps, even further afield. SADC is already at an advanced stage in building the capacity of the sub-region to deploy peacekeeping forces. Proof lies in the success of training exercises such as Exercise Blue Hungwe in 1997 and Operation Blue Crane in 1999.[12]

Zimbabwe was given the mandate by the ISDSC to coordinate and harmonize peacekeeping in SADC. In 1998 SADC Ministers of Defense and Foreign Affairs and high-level military teams visited Denmark and Bosnia to evaluate the feasibility of, and to lay the foundations for, a SADC peacekeeping force, probably of brigade strength. The high-level military team judged that a SADC peacekeeping brigade was feasible and recommended setting up a steering group on policy formulation and a working group to formulate detailed work plans. The team's recommendations are now being studied by SADC Ministers of Defence and Foreign Affairs. Progress on these lines should yield a sub-regional peacekeeping force in approximately five years. These developments put the question of the feasibility of having African peacekeeping forces beyond academic debate. The issue now is how to proceed with the process.

It should be noted, however, that there are also drawbacks to the use of African forces. The OAU and sub-regional organization have been greatly hindered in their operations by logistical and financial constraints, as well as by political rivalries and the negative legacy of colonialism. The OAU, unlike organizations such as the European Union or NATO, is a weak association of states. The commitment of some of its members is questionable. Countries have very different opinions even as to which nations should be involved in efforts to resolve particular conflicts.

There has sometimes been a visible rift in Africa between anglophone and francophone nations. At the ECOWAS meeting in March 1998, for example, there was an acrimonious debate between the Nigerian-led bloc of anglophone states, which favored the expansion of ECOMOG, and the francophone bloc, which advocated for a loose structure similar to the one that existed among former French colonies in the Central African Republic. This is characteristic of the lack of consensus and common approach within the sub-regions.

Further, while the training of most militaries of the developed world is standardized through membership in alliances like NATO, this is not the case in Africa. This fact has a negative impact on the performance of contingents and on force cohesion. In addition, the provision of base-level facilities, such as repair and recovery, mobile field hospitals, and plants for field engineers, is out of the financial reach of most African countries. Africa, moreover, does not have an effective media strategy. The constant intervention of foreign media may frustrate many gains.

A Framework for Future African Peace Operations

The need for Africa to take charge of its future, particularly where peace operations are concerned, has been gathering momentum. In 1998, at a seminar of the High-Level SADC Military Visit to Denmark and Bosnia, the Minister of Foreign Affairs of Zimbabwe, Stan Mudenge, articulated key recommendations for peace support operations in Africa:

—The various sub-regional groupings in Africa should set up regional peacekeeping brigades.

—UN peacekeeping doctrine should be adopted by Africa as its peacekeeping doctrine.

—Africans should ensure ownership of peacekeeping in Africa by retaining command, control, and communications of peacekeeping operations, including training in Africa.

—Where budget and logistical issues are concerned, Africa should recognize its limited resource capacity and accept outside assistance.[13]

These recommendations undoubtedly influence the debate and development of African capability in peace support operations. Taking each recommendation in turn, one can see the wisdom and realism of this approach. First, a force of brigade strength, properly trained and equipped, is achievable for most of the sub-regional groupings of Africa. Indeed, a brigade is a force that is able, once deployed, to have a tangible effect on a conflict situation, particularly considering the types of African conflicts, force levels, and armaments of belligerents. A battalion would in many cases be too small. While it is accepted that even the brigade can be on the small side in major conflicts, a brigade can be complemented by the deployment of brigades from other sub-regions or outside Africa. Planning for a force above brigade strength would unduly stretch the resources of countries involved.

Second, adopting the UN doctrine gives African forces the ability to operate together with forces from outside Africa. And, as UN doctrine is well known, following it would avoid "reinventing the wheel" for Africa. As Africa is part of the international community, this approach would also mean that African forces could be deployed outside Africa, something that has happened in the past.

Third, the issue of ownership of peacekeeping operations on the African continent is tied to the desire on the part of Africans to have more control over their political destinies and not to be entirely dependent on the international community to intervene in African conflicts on their behalf. In practical terms, however, this recommendation has to do mainly with forging effective command, control, and communications capabilities. Absence of effective capabilities in these areas would undermine the ability of African forces to conduct an operation without foreign assistance. Internal African capability adds flexibility to operations and facilitates speedy deployment. This is useful considering that the UN has failed in the past to deploy forces timeously in certain conflict situations, resulting in considerable suffering and loss of life.

Fourth, the issue of having the North provide assistance to African countries in the area of logistics and resources is straightforward. Needs are quite varied, including training, provision of information and intelligence, and material and financial assistance. Insufficient national funding has had a negative impact on the OAU's ability to mount effective operations. In contrast, the UN system provides troop-contributing countries with reimbursements for equipment employed in operations and with allowances for personnel. One related question has to do with whether foreign assistance should be bilateral (to countries individually) or multilateral (to sub-regional groupings). Both types of arrangements are possible. The United States African Crisis Response Initiative's (ACRI) training of African battalions is done under bilateral arrangements. The Danish-Zimbabwean agreement, which calls for regional peacekeeping courses in Harare, is also a bilateral agreement with many benefits for the fourteen SADC countries. It seems likely that Denmark's willingness to provide funding is influenced in large measure by the fact that courses are conducted for the benefit of all fourteen countries of SADC and not for the benefit of a single country.

The Way Forward

The growing involvement of the OAU in peace efforts on the continent, the emergence of sub-regional organizations and the creation of sub-regional peace-keeping forces, and operations already undertaken by ECOWAS point toward a future in which African peace support forces have a greater role in peace operations on the continent. It is clearly feasible to have African military forces undertake peace operations in Africa. The debate thus concerns when, where, how, and in what strength the forces should be employed. Indeed, researchers, academics, and military practitioners in the years to come will focus on how to enhance the capabilities of African military forces in very practical ways. As a first step, the rest of this chapter discusses how Foreign Minister Stanley Mudenge's recommendations can be translated into reality within SADC.

Force Composition

Building on the relative sizes of the SADC member countries, a force of brigade strength in southern Africa might include a South African logistics battalion and air transport and support; Tanzanian, Zambian, and Zimbabwean infantry battalions; a Botswanan signals contingent; a Namibian field engineer squadron; a Swaziland field medical company; a Malawian military police platoon or detachment; Angolan field engineers for mine clearance; a Mozambican boat squadron; a Lesotho contingent of military observers; and a Mauritian contingent of civilian police.[14] The combat brigade could be manned by about 5,000 officers and men when summoned. The detailed order of battle is something to be worked out.

Although there is a temptation for countries that have more military and economic power in a sub-region to monopolize the key posts and to contribute more, such an approach should be avoided. The position of the force will be strengthened politically by the number of countries participating. Smaller countries should be encouraged to play a meaningful part in any sub-regional force. There are many possibilities, even in combat battalions. For example, following the BALTBAT example, smaller countries like Lesotho, Swaziland, and the Seychelles could contribute a motorized infantry company each and, together, a battalion headquarters staffed by officers from all three countries. Indeed, a fourth country could even join this arrangement.

The creation of a force as described above would not mean the creation of a standing brigade. What would be essential would be to have the brigade head-quarters be permanent, along the lines of the SHIRBRIG example, to allow for planning and training. The components of the brigade would be resident in their own countries and would also be part of the UN Standby Arrangements System. Each country would undertake to keep its contribution at an agreed state of readi-ness. Ideally, more forces than those required for a single brigade would be iden-tified. In order to guarantee a force of brigade strength, duplication should be the planning norm because, in some instances, a country may choose not to deploy as part of a particular operation. In SHIRBRIG, the core components of the brigade are duplicated.

Command and Control

At the political strategic level, a sub-region such as SADC may not need addi-tional political structures to implement a regional peace operations concept. The outcome of the debate on the relationship between the SADC Development Com-munity and the SADC Organ on Politics, Defence and Security will have a bear-ing on this decision. As things stand, the Organ is the one that would take charge of operations at the political level. However, the development of a clear link between sub-regional leaders, the OAU Secretary-General, and the UN Secretary-General is required.

The ISDSC could assume the responsibilities of a strategic headquarters pro-viding the strategic direction for peace support operations in the sub-region. To link the strategic and operational levels, national commanders (Defence Forces Commanders) should continue to play their role by making sure that those con-tingents taking part are well trained and immediately available. National com-manders should also ensure that units earmarked for the sub-regional force are appropriately and adequately equipped.

At the operational level, the ISDSC may create a military staff group working for the ISDSC but above the brigade headquarters. For this requirement, if the need is identified, certain officers should be earmarked to become part of the future sub-regional force's operational headquarters. This group could be formed from the proposed Steering and Working Groups on the SADC peacekeeping capacity building initiative discussed earlier. The staff group, which should be composed of potential force commanders and their staff, should be able to assemble quickly to plan operations and should continuously train together. During training, the group should have a component of civilians and non-governmental organizations (NGOs). The operational level headquarters should be linked to standby units in different countries.

When deployed, the brigade commander of the sub-regional peacekeeping brigade (who may be appointed force commander in a sub-regional or regional operation or until a UN-appointed force commander arrives) must have operational control of the regional force, while administration and logistics can be referred to national command authorities. The selection of the force commander must be based on ability and experience. Countries should also rotate in providing a force commander, as this will help to spread experience and to reduce friction among countries.

At the tactical, battalion level, command should not be a problem since units would be commanded by their national commanders. The units would remain under national command engaged in their normal duties and only assemble when there is a problem. Battalion headquarters would be staffed by officers from the countries contributing the companies of the battalion, with command being for a stipulated period and on a rotational basis.

The discussion in this section is shown diagrammatically in the appendix.

Summoning, Response Time, and Readiness

Timely warning of potential crises or humanitarian disasters is essential. An early warning center could be established in one of the countries. (One drawback is that the development of such a center may be viewed negatively as early warning is essentially intelligence work.) The efficient summoning of the brigade and its deployment at short notice hinges on the establishment of an early warning center. In the case of SADC, the center could be either with the SADC Secretariat or with the headquarters of the peacekeeping brigade. Once established, the center could be linked to the proposed OAU early warning center and eventually the UN situation center. The center should realize the important role played by NGOs and UN agencies, which have the ability to deploy in areas often ignored by governments. The deployment of, say, a SADC Brigade would require the political green light from the SADC Organ on Politics, Defence, and Security as well.

Recommendations

While Africa remains part of the community of nations, the idea of having African forces undertake peace support operations in Africa and elsewhere deserves attention. It may be the only way to avoid catastrophe in Africa, as the developed world has shown clear signs of reluctance to intervene in many conflicts on the continent. Success in developing effective peace support operations capability will come from sharing of tasks by member states on the basis of comparative advantage in specialization and resource capacity. The following conclusions emerge from the discussion above:

—Employing African military forces in peace support missions in Africa is feasible and can be realized. It should be primarily in the context of sub-regional groupings. The proposed SADC Peacekeeping Brigade is a case in point.

—African forces need to adopt UN doctrine in training and to be part of UN standby arrangements.

—Sub-regional early warning centers, linked with the OAU and UN, should also be established. Such centers will assist in the summoning of forces.

—African countries should seek logistical support from the northern hemisphere through bilateral and multilateral arrangements as necessary and appropriate.

Notes

1. Examples include the United States African Crisis Response Initiative (ACRI), the French African Response Initiative (the Re-camp Concept), and various seminars (for example, the World Peace Foundation Seminar held in Malawi from May 14 to May 16, 1998) conducted on the subject of peacekeeping and enforcement action in Africa.

2. See United Nations, Department of Peacekeeping Operations, "Completed Peacekeeping Operations" and "Current Peacekeeping Operations," located at www.un.org/Depts/DPKO/p_miss.htm and www.un.org/Depts/DPKO/c_miss/htm, 5/23/00.

3. Kofi Annan, "Renewing the United Nations: A Programme for Reform," Report of the Secretary General, UN Document A/51/950 (July 14, 1997), located at www.un.org/reform/track2/focus.htm, 5/1/00. See also the discussion of this quote in Mark Malan, "Peacekeeping in Africa—Trends and Responses," Institute of Security Studies Occasional Paper 31 (June 1998), located at www.iss.co.za/Pubs/PAPERS/31/Paper31.html, 5/2/00.

4. Salim Ahmed Salim, Opening Address to the Second Meeting of the Chiefs of Defence Staff of Member States of the OAU Central Organ, Harare, Oct. 25, 1997, as quoted in Malan, "Peacekeeping," 1.

5. For further discussion see Chris Alden, "United Nations Peacekeeping in Africa: Lessons for the OAU and SADC," ACCORD Occasional Paper (January 1997), located at www.accord.org.za/publications/papers/97-1.htm, 5/2/00, 1–3, and A.J. Rossouw, "Towards a New Understanding of the Terms and Definitions for International Peace Missions," ACCORD Occasional Paper (Feb. 1998), located at www.accord.org.za/publications/papers/98-2.htm, 5/2/00.

6. *Charter of the United Nations,* Chapter VI, Article 33, located at www.un.org/aboutun/charter/chapter6.htm, 5/2/00.

7. *Charter of the United Nations,* Chapter VII, located at www.un.org/aboutun/charter/chapter7.htm, 5/2/00.

8. United Nations, "Press Briefing by Head of Standby Arrangements Unit" (March 14, 2000), located at www.un.org/News/briefings, 5/11/00.

96   HAPPYTON M. BONYONGWE

9. See United Nations, "Progress Report of the Secretary-General on Standby Arrangements for Peacekeeping," S/1999/361 (March 30, 1999), located at www.un.org/Docs/sc/reports/1999/ s1999361.htm, 5/11/00.

10. United Nations, "Press Briefing, March 14, 2000."

11. See William Nhara, "OAU Perspectives for Africa's Conflict Resolution Mechanism and the Manner in Which Peacekeeping Training Should Proceed on the Continent," unpublished paper (1998).

12. Exercise Blue Hungwe was a battalion-level multinational peacekeeping exercise held in Zimbabwe. The aim was to enhance regional African liaison, cooperation, exchange of military skills, and interoperability by means of a multinational joint field training exercise in tactics and techniques of international peacekeeping. Eight SADC countries participated. Operation Blue Crane was a brigade-level peacekeeping exercise held in South Africa. The aim of the exercise was to enhance the capacity of SADC/ISDSC military forces in peacekeeping operations.

13. See "SADC Officers to Tour Europe," *Herald* (Zimbabwe) (May 5, 1998), 9.

14. See also Stanford Khumalo, "Forging A Regional Peacekeeping Partnership in Southern Africa," Institute of Defence Policy Monograph Series, V (July 1996), 30.

Appendix

Diagrammatic Presentation of Political Direction, Command, and Control for an SADC Peacekeeping Operation

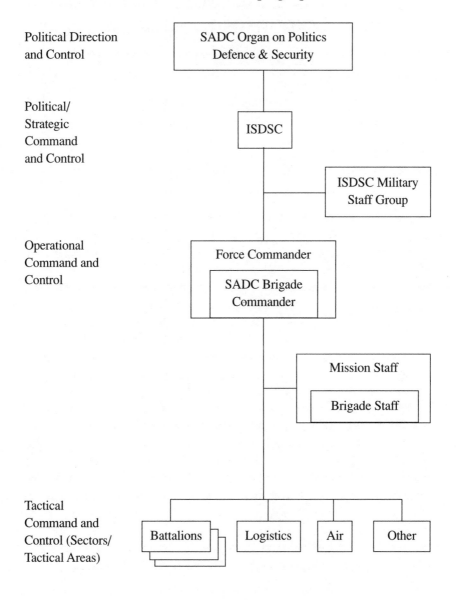

CHAPTER SIX

African Responses to African Crises: Creating a Military Response

Robert I. Rotberg

INTRASTATE CONFLICT is the bane of West, Northeast, and middle Africa, especially the Great Lakes region, but no area is immune from the corrosive appeals of ethnic, linguistic, religious, or racial rivalry. Indeed, even where there appear to outsiders to be no true markers of difference, Africans can find them; intercommunal mayhem has been a growing feature of modern Africa. From the Biafran war to the Congo implosion, there seems no end to the races for resources and the arousals of fear that have fueled intramural African antagonisms.[1]

Africa boasted large empires and vast city-states as early as the eighth century A.D. Those early ethnic conglomerates and their many and varied successors comprised competing peoples, linguistically and ethnically diverse. The colonial empires eventually carved up Africa according to European as well as local geographical mandates. In so doing they, like their indigenous imperial predecessors, bundled peoples together who had nothing in common but accidental territorial contiguity. Thus, many of the post-colonial independent states inevitably included a mishmash of peoples, some not even of similar linguistic and ethnic origins. The larger the new state, the more numerous its component parts and, frequently, the more those components differed in culture, outlook, education, and political attitudes. Even small states, like Rwanda and Burundi, could harbor ethnic groups that considered themselves enduring rivals. Only Swaziland, Lesotho, Botswana, and Somalia could have been considered homogenous, but the Somali clans ultimately proved just as fractious as distinctive ethnic groups elsewhere.

Some modern African states, like Tanzania, have largely avoided contentions between ethnic entities, either because of the unusual character of their colonial experiences or because of the rough equality and similarity of the entities. Tanzania, Senegal, and the Central African Republic (among others) may have been blessed in that manner, but Namibia and Botswana, with large dominant groups and numerically weak minorities, provide another significant model. Precolonial and colonial intraterritorial rivalries, however, have not necessarily proven the fodder of modern civil wars. Nor has post-colonial mismanagement of communal fears been the only key variable, albeit an inescapable one.

The indigenous and foreign empires in Africa kept the peace, however partial to one or another group they were perceived to be. Most of all, they reduced intergroup hostility by minimizing the potential fears of less-favored, fragile, ethnic, and other groupings within a territory.[2] With the end of empire and colonialism, the governments and leaders of successor states aroused the anxieties of many of their constituents. Sometimes they pitted group against group, sometimes they favored their own group and disenfranchised or weakened their obvious rivals. New states discriminated economically and politically. Before long, in so many states, the fear of being deprived of current or future resources, or of being denied equal shares of a national patrimony, was commonplace.

This oversimplified analysis of the African condition permits two conclusions:

1. that the bitter civil wars of Africa are largely a modern phenomenon, with multiple causes and complicated remedies; and

2. that intrastate conflict is not apt to disappear in this millennium.

For that latter reason, if for no other, it is essential that Africans find ways to manage their continuing and incipient communal conflicts more effectively than hitherto. In the early decades of independence the former colonial powers rushed back to Africa to dampen fratricide, as the French did so many times in West, Central, and East Africa, and as the British did on several occasions. More recently, in Somalia, the West intervened for humanitarian purposes at a time of great human loss and unexpected ethnic carnage. But its operations, no matter how initially successful, did nothing to restore national order or reduce the likelihood of interclan hostilities. To have overcome warlordism, the United States and other intervenors would have needed to disarm the contenders and impose a new suzerainty.[3] This opportunity was soon lost as the peacemakers became, or were seen to be, contenders for local power. As a tragic result, when Rwanda exploded into genocide in 1994, neither the United States nor the United Nations was capable of acting rapidly or effectively. Preventing massacres, much less genocide, was no longer perceived to be a Western responsibility. In the inexperienced eyes of Western statesmen, Africa had descended into a bitter chaos from which only

Africans could extricate themselves. At least that was the unfortunate view, here abbreviated, that captured Washington and other Western capitals.

But Africans on a national basis were not ready to separate battling parties within sovereign states (or even between states). Africans had been unable even to eliminate the outrages of dictator Jean-Bédel Bokassa's Central African Empire or Idi Amin's Uganda until Tanzania's patience was finally taxed beyond limit in 1979. Since then, Africans in large have too rarely intervened militarily to prevent intrastate conflicts, although Nigeria led the Military Observer Group into Liberia in 1990 and Sierra Leone in 1997, post-apartheid South Africa led an intervention in 1998 to curtail a mutiny in tiny Lesotho, and Tanzania had much earlier sent troops to quell insurrections in both the Seychelles and the Comoros. Senegalese troops had helped to keep the peace in 1998 in Guinea-Bissau. But there has been no pan-African attempt to intervene physically between the warring parties in Angola, Burundi, the Central African Republic, Chad, Congo (Brazzaville), Kenya (in the Rift Valley), Mozambique, Rwanda, Senegal (in Casamance), Somalia, the Sudan, or Uganda (in the north and west). Nor has Africa as a collectivity been able militarily to separate the warring sides in Congo (Kinshasa), and impose the peace that its diplomats have sought time and again. Indeed, with Angola, Chad, Namibia, and Zimbabwe arrayed on the side of President Laurent Kabila's Congo and Rwanda and Uganda the principal backers of an eastern Congolese anti-Kabila insurgency, no easy end to the Congo's widespread, externally fueled civil war was possible.

Since future Congos and Rwandas are unlikely to be rare, and since Burundi is a continuing calamity, an overriding issue for Africa, and for the West, has been how to restore and keep the peace. The motives for doing so are obvious: to save lives and boost the possibility of economic development, and to achieve a greater than present prosperity for Africans and Africa. The absence of civil war would encourage national and continental opportunities for growth. Human and economic potentials would be unlocked after years, if not decades (in some cases), of destruction.

Africans could take charge of their own conflict prevention and peace enforcement. For decades, contingents from a number of African countries, especially Ghana, Senegal, and Botswana, have been deployed in UN peacekeeping operations, outside as well as within Africa.[4] They have served in South Lebanon, Somalia, Angola, and elsewhere. But peacekeeping occurs after a brokered ceasefire is in place. Peacekeepers observe violations of ceasefires and seek to reduce other breaches of the peace.

Africa's problems are primarily of the type III pre-ceasefire kind. How to persuade or compel warring parties to lay down their arms and resolve conflicts peacefully is the overriding question. Thus, if a rapid reaction force of African soldiers could be formed to create the peace, and to minimize the spread of hostilities, fewer lives would be lost and fewer internecine antagonisms would transform themselves into all-out civil wars. At least that is the hypothesis that motivated the World Peace Foundation, beginning in 1997, to explore how an African-controlled force could be used to prevent conflict and strengthen the pursuit of peace on the continent.

U.S. Secretary of State Warren Christopher had similar goals in mind when he enunciated the ill-fated African Crisis Response Force (ACRF) doctrine in 1996, although without undertaking widespread consultation in Africa. Since the West could no longer be relied upon to forestall massacres in Africa, and since the likelihood of continued massacres was not inconsiderable, Christopher advised Africans to form a rapid reaction brigade (like that originally contemplated globally by the UN Charter). The United States pledged to fund and train such a force if Africans would organize it and assume their responsibilities in a serious manner.[5]

Christopher's initiative responded to an acute need, given the plethora of civil wars and ethnic and intercommunal hostilities in Africa. Massacres had already occurred in Burundi before and after the Rwandan genocide. Christopher and others rightly feared further massacres, renewed implosions of states (as in Somalia, Liberia, and Sierra Leone), episodes of brutal intrastate rivalry like those that have occurred in Guinea-Bissau and Congo (Brazzaville), not to mention the Comoros, Lesotho, and Niger. Kenya, and even Zambia and Malawi, continue to merit attention, as does Nigeria, with its multiethnic composition and its myriad internal tensions.

Africans have long recognized the great need for conflict prevention and appropriate military intervention on their continent. Some of their savvy statesmen have often sought to reduce threats to peace and have employed the usual concatenation of diplomatic means to limit the spread of internecine imbroglios. The Organization of African Unity (OAU) in theory exists to perform precisely such roles, but unanimity of decisionmaking hinders any decisive action, as does the inviolable doctrine of non-interference in sovereign states. Moreover, the OAU has had no effective early warning or early action capacity; nor has it had any military capability.[6] Only when Tanzania ousted Amin in 1979 and when a frustrated Economic Community of West African States (ECOWAS) formed the expeditionary force known as ECOMOG to intervene in Liberia, and later in Sierra Leone, did Africa exhibit any broad willingness to limit the killing fields of the continent.

In both cases, strong personalities decided that intervention was essential: President Julius Nyerere of Tanzania in 1979 and General Sani Abacha of Nigeria in 1990 and 1997. No African leader has yet said "enough is enough" in Somalia, the Sudan, Angola, or Burundi, and despatched sufficient troops to end hostilities and bring opposing sides together. Nor, except in the purlieu of South Africa, where an unofficial *pax azania* exists, and in West Africa, where the ECOMOG precedent is strong, can such interventions be anticipated. Absent a new force or forces and a readiness to act, all the other existing and likely future eruptions of ethnic and intercommunal violence are apt to be ignored, or responded to in ad hoc self-interest, as five countries did in the Congo in 1998 and 1999.

The West stands by, wringing its hands. The UN evinces concern. Donors attempt to assist the OAU in developing a capacity—any capacity—to respond diplomatically and effectively to crises within, as well as between, states. Meanwhile, the United States, Britain, France, and the Nordic countries have all actively been strengthening African armies, improving their peacekeeping potential, upgrading their communications and logistical capabilities, and assisting in joint training exercises. Christopher's ACRF has become the African Crisis Response Initiative (ACRI), with its State Department-led emphasis on helping African militaries prepare themselves for the tasks of peacekeeping.[7]

Do Africans want more? Do they want to keep their own peace by developing peace intervention and peace enforcement capacity? Do they want to limit the carnage currently wreaked on hapless populations by intercommunal conflict? Are they anxious to reduce hostilities fueled by ethnic enmity? Can they envisage a force or forces ready to be mobilized at the onset of an intrastate crisis?

If the strong recent responses to these and similar questions by an African prime minister, about twenty African ministers of defense, and about thirty African chiefs of staff and their deputies are at all representative, then the answer to each question clearly is affirmative. During the course of three large meetings (1997–1999) in the United States, Malawi, and Tanzania, military and political leaders from as many as fifteen African states appeared ready to embrace the notion that collective African–controlled peace intervention methods were desirable, even possible. Western financial and other support would be essential. Western direct logistical assistance would be critical. Those who attended the three meetings also decided that Africa was a continent of sub-regions, and that the crisis response forces should be organized roughly along sub-regional lines. That is, instead of a single, continental army of questionable quality, there should be four or five sub-regional crisis reaction forces, each with its own mandate, derived from the nations it would serve.

There is broad agreement about the utility of such forces. Raising them through secondments from existing operational military units would not be difficult. Choosing commanders would not prove a stumbling block; indeed, the African military leaders at the Foundation-sponsored meetings were sanguine about battalions from disparate countries working easily together for the common cause of sub-regional peace. The problem was not technical or professional. It was distinctly political.

Conceptualizing a Southern African Development Community (SADC) sub-regional crisis response force appeared straightforward. As an example of what could be duplicated in other African sub-regions, the states of SADC (from Tanzania and Congo southward to South Africa, plus the Seychelles and Mauritius) would agree to contribute battalions or companies to a brigade-sized force. That force would be summonable; it would not be a permanent, standing entity. For that reason, SADC would agree beforehand about command and control issues; select a commander and deputy commander; decide on standard issues of nomenclature, uniforms, catering, communications, languages, and so on; and allocate fixed responsibilities to the constituent states. There would be a headquarters and administrative capacity. Absolutely critical would be regular joint training exercises, where the SADC sub-regional crisis response intervention force would demonstrate how well and how quickly a concerted military operation could be mounted by battalions and companies from different backgrounds. When emergencies mandated the deployment of the force, its constituent parts would be brought together under the designated commander and sent into the field as an interposition and prevention agency.

How the force physically came together would be no easy exercise. It has always been assumed that providing the aircraft and underwriting the costs of force deployment would be a Western responsibility. No set of African countries, not even South Africa plus others, could spare resources sufficient to transform such a virtual ready-response brigade into a reality on the ground. At the three Foundation-sponsored conferences, official representatives of Western nations pledged their financial backing and their military technical assistance to move and position African troops. Building upon their existing training of Africans in peacekeeping methods, they also promised to do more: to provide communications and signaling capacity (as the Canadians did in the Central African Republic), to provide heavy equipment like the trucks and personnel carriers that the African armies largely lack, and to assist in every other possible logistical way. In asserting their willingness to help, Westerners reiterated one fundamental underpinning of their aid: Africans would be in command; the interventions would be African-directed, planned, and executed, albeit with technical assistance from the West.

African chiefs of staff were hardly reluctant to join such enterprises. They saw the importance of attempting to reduce conflict by intervening militarily and also by brandishing the threat of such an intervention. East Africa's armies are moving closer together and adopting joint doctrines and mutual training. The southern Africans have already cooperated militarily. ECOMOG, originally and in theory, was a multilateral force. So the soldiers everywhere are well ahead of the politicians. For many chiefs of staff, acting together sub-regionally in order to improve the chances for peace in Africa is appropriate. They look forward to creating larger-than-national forces in the interests of sustainable peace.

The difficult questions are all political. Which crises merit the attention and intervention of a sub-regional force? Are they to be restricted to the Lesotho-type scenarios, where the elected government of Prime Minister Pakalitha Mosisili was threatened by mutinous soldiers and defeated politicians, perhaps in league with the monarch? Or could a force of the kind contemplated have been used to impose peace on Somalia, prevent genocide in Rwanda, and reduce the threat of a rebellion in the Democratic Republic of the Congo? Those models of larger crises would, in retrospect, have been desirable settings for such peace enforcement strategies. In theory, a rapidly mobilizable multinational brigade could have dampened those conflicts, obviating death, misery, and the spread of instability. With the will of Africa behind it, such a force could have disarmed the feuding Somalis before the warlords gained strength, prevented the Hutu Interahamwe from rounding up and then massacring Tutsi in the first month of the genocide, and separated the warring sides in the Congo early enough to have made a peaceful difference.[8]

The thorny questions of when and where to intervene also raise the critical question of who decides? How does the peace enforcement operation commence? Whose fingers are on the trigger of intervention? Who summons the SADC or the East African or the ECOWAS force together? Who tells the commander of one of the forces to mobilize his multinational troops? The same mechanism, organization, or person that recognizes an incipient or actual conflagration within a state (or between states) as worthy of peace intervention also calls in the previously arranged response: the sub-regional brigade. But what or who could do it?

Africa has a regional organization, the OAU, but nearly every observer of the OAU, and even its own officers and staff, despair of the OAU ever being able to act decisively against one of its members. Given the operational tradition of unanimity, building consensus for a serious intervention would take too long and be unlikely ever to be accomplished.

If not the OAU, perhaps decisions of the kinds contemplated could be devolved to the sub-regions. Not all the sub-regions have working forums like SADC and ECOWAS. In the Great Lakes or the Horn there is too little cohesion and sense of common purpose. In southern Africa, in theory, there is both the will and modalities sufficient to bring about the decisionmaking processes that will be necessary. But that depends entirely on the pleasure of South Africa, SADC's largest and wealthiest member and its natural leader. South Africa already acts directly when it needs to, as in Lesotho. It has chosen not to exercise any military might in Angola, the Congo, or even Burundi (despite talk of doing so and a keen diplomatic involvement in all three zones of conflict).

It is not as yet evident (and participants from Africa at the Foundation meetings all evaded closure on this question) that there exists either the capacity to make such decisions multilaterally in Africa, or to have them taken by individuals for the common good. President Robert Mugabe of Zimbabwe was decisive regarding the Congo, and intervened on behalf of President Kabila. But no state, not even Namibia and Angola, which also took Kabila's side, let Mugabe's decision substitute for its own judgment. Indeed, President Nelson Mandela of South Africa opposed Mugabe's lead, and said so. Former President Nyerere of Tanzania telephoned Mugabe with a similar message—but to no avail. Likewise, in ECO-MOG, Abacha ultimately made the decisions, not always with the support of his fellow West African presidents, or to their liking.

President Thabo Mbeki of South Africa may in future make some of the critical decisions about whether to intervene to keep the peace, and where and when. But even Mbeki is unlikely to command the acquiescence of his fellow African or southern African presidents. He will be unable to commit any expeditionary force that includes the troops of nations other than his own. However, he might be able to fashion a SADC response, guided by South Africa, which performs the same function, and is operationally effective.

Until the time when an African capacity for making these kinds of decisions is fully developed, a crisis response force for Africa could conceivably be mobilized by the Secretary-General of the United Nations. His or her stature and impartiality would be recognized widely in Africa, whether or not the incumbent were an African. The Secretary-General would have access to early warning information (currently collected by the UN Department of Peacekeeping Operations) and be privy to the concerns of the OAU and sub-regional organizations. He or she might even gain access to intelligence on such matters of individual powers. A Secretary-General could, in theory, be perfectly placed to decide when to pull an interventionist trigger. But the Secretary-General works for the UN and for the Security Council. In the Rwandan crisis of 1994, the Security Council prevented action by representatives of the Secretary-General until it was too late. In the Congo, and elsewhere, the mandate of the Secretary-General was ignored. The UN usually respects the sovereignty of its members, despite the possibilities provided by Chapter VII of the Charter.

There is no perfect, no realistic, decisionmaking apparatus around which the participants in the Foundation meetings were prepared to rally. The instrument of the Secretary-General of the UN seemed the best possibility, despite its obvious structural flaws. Certainly, as far as the participants were concerned, no African individual or organizational modality offered any higher decisionmaking ability in this regard.

But imagine that a readied force of sufficient size and ability actually were summoned, flown in Western aircraft to the center of a crisis, provided with appropriate intelligence and logistical support, and directed into the field to reduce or eliminate shooting between two contending parties. Suppose this intervention restored the status quo ante and was therefore successful. What then? What would be its mandate? Who supplies that mandate? Would the force be instructed to halt the fighting and keep it halted until diplomats could negotiate a ceasefire? Or would the force be instructed to stay and enforce a ceasefire and militantly to put down threats against that ceasefire? How militantly? With how much force?

Once a ceasefire is in place, what should the force do? Should it prepare to reinvigorate or reconstruct a country or a country's government politically? Should it bring in political specialists to impose democracy? Should it be followed by a military police or a regular police force? To whom should this interventionist operation report? Should it report to the existing authorities even though they have been a part of the problem? Or should it report back to the sub-regional organization, to the OAU, or only to the UN and its Secretary-General?

Few African leaders are comfortable with these questions, much less the potential answers to them. Hence, though nearly everyone understands the nature of the problem, few are prepared to accept answers that would diminish state sovereignty or transfer authority for a country, even a country that has ceased to exist (like Somalia), to outsiders. Or even to themselves. As welcome as the notion of a sub-regional crisis response force is to Africans, especially African ministers of defense and their chiefs of staff, and as welcome as conflict prevention through concerted force is to the same persons, the necessary political creativity—really the capacity to imagine transferring authority for action to the Secretary-General or to a SADC—is not yet fully available.

The purpose of convening three consecutive meetings of African ministers of defense and chiefs of staff, together with officers, diplomats, and scholars from Europe and America, was to solve both the technical problems and answer the relevant political questions. The first meeting, at Harvard University, evaluated existing Western initiatives, found them wanting in terms of conflict prevention and serious peace enforcement, and emphasized the need for African ownership of conflict prevention in Africa and any forcible kinds of intervention for peace. Jeffrey Herbst's report of that meeting, *Securing Peace in Africa: An Analysis of Peacekeeping & Peace Enforcement Potential*, WPF Reports 17 (Cambridge, Mass., 1998) underscored the difficulties. He suggested that traditional peace-keeping was irrelevant to Africa. Instead, peace enforcement of the kind anticipated by Chapter VII of the UN Charter was needed to deter bloodshed in a country that was "at war with itself."[9] Ending hostilities—not reinforcing an existing peace—was and would be the object in Africa.

Herbst predicted that there would be recurring African situations where multiple armed groups would be attacking each other within a state. Those groups would be indistinguishable from the local populations, the lines of battle would be fluid, and long-standing grievances would motivate the antagonists "to try simply to outlast the intervenors through wars of attrition." There was a continuing demand for some kind of intervention capability, even if peace intervention by soldiers could only be one of the many ways of minimizing conflicts and preventing conflicts in Africa. What was needed, Herbst suggested, was the UN volunteer force contemplated in Article 43 of the Charter. But that has not and will not be realized; nor had he any faith in Africans taking upon themselves an effective primary responsibility for their own wars. African problems could not be left exclusively to Africans: "the gross violations of human rights occurring in parts of Africa demand the resources and attention of the whole world."[10]

The second meeting in this series took place at the invitation of and with the co-sponsorship of the Ministry of Defence of Malawi. Along the shores of Lake Malawi, ministers of defense, chiefs of staff, and former military leaders from Senegal, Ghana, Uganda, Kenya, and virtually all the members of SADC, excepting South Africa and the Congo, decided that crisis response forces, organized sub-regionally, were a good idea. Unlike Herbst, they believed that they could assume primary responsibility for preventing their own internal wars. Properly trained and equipped African fire brigades, funded and assisted by the West, could greatly improve Africa's ability to reduce intrastate conflict and civilian deaths. Military and diplomatic officials from Britain, Denmark, France, Canada, and the United States, at the meeting in Malawi, welcomed these decisions and promised to back the creation and support the operations of sub-regional crisis response forces. Those warm words went beyond existing and continuing cooperation with African armies. Dana Francis's report of the Malawi meeting, *Peacekeeping or Peace Enforcement? Conflict Intervention in Africa*, WPF Report 21 (Cambridge, Mass., 1998) summarized its accomplishments and emphasized the large extent to which answering the key political questions had been gently avoided.

Francis reported that Africans felt a neighborly obligation to involve themselves in sub-regional conflicts. The African participants at the Malawi conference said that they were "tired of relying on the West." They had the manpower and the will to intervene in their own conflicts, but they lacked money, equipment, and technical capability. Since the West no longer wished to involve itself directly in these same conflicts, Francis suggested that a "balanced partnership" could result.[11]

At the Malawi meeting, the participants described that partnership. Francis outlined a consensus among the participants that included:

—a willingness of Africans to do their own peacekeeping and peace enforcement, with substantial help from the West.

—an African desire to train and organize peace enforcers systematically.

—the strong belief that peace enforcement should be developed sub-regionally.

—an assertion that battalion strength troops should remain in their own countries until called upon to intervene, coming together in brigade-sized (4,000–5,000 person) strength.

—the belief that Africa needed a classification method for early warning of dangerous conflicts. African countries should be ranked according to their potential for conflict, and attention sub-regionally should be focused on those with the highest scores.

Francis reported a long series of discussions in Malawi about how these proposed crisis response forces would best be commanded, controlled, and trained. African peace enforcers would have to overcome a legacy of weak command and control structures, major logistical weaknesses (few transport aircraft and tracked vehicles), primitive communications equipment, medical care insufficiencies, intelligence inadequacies, an absence of policing capabilities, and few opportunities for intensive training.

The ministers and chiefs of staff demanded a further opportunity to address these lingering issues, especially the tough ones that had been raised without answers being forthcoming. The Ministry of Defence of Tanzania decided to co-host a third meeting to create a broader consensus, especially on the unresolved questions: Which crises? Who summons? Who develops the mandate?

The third conference was held in the middle of a national park in western Tanzania. This time, in 1999, nearly 70 participants represented the countries of the Malawi conclave, plus Namibia, Nigeria, and Norway (which had also been represented at the initial session at Harvard). Many of the officials who came to Tanzania were new to their posts owing to reshuffled cabinets and changes in staff assignments since the Malawi assembly in 1998. This time, although assumptions about what could be accomplished militarily through crisis response forces remained consistent, doubts about the ability of African political leaders to resolve the critical political issues were articulated even more forcefully and candidly than at the previous meeting on African soil.

Between the discussions in Malawi and Tanzania, optimism about Africa's capacity to cope effectively with its own mayhem, and organize peace more effectively than war, had been replaced by a profound pessimism. Two major events had catalyzed Africa. At the Malawi meeting, participants had Rwanda and Burundi on their minds. A year later, in Tanzania, participants could not help but reflect upon the failure of Africa to achieve peace in the Democratic Republic of the Congo and along the Ethiopian-Eritrean border. Angola and the Sudan had been running sores throughout, and in both cases for so many years that at both meetings (the first attended by Angolan generals) those wars were regarded as exceptions to what could become a general rule. Not so in 1999, when Africa had once more descended of its own volition into what many were calling chaos. The Congo seemed a quagmire, and one from which extrication would not prove easy.

The 1999 discussions covered all of the critical areas summarized above. No summary, however, can do justice to the ways in which African, American, and European participants expressed themselves on each point, and how individually and collectively they approached the central questions of peace intervention, political will, the despatch and the command and control of sub-regional rapid response forces, and the contributions to African peace enforcement of the wealthier powers of the West.

The conversations that took place in Tanzania extend and elaborate the ideas and conclusions of this chapter. They follow, and are organized topically rather than in their original sequence; each is an authentic summary but not necessarily a verbatim reproduction of the actual words employed. The candor of the meeting is evident; the atmosphere was positive, and there was much more widespread and general participation than is apparent from the frequency with which the remarks of some individuals are represented in the summary. Each section is prefaced by a brief introduction so as to place the ensuing dialogue in context. (Ericka A. Albaugh produced the summary, and David W. Kearn Jr. and Rachel M. Gisselquist helped significantly to put it into its final form.)

The soldiers in Africa want their civilian masters to initiate peace enforcement and peace building activities. They are ready to create crisis response forces and engage in collective readiness and intervention actions. They are confident that they could without difficulty organize themselves sub-regionally or otherwise to deal effectively with the kinds of intrastate crises that have already disturbed the peace of Africa. They could interpose themselves as the Nigerians did in Liberia and Sierra Leone, Tanzanians in Uganda, and South Africans in Lesotho. They know, too, that no such forceful effort at conflict reduction would prove easy. But with sufficient firepower and manpower, and with Western financial backing, they could imagine controlling most intrastate implosions. Technically, their issues are all challenges to be met.

But they doubt the existence of sufficiently strong political will in Africa, either at the OAU or the sub-regional levels, to direct the generals and their soldiers appropriately. Strong leaders of strong countries are the only hope. So military persons are doubtful that Africa will ever organize itself as this report and its predecessors have contemplated, and advocated. The dream of conflict prevention by Africans in their sub-regional crisis response forces remains an ideal searching for one or more visionary indigenous leaders, and subtle Western diplomacy, to appreciate its merit and put it into practice.

Notes

1. This chapter is a revised version of the opening part of Robert I. Rotberg and Ericka A. Albaugh, *Preventing Conflict in Africa: Possibilities of Peace Enforcement*, WPF Report 24 (Cambridge, Mass., 1999).

2. David Lake and Donald Rothchild, "Containing Fear: The Origin and Management of Ethnic Conflict," *International Security*, XXI (1996), 41–75.

3. Walter Clarke and Jeffrey Herbst, *Learning from Somalia* (Boulder, Colo., 1997).

4. For a list, see *Peace, Security and Conflict Resolution*, SIPRI-UNESCO Handbook (Oxford, 1998), 13–36.

5. "Five Nations Reportedly Lined Up for African Force," *Boston Globe,* October 10, 1996.

6. See Jeffrey Herbst, *Securing Peace in Africa: An Analysis of Peacekeeping and Peace Enforcement Potential*, WPF Report 17 (Cambridge, Mass., 1998); Robert I. Rotberg, "NGOs, Early Warning, Early Action, and Preventive Diplomacy," in Rotberg (ed.), *Vigilance and Vengeance: NGOs Preventing Ethnic Conflict in Divided Societies* (Washington, D.C., 1996), 263–68.

7. See Herbst, *Securing Peace*, 22-29; Dana Francis, *Peacekeeping or Peace Enforcement? Conflict Intervention in Africa*, WPF Report 21 (Cambridge, Mass., 1998), 10.

8. Alison Des Forges, *Leave None to Tell the Story: Genocide in Rwanda* (New York, 1999), 21–24, 180–219.

9. Herbst, *Securing Peace*, 9.

10. Ibid., 9, 31.

11. Francis, *Peacekeeping,* 11.

CHAPTER SEVEN

Preventing Conflict in Africa: Possibilities of Peace Enforcement

Edited by Ericka A. Albaugh

I. African Responsibility

Conflict prevention in Africa is the responsibility of Africans. The states of Africa should not ask outsiders to bring peace. Africans must do that themselves, in determined ways. African nations are now more mature than they were; so are their sub-regional organizations. Although African leaders have depended often on Western intervention in the continent's troubles, that era ought to be over. Africans must take charge.

Minister of Defence Edgar Maokola-Majogo [Tanzania]: The latest developments have shown that solutions may be attained, though more efforts and commitment are needed. African countries, not the West or the UN, should take a leading role in finding solutions to interstate conflicts through diplomacy. In this sub-region we are making more efforts to find peace without interference except advice and technical support. We should take note of this significant development.

Deputy Minister of Defence Mike Mulongoti [Zambia]: As an African, my biggest worry is that we have to build confidence in the way we interact with one another. We have to move away from suspicion. When people move in, stop asking immediately why they did it. If we keep saying, "Africa has no resources," we have to admit that whatever little resources we have, they must be employed in

This chapter is a revised summary of the discussions at the World Peace Foundation's June 6–9, 1999, meeting in Tarangire, Tanzania. The italicized introductory paragraphs provide context for the summaries. They were written by Robert I. Rotberg.

solving our problems. In Zambia, if we had to wait for the UN or the EU, there
would be no start. But we said, "What can we do before that?" Pleading no
resources all the time won't take us anywhere. We also have to show commitment
to our own problems and be grateful to others who help us. Problems that are ours,
are ours. We can't continue to point fingers at people who died years ago. If so,
we invite them in to help re-partition us because of our inadequacies. They will
re-draw boundaries based on economics—diamonds here, oil here, etc. Develop
pride in finding solutions that are African. Ask for support, yes, but the solution
must be one cooked in an African pot. Political will, determination, pride. Whatever help we get must be in addition to our own ideas. Africa is coming of age. If
we don't do that, there will be no globalization.

General David R. C. Tonje [Kenya]: I want to provoke discussion by posing
a few questions. We have talked about African response forces, but I haven't heard
anyone define what "African" is. I'm a Kenyan and I look at things from a Kenyan
perspective. There are fifty-three others. Who is this African we're talking about?
Are there common characteristics? Do they have common interests? Have they
got the values that we need, if necessary, to fight and die for? If there are clear
conclusions on these issues, and we arrive at a position that there is such an entity,
such a people with values, then maybe there is a need for an African defense force.
We have to look at it by way of military, as well as diplomatic, cultural, and social
values. All of it needs to be put together.

Throughout the discussions, it has been suggested that we need financial support, that Africa is incapable of doing things on its own. I've even heard proposals that sound like selling raffle tickets to support our organ for conflict
management. Yes, Europe was developed on our shoulders. Yes, I know we were
short-changed. But most of the companies that survive today, like Barclays Bank,
for example, would have been there without us. Is it really resources we need, or
something else? It's really a question of priorities. Where are our priorities? If we
feel that they are in this area of conflict resolution, then we have what it takes to
solve these problems.

To what end are we putting all this energy, time, and effort? Where do we see
Africa ten, twenty years from now? What is the end-state we desire that can ener-
gize us to apply all the resources we have to achieve? This takes us back to the
first question: Who are we? What we are is defined by others. We haven't defined
ourselves. Even our names—others called us by their names. The structures that
we have are by and large imposed. Our boundaries are not there by our own choice.
For how long will we continue to be defined by others? When will we define ourselves? The world is moving at supersonic speed in almost every facet of our
lives...but we haven't gone through an agrarian or an industrial revolution! We
face the information age. There is a desire by us to catch up. We are forced to

build or act—"to democratize." This is part of the continuous drain of resources that has gone on. We've been asked to come onto a playing field—I'm not sure it is level—by lowering the barriers of trade, etc. How can we compete with the organs that we helped to bring about 400 years ago? We haven't been at this thirty years. We've been dragged by the scruff of our necks into a new arena, and we therefore have to live through many revolutions that have gone on elsewhere— all at one go. It is in our interest to do so—to catch up to the information age— but how, with some states that are only 1 million people? The question of defining ourselves is important. We must set a goal and determine a desired end-state.

We should leave the baggage of history behind. Leave tinkering with what has been imposed on us. As for the boundaries that have been imposed, satellites don't respect boundaries. Let those states that may have fought and survived colonial history forget about it. We should join with other African countries, pool our resources, and start anew in redefining who we are and where we're going. We need to put our resources to optimum use in catching up with the rest of the world.

Maj. Gen. Martin Shalli [Namibia]: In the 1960s, we used to hear about pan-Africanism. In the 1970s, we heard about humanism. Now we hear about an African renaissance. Maybe that is another concept. I just attended a conference at Windhoek on the subject of renaissance. African relations can be frightening to others if they don't understand. Maybe we have to start by understanding who Africans are. If not, we won't know what African solutions should be.

Tonje: We can't pre-judge the solution to various states' problems. We have to take into account the environment. Africans want their own solution to problems, often distancing away anyone else who wants to participate. There is a song that says, "Don't come—" But we are not prepared to solve the problems ourselves.

Professor Jeffrey Herbst [USA]: I am going to reflect on what I've learned in Malawi and in Cambridge, Massachusetts. A surprising amount has also occurred between May 1998 and this time: Lesotho, Democratic Republic of Congo (DRC), Guinea-Bissau, and Ethiopia and Eritrea.

African conflicts share two negative characteristics, both non-ideological. This is different from some conflicts in Central America, which ended after the global ideological conflict subsided. In Africa, most conflicts (except for the Great Lakes) were fully dependent on outside powers. That certainly played a role. But they continue even once the original patrons have changed.

Wars originate from a variety of sources. It is often in the context of reinventing politically, where the losers don't accept it. It also occurs where African governments only have incomplete control. In this environment, there are places for those who disagree to go. Further, weapons are everywhere. Alienated men can find both the space to create a force to challenge leadership and the weapons to arm themselves well.

The political science literature says that the conflicts will continue until one side or the other wins a military victory. There is little hope of an interim agreement because there is no outside referee that can bring all sides to the table. Part of the charge is to get away from the solution being outright military victory. This can be done with a neutral arbiter, an outside force, so fighting it out to the end is not the only alternative. To be the kind of intervenor that would solve military and underlying political issues, the intervenor has to have military dominance, a strategy, and a willingness to stay in and operate in difficult circumstances.

For a long time, the UN attempted traditional Chapter VI intervention: Blue Helmets in between warring armies that had already agreed to a cease-fire. After the Cold War, starting with Somalia, the second era began. In this decade, Somalia and Angola stand as stark failures of a new Chapter VII robust peacekeeping strategy. Both operations cost over 1 billion dollars, involved thousands of troops, and did not meet their final objectives. There has been some success—in Mozambique—but the stark failures have led to a new era. Today, there are only 2,000 Blue Helmets in Africa: in Angola, Sierra Leone, the Central African Republic, and Western Sahara (which is traditional de-colonization). The world has come to a halting consensus that the 1990s' method of large numbers of troops sent and guided from the outside cannot meet the challenges. They cannot meet the requirement for military dominance.

So the third era has African self-help, African initiative, as its defining characteristic. In some cases, unilateral action by an African country is later endorsed (for example, that by South Africa in Lesotho or Nigeria in Liberia); in others, it is not later endorsed (for example, that by Angola in the Democratic Republic of Congo). African countries are now taking the lead in peace making. It actually looks much like traditional international relations: neighbors reacting to a political vacuum. First, it is not neutral; the intervenor wants one side to win. Second, it is robust, particularly in Chapter VII-type operations. And finally, it is problematic, because the intervenors face the same logistical, political, and financial problems as Western countries that had previously tried to intervene.

II. Crises Ripe for Action: Who Decides, Who Triggers?

Within Africa, sub-regions like the Southern African Development Community (SADC) and the Economic Community of West African States (ECOWAS) have the demonstrated capacity to begin to forge their own peace enforcement regimes. They already have shown a capacity beyond peacekeeping (see below); the potential for cohesive responses is more attainable in the sub-regions. Collective respon-

*sibility is more realizable there than in Africa as a whole, as the failure of the
Organization of African Unity (OAU) over decades to play a meaningful role in
concerted peace enforcement makes clear. It is the sub-regions that have the clout.
But within those sub-regions, it is the hegemons—the larger and more powerful
states—that can, have, and will motivate sub-regional responses. Hegemons have
acted in place of or on behalf of sub-regional and regional organizations. They
have done so without explicit reference to the UN, but often in cooperation with
other African states. Logistical and other kinds of support have come from the
West. There is also a possible role for coalitions of the willing—hegemons and
smaller states or a collection of medium-sized states. But there exists no mechanism as yet to organize or recognize when hegemons, coalitions, or sub-regional
responses should be launched. The UN's imprimatur remains important, and sub-
regional activities may best be regulated or legitimated within a UN framework.*

*The kinds of internal conflicts that merit intervention by an African force or
forces include those where the state has become the oppressor, where ethnic or
other kinds of intercommunal hostility have degenerated into massacres of civilians, where gross violations of human rights are common, where the state itself
has collapsed and cannot maintain order, and much more. Hitherto, strong leaders have sent their soldiers into action to limit mayhem or restore peace and order.
So far there is no mechanism to choose the crises that merit intervention or to
send troops into conflict areas on short notice. In each sub-region, at least, that
mechanism must be created.*

Minister of State for Defence Steven Kavuma [Uganda]: President Yoweri
Museveni decided to challenge the OAU in 1987 because we had suffered under
the regime of Idi Amin and no one would come to our rescue. Only our brothers
from Tanzania responded in 1979, and I want to thank them for laying a good
precedent. We don't want to sit aside and watch while serious crimes are being
committed under the principle of non-intervention. What are the justifying circumstances?

1. Genocide: crimes against humanity. It wouldn't be proper for anyone to look
on when people are being killed en masse, doing nothing simply because there is
a government.

2. Endless civil war (for example, Liberia). If you don't see an end coming,
you might want to think about the need for generating consensus to end it.

3. Massive killings of people by their own state. Uganda under Amin is an example.

4. Massive displacement of persons, either internally or externally. In the 1980s,
this happened to a small extent in Uganda. If people are ordered to leave, told that
they belong somewhere else, the world should know that a catastrophe will happen.

5. Failure by a state to control its territory effectively. We see examples in the

Great Lakes region. Here, there is intervention to prevent catastrophe. When you
have rebels, and they are armed, trained, and allowed to cross into your country,
it is difficult to live with that without allowing it to come to an end. The DRC's
border with Uganda is an example.

What are the constraints? We are all constrained financially, but I think a government worth being called a government must take as a priority that the lives of
people and property are properly secured. Whatever meager resources they have,
they must be prepared to meet the needs of their people. And they should be prepared to stop catastrophes once they happen. That is our primary responsibility.
Support is needed, but we have to take the initiative. A number of things have
evolved after Cold War; it is not a positive situation for aid. The time has come
for us to act: act now.

Prime Minister Pakalitha Mosisili [Lesotho]: Regarding the "common values" that Tonje described: That is important. In the case of SADC, I think we've
gotten to a point where we have certain values we share. One such value is a belief
in democracy and democratically elected governments. We will not allow a democratically elected government to be overthrown by force. We will intervene in such
cases. So it wasn't difficult to agree on intervening in Lesotho. Second, I observed
that the admission of the DRC into SADC was indeed very problematic, precisely
because of the democracy issue. Some of us argued that it wasn't yet time for it
to be admitted into SADC because the government hadn't come into power democratically. But that is water under the bridge; it did get in. And see what it has led
us to! Third, much has been made of the need for a legitimate government invit-
ing forces to intervene. That can only hold in certain cases, because what if the
legitimate government is the perpetrator of atrocities? Will you wait and say, "We
won't intervene unless they invite us in?" Also, much has been said about how
South Africa invaded Lesotho. I appealed to the four presidents whose countries
had been mandated by SADC. I haven't hesitated in any forum to take full responsibility for the forces in Lesotho. I invited them in and would re-invite them tomor-
row. [See also below.]

Herbst: The question is, how can African countries work together with other
nations to undertake peacekeeping and peacemaking operations, rather than acting in self-interested, traditional international relations behavior?

My understanding is that intervening countries want international legitimacy
for these operations, but are often willing to act without legitimacy beforehand.
They understand the importance of some kind of sub-regional operation. There is
consensus that the West must provide military assets, logistics, and financing, as
well as reconstruction efforts afterward.

But there is a contradiction between sub-regional organizations and neutral peacekeeping. If neighbors are going to intervene because they are at risk, it invariably involves a question of self-interest. The intervention could cause disaster or be little more than a cloak for self-interested foreign policy. To complicate the situation, some countries dominate the regional organizations that are later asked to legitimate their action (for example, Nigeria and South Africa). Regional organizations are weak, and not designed to handle mandate or trigger questions. They have to determine how those will be answered from beginning.

Nicholas Normand [France]: France no longer has a strategic interest in Africa. There was one during the Cold War. Now it is difficult to say that France or any country has a strategic interest in a specific African country. Most, if not every, time France, the U.S. and Britain do not try to protect their own interests in intervening. As proof, we insist on transparent discussion within the Security Council. True, peacekeeping is hostage to those who provide the money. These countries do try to protect their money. The U.S. should provide 25 percent, France 6 percent [of the UN peacekeeping budget]. It is not a political obstacle, though a financial one.

Tonje: Coming back to the idea of self-interest: No one will invest resources without considering the costs to its own people.

Shalli: Herbst mentioned self-interest. Can a head of state commit a country's resources to protect his personal interests? That would be intervening for self-interest. Why is it called self-interest in Africa and national interest outside Africa?

Herbst: There are national interests. I think sub-regional organizations intervening in their neighbors is a bad idea because they can't be neutral. Senegal can't be neutral in Guinea-Bissau. However, no one has said anything yet about sub-regional organizations as the only solution, because no one else has the interest or quickness to address the problems. So in principle, I'm uncomfortable with sub-regional organizations, but no one has told me why any other set of countries is willing to address the conflicts.

This raises the question of the responsibility of large nations within each of the regions and how they act. Large nations have particular problems in regards to regional interests.

Normand: I agree that it may be risky to give responsibility to a sub-regional organization to intervene in its own region. The goal of providing assistance to sub-regional organizations is to allow them to participate in peacekeeping operations in the framework of the UN *outside* of their region, even outside Africa. They may be more apt to participate outside the continent. It is risky to participate in a place where they are not neutral.

Minister of Defence Joseph Kubwalo [Malawi]: I disagree. It depends on the magnitude of conflict. On smaller ones, there should be a sub-regional responsibility. It is high time we learned to solve our own problems.

Lucy M. T. Dlamini [Swaziland]: In the case of Lesotho, it was good that South Africa and Botswana could intervene. The situation might have been worse and spread to South Africa. They certainly had to intervene. We really should take part in our own regions; then we can go abroad.

Tonje: How about the power of the UN beside other forces that we know are in the game? The idea of the sub-region arose from the fact that the OAU and the UN were not providing satisfactory responses. The UN is under the control of powerful nations; they act in their interests. So if their interest is not there, the UN is sidelined. Lesotho proves that point. An action might require an interested party to go in under certain conditions. As far back as Korea, resolutions were taken that bypassed the Security Council. We're now scuttling some organizations. There is another option: states themselves. Should we not therefore be discussing the place of those states as well? The bottom line is the nation-state. Don't necessarily try to downplay interests. States have interests beyond their borders. We can't run away from the nation-state and from powers held by those in control of nation-states. So the question of sovereignty must be discussed. If powerful, can one state ride roughshod over others?

Maj. Gen. Ishola Williams [Nigeria]: As for the subject of the national interest, take the case of Nigeria in the Guinea-Bissau crisis. No one wanted to do anything at first. Then Senegal and Guinea moved in for their national interest. But because ECOWAS couldn't react quickly, the Commonwealth decided to come together and act. This created a problem between ECOWAS and the Commonwealth countries. Then Nigeria was asked to take responsibility. It refused, since it was over-committed to Liberia and to Sierra Leone. France said they would pay for troops and transportation, and the problem was solved. So sometimes it is not necessarily national interest that provokes a response.

Hegemons

Williams: We always have internal problems, crises and conflicts in Africa, and then knowingly wait for an outsider to intervene to manage or resolve our conflict, because Africans claim to respect sovereignty. Formerly, when the UN was created, the emphasis was on sovereignty—the idea that nothing must be done to compromise the territorial integrity. Right from its inception, the OAU accepted that African strategists would solve their problems.

But they were looking at the issue of someone coming from the outside only as a problem of interstate intervention. They didn't recognize problems as *intra*state. Many countries are still very scared about anyone trying to interfere with their internal problems.

We have now reached a situation where that can't go on any more. We are having a lot of problems with preventing conflict in African countries. There is not a
conflict where we didn't see smoke before fire started. But we only decided to act
when there was fire. We have to ask, when does the internal crisis reach a stage in
which something has got to be done to prevent the smoke from becoming a fire?

Now in West Africa, Liberia presented an opportunity. The case of Chad, too,
was a test of African intervention in an African problem. Nigeria went into Chad
much earlier than the OAU intervention. But this was at the request of France, the
U.S., and Britain and was not an African initiative. Liberia for the first time gave
room for African intervention based on African initiative. The question in such a
situation is who decides and who triggers? It has to be a hegemon. It was not that
Nigeria was interested in being a hegemon. It was President Museveni of Uganda
(then OAU chairman) who, believing that one could not look at the events then
in Liberia and remain aloof, urged General [Ibrahim Badamosi] Babangida to intervene. Even Angola, with its own wars, is a hegemon in the Democratic Republic
of Congo and Congo-Brazzaville. Once you have a hegemon with political will,
it can be the trigger. Acting in a sensible manner, the hegemon gives legitimacy.
We have to accept that hegemons have responsibilities. When you have resources,
you have to intervene.

But then there is the question of staying power. Here we need the international
community to help. Also let us remember that when the traditional and national
institutions for conflict management and resolution fail in an African country, the
country can no longer run normally. When can you intervene as the situation in a
country degenerates into chaos and anarchy? ECOWAS has found the answer in
its revised treaty. It can now intervene when it sees that a country is going to descend
into chaos, no matter who is responsible. A lot of times it is obvious that a country can no longer provide adequate security for its own citizens while the government has lost control of the administration. Hence, the question of intervention
is made easier and easier.

Taking the case of the UN or the OAU in the realistic sense, pragmatically they
cannot take care of the problems we have with respect to Africa. The process is
too long and bureaucratic. In Cairo in 1994, before the Rwanda genocide, there
was a meeting of military leaders and diplomats. We asked, "What do we do about
Rwanda?" A committee was formed, and it worked through the night to try to find
a response. We worked out a force structure, and asked African countries to volunteer. We wanted to create a place for refugees to go. There were only one or
two volunteers.

Ultimately, you have to depend on one or two countries who can make their
decision, who say, "We have to do something and do something quickly." We talked

and talked and talked. Britain and Nigeria worked out a proposal on peacekeeping that was sent to the Security Council. But it was impossible. [UN Secretary-General] Kofi Annan said to ECOWAS that the sub-regional organizations had to accept responsibilities. Only then can the UN and the OAU come in and help. "Take care of the problem first, and then we can come in and help." The grand truth is that it is only a hegemon and consensus-building within a sub-region that can trigger a [quick and helpful] response.

Tonje: I am uncomfortable with the hegemon theory. All countries are sovereign. But I have come around over a few days to the idea that the OAU can be changed regarding non-intervention. We're being driven to a position where we have to make choices. Small countries may be able to do it themselves. The UN, the OAU, and sub-regional organizations are not structured to solve problems. There have to be other interests. It's more of a political nature. It has to come to the neighboring countries. Kenya didn't get involved in Somalia. Since it had had problems for so long, we didn't want to touch it. But because of the effects of problems on us, we are inclined to think there ought to be something done about the restoration of order. We can't do it alone. But if there is a consensus of countries, maybe something can be done.

Lt. Gen. L. M. Fisher [Botswana]: As for a hegemon, when it represents a translation of access to resources, then the bigger countries that make resources available can give confidence to others. Convincing them that we can do this can create a catalyst. But there still remains the problem of internal constituencies' support. You ignore your constituency at your own peril.

And unless those bigger countries can convert their participation into access to resources, I still see that in the future there will be a coalition approach to conflict resolution. We have to be careful if we're going to portray larger countries in a way that says they don't need other countries. These are sovereign countries that should seek consensus. The longer you stay in a country, the more resources you're going to require. A coalition can help in this regard, as we saw with ECOMOG. One country could act by providing the immediate access to troops, while the diffusion of logistical support by Americans allowed the troops to cover an area.

Professor Christopher Clapham [U.K.]: I would like to comment on hegemony from the point of view of a Western European. We have lived under the shadow of hegemony for fifty years. We moan about the arrogant, bloody Yankees. But we would recognize that it has been enormously helpful to the security and welfare of Western Europe. Hegemony is not necessarily something to be feared by other states. It does depend on shared values and institutions that link the hegemon and smaller states into a real alliance for real discussion. That is the only way it would work in Africa too.

Rotberg: I am puzzled as to whether this group accepts one conclusion of some of the speakers so far: that the only effective peace intervention is almost always bound to be ad hoc and totally unplanned. This conclusion is based on a "large African power" perception of national interest. This would imply that sub-regional organizations are not going to be able to gain a handle on a conflict unless the large African power in that region has a national interest and agrees. That is a pessimistic conclusion. I hope it is false. I hope you will disagree and provide evidence that it is false; that you will offer a better paradigm and an answer to those conflicts that exist.

Ambassador Robert Houdek [USA]: I don't think African hegemons themselves will be able financially to carry out those interventions in the future.

Rotberg: Nigeria in Sierra Leone and Liberia won't repeat itself?

Houdek: I don't think so. $4 billion was spent over seven years. That's real money. And Nigeria has serious internal demands. To commit those kinds of resources in territories that are not even contiguous is not very likely. Successful efforts will require coalition building, regional groupings. I don't know if we'll have General Alain Faupin's direct chain of command from states to sub-regional organizations to regional organizations to the UN. But we will need serious consultation. We had a leadership role in Desert Storm, but it took time to build the coalition. The U.S. needed various Arab countries on board.

Mosisili: I feel rather constrained, as the only head of government in the room, and I prefer to sit back and listen to wisdom. On a number of occasions, I have seen that some have been looking this way. So I would like to say something. We are the beneficiaries of an intervention exercise under the auspices of SADC, but strictly speaking through the governments of South Africa and Botswana. What our experience in Lesotho has taught us is that yes, indeed, sub-regional structures are very important. But then, SADC has this Interstate Defense and Security Committee (IDSC), but that structure does not have the financial resources that can enable it to carry out its mandate. The example of Lesotho has led to a lot of observations about exactly who has intervened in Lesotho. We argue that it is SADC; other people think it is South Africa or Botswana. When you look at the situation closely, you have to agree with the latter. Those two republics sent in their own forces at their own expense; there has been not a cent from SADC or Lesotho. So it is a question of someone who sees a problem and thinks that it is a problem serious enough to do something about it, being prepared to spend not only human but financial resources in that exercise. The sub-regional structures are crucial, but there is also the question of whether those are being properly resourced to carry out their mandate.

Rotberg: The prime minister has just challenged us: Is the South African method the only method? Can we develop a sub-regional method instead of one or two individual countries taking up the cudgel to act?

Sub-regional Organizations

Maj. Gen. Michael R. Nyambuya [Zimbabwe]: I am fully behind these noble efforts which empower the sub-regions to help themselves. It is within the spirit of what we've been saying. If we wait for someone, there might be no one there when we need them. We have to help ourselves. I have a question, though, about the business of peacekeeping. It is not clear what the idea of bilateral peacekeeping is. If training is done bilaterally, do we expect that country will engage in peacekeeping? Is it not better for these initiatives to be coordinated within a sub-regional context?

Rotberg: "Is it better to coordinate these efforts within a sub-region?"—is that not your proposition?

Kavuma [Uganda]: It is better to coordinate within a sub-region. But everything needs to start. We thought we'd be first. Now it is time for us to do it together. We've been talking for three years...can't we get going? We have a battalion ready, what next?

Gen. Fisher: Looking in the context of SADC as a region, we've tended to assign responsibilities as far as countries. Zimbabwe has been assigned to peacekeeping efforts and training in the region. That's why the peacekeeping training center will be in Zimbabwe. As a region, we can send peacekeepers for training there. The fundamental factor is that these efforts are multinational. We have to go there as a group of countries.

Harmonization has been mentioned. In the SADC region, the British come up with their proposals, then the Scandinavians, then the Canadians, then the French. At the end of day, you don't know which peacekeeping conference to go to. Look at African Crisis Response Initiative (ACRI) in SADC. The feeling of SADC is that some of these initiatives must come to the sub-region, and the sub-region as an entity must move in and utilize these initiatives. But we get a feeling that these are competing with each other. Somewhere along the line, you need to coordinate, channel them. They should not be competing efforts. This is where Nyambuya was coming from. There is a concern that these initiatives are competing, and we need coordination.

Nyambuya: I am a sincere and ardent fan of the concept of sub-regional organizations. The world does not owe us anything. We must be seen to be doing something about our own problems. We should be seen making bold attempts to address some of the major issues. Hiding from them is a shameful act of omission. At the same time, I feel that the UN Security Council should not be kept from the responsibility of addressing security conflicts. We fought in many wars, for example the UN peacekeeping operation in Haiti. Further, some of the problems we're facing are a result of acts of commission from outsiders: imposed borders, ideological intervention during the Cold War, conveniently looking aside while people are suffering. We need to focus on sub-regions, plus whatever structures and mechanisms are needed to activate those sub-regional arrangements. We need to address them with input from outsiders.

Rotberg: What arrangements might be made?

Nyambuya: Already under discussion are concepts such as P3 [Three Powers: United States, Britain, and France] and the African Crisis Response Initiative. We already have organizations within the UN. Perhaps there needs to be more time and research on how to create structures, how to put them into the field, how to activate sub-regional arrangements, and how to operationalize the strategic effort.

Tonje: Regarding subgroupings: Are they appropriate for solving the problems? Mention was made of the condition of Africa: ethnic identities with boundaries imposed that aren't in keeping with nation building. In Europe, you have nation-states. In Africa, we have nations within the states. Are these not the problems that we should be tackling in Africa? We can't differentiate ourselves from the rest of the world; we are connected, they are connected, to the rest of the world. Does it not require us to go to first principles? What are the real problems? Is Africa prepared to rewrite the boundaries imposed? What is it we want to achieve? Are we willing to invest in that objective? What do we actually mean by the solutions?

Gen. Fisher: Regarding regional organizations and their financial limitations. Herbst used the words "ability or willingness" to stay on. This also has financial implications. The longer you stay, the more resources you require. You get sucked into the conflict. Sub-regional organizations may have the advantage of quicker reaction. But only in the short term. In the long term, they have limitations, especially financial. For the short run, there is a sub-regional advantage; for the long-term, we need the UN.

Kubwalo: I concur. We are meeting for the third time in three years. The fact that South Africa and Botswana went to help in Lesotho means that only able countries are intervening. We need assistance for SADC for its own force, or we are not moving anywhere.

Rotberg: Is it a problem of finance only, or of political will?

Kubwalo: We have done joint exercises in preparation, but things just keep going around and around. When will we come up with the real thing?

Majogo: Financial resources are a big thing; but it is also a question of speed. We need assistance now. We need something that can be convened at a quick moment. There is a political problem there. But for a legitimate government, when facing a problem, fast decisionmaking must be synchronized.

Rotberg: In a zone of states with no government, sub-regional intervention might be helpful.

Majogo: It is important to look at who triggers and who decides to intervene. Since the UN has ultimate responsibility over the security of the world, the Security Council has a role. Likewise, the OAU and the sub-regions. It is good to have a principle of noninterference. But let's face reality, if you want to intervene, there must be a political will first. The answer to the question is that the Secretary-General of the OAU can be empowered to trigger a response, but it is a fact of life that without heads of states themselves having the political will to intervene and deciding on assistance, nothing will happen. Even in the U.S. itself, the president comes forward and gives reasons for intervention. There is no way anyone below a head of state can trigger this.

If we come to sub-regional organizations, the commander in chief makes the decision to commit troops. That is embodied in the constitution. We can make decisions, but without heads of states, nothing can take place. This is the reality, because the head of state is the commander in chief. When you see a minister of defense, he may be a head of state himself or he may be a prime minister. If he is not, like myself, he can never make decisions to intervene. Heads of states, properly and quickly advised, make the decisions.

Rotberg: We've certainly discussed many of the parameters of the problem. Heads of state have to act, yes, but what if they disagree within a sub-region, even? Or what if there is only one dominant hegemon? How are decisions to be made? I hope we can come back to these questions.

Kavuma: In the context of small states, we can enhance the capacity of people to hold leaders responsible. The majority of our people are illiterate, but that doesn't mean they can't be mobilized to represent their interests. To know their interests in security, to own them, means to call their leaders to accountability. That won't be easy, but that is a first step. Secondly, the element of mutual respect among states is very important. It helps to achieve consensus. We must also have the criteria spelled out about how our peace mission should be conducted—the structures, mechanisms, and steps. Leaders must be strongly committed to regional grouping charters. We can't say that this is a problem too big that we can't help. History will judge us. We have to put into place mechanisms that will work in the future. We have no choice but to put in place the steps.

Nyambuya: One of the problems in Africa is mistrust, suspicion among ourselves. We hold conferences, and it keeps coming up that we need some confidence-building measures. On the basis of that, I believe we should go in the way of a regional, instead of a "big-power" concept. The latter would increase mistrust, creating the ground for further problems. Coalitional, sub-regional action is a basis for trust.

Majogo: It would be unfair if I did not comment on what Nyambuya has just said. As a soldier, it is a good observation. From a political point of view, some conflicts are accentuated by the fact that there is no mutual trust among top and lower leadership. Sometimes we go to international meetings with suspicions. Sometimes we also go with two versions of the same subject: one for the consumption of the conference, one for implementation on the ground. This is bad. At the meeting in Lusaka [to discuss the war in the Democratic Republic of the Congo], among the ministers of foreign affairs, we agreed we should always go to meetings with only one version: the truth of the matter. Be frank. From there, we can evolve a solution. Or we will waste lots of resources. Particularly on the Congo issue, we have made some progress toward a cease-fire and an understanding of the issues involved. All interests can be genuine. They need to be discussed frankly, and then we can have solutions.

OAU

Dr. K. Scott Fisher [USA]: I want to speak about the OAU and modestly about the UN. I come with some humility to express these views. They are issues that need discussion. Take Williams's point, for example. There has been an evolution of thinking regarding the OAU's role. The emphasis has generally moved away from the OAU. But I want to look at the half-full part of the glass, not the half-empty.

It has only been six years since the Cairo agreement, and seven years since a son of Tanzania took up the idea that African peace could be carried forward under the umbrella of the OAU. The Arusha Accord, even if abrogated the following year, represented a success. The Observer Mission in Rwanda kept a lid on hostilities as they existed. It was very useful in that context. These are things that the OAU must build upon in terms of successes. And heeding Museveni's views about early intervention in Liberia, not all interventions are successful, but some are, and we need to build on them.

For the near term, the OAU's role will be modest—confined to conflict resolution, mediation, sending persons like Julius Nyerere to the Burundi talks, and observer missions. It exercises great political authority, but that is not always translated into [military power].

The strengths of the OAU are three: First, it has political authority. It has called an important meeting with African chiefs of defense staff. Though not enough, this can be useful in providing information. Second, it has a Conflict Management Center with an observer capacity. Third, it has responsibility for issues in areas where there is no competence sub-regionally—in the Great Lakes and the Horn (Eritrea, Somalia, Sudan), for example. In these areas, security matters can't be handled by a sub-regional organization.

The constraints of the OAU are also three: First, fiscal. Secretary-General Salim Ahmed Salim has won agreement for a 5 percent decrement against assessments for conflict resolution. But this is quite modest. Second, billets. The U.S. government has funded materiel that would supply a 100-man observer mission. But there are no men behind the commitment who are trained on processes and procedures. Third, problems with political authority. There is a basic difference between the conflict management mechanism and the Secretary-General as against the Central Organ decisionmaking process. It is a forward-leaning Secretary-General against a more reticent central organ.

So, what to do to strengthen the OAU? First, consider appointing people of civil and military competence to the OAU. The current staff is fourteen to fifteen individuals. The OAU needs thirty-five or thirty-six people for 24-hour-a-day operation. There is no 100-man observer mission. Second, pay assessments. Some are grossly overdue. I speak with humility, as I represent the United States. Third, for the West, approach the OAU with a continuation of support. Work with the conflict management mechanism. The British team is continuing to work with it. The United States should continue financing, and work with its observer capacity. Fourth, for the OAU, is it time to revise those clauses of the OAU Charter that inhibit the effectiveness of the central mechanism? There is some degree of authority for the Secretary-General to intervene in the case of severe human rights or refugee problems. But should the Secretary-General be provided with more authority?

There is a peacekeeping planning questionnaire put forward to member countries on an annual basis. It assesses the willingness of countries to commit, for example, two radio operators, a Lusophone trainer, a battalion, or observers. If those commitments could come forward on an annual basis, the OAU could make known its commitment to sub-regional forces. The OAU Mechanism [for Conflict Prevention, Management and Resolution] itself must be exercised, as should its observer capacity. Linkages to sub-regionals must be created and expanded. As the sub-regionals are accorded status, there must be communication and regular information exchange. This could be done at the OAU and would have great influence on the issues we're here discussing. At all levels of mandates we're discussing—from the UN to the OAU to sub-regionals to "coalitions of the willing"— all could be more effectively informed and better put to use.

Houdek: I have had some experience in Ethiopia and Eritrea. I was ambas-

sador to Eritrea at the time of the war. So I was invited back by the assistant secretary to be a facilitator (at the invitation of the parties) to help with bringing about
an agreement. Despite some mistakes we made, there was a great deal of progress.
Throughout the period of shuttling back and forth, we had the closest consultation with the OAU. At one point, we thought we were close to providing an
observer force; we would be able to bring Rwandans in as part of it. The U.S. was
prepared to provide airlift and minimal supplies for the forces to go in. The OAU
made a commitment to provide equipment of humvees and communications gear.
It would have been a noteworthy and timely contribution [had the intervention
occurred]. So I don't want to make light of the OAU. Little by little, we're getting there. It is a building block approach. We may leave asking how much we
achieved, but I know we've been learning from our errors. I am heartened by other
delegates. I'm pleased to see how France has broadened its activity. The new French
training school in Abidjan will have Ghanaian teachers, demonstrating that it is
not just a francophone, but an African-wide effort. There has been openness and
a willingness to accept advice and criticism.

Nyambuya: Regarding the role of sub-regional organizations in command and
control, communication and transportation: I am really saddened that the OAU is
not here. The OAU, to a large extent, is responsible for incapacitating itself. It
starts and doesn't follow up. Heads of state created the present conflict response
mechanism. At the 1997 meeting in Harare, the concept of an African peace
enforcement force was central. We talked about command and control. A document was produced, but there was no follow-up. The "within sub-region" concept
is a good one. SADC could have a sub-regional training center, operating from
staff colleges, to train peacekeepers and logisticians. It would be staffed by people from our sub-region. I believe we should have a sustained approach to the
issue of sub-regional security. Sub-regionally, we should accept that the UN is
sluggish. So let's have something to help us. The overall structure is already there.
It is a question of perfecting it.

The United Nations

Williams: The UN has already abdicated responsibility toward Africa. In the
end, anything that the UN is going to do for Africa has to go back to the USA,
France, and Britain for approval. If they refuse, the UN can't do anything. When
you hear [OAU] Secretary-General Salim speak, he talks about help from the UN.
Without help from the UN, he is helpless. It appears that we Africans cannot manage or resolve our conflicts without Western support. Therefore we need an African
agenda. There is an OAU umbrella, there is ECOWAS, and, depending on whether

the Great Lakes is going to come together, there can be a collective security mechanism. We already have these frameworks. The frameworks exist, but the way the OAU continues to act, these frameworks cannot be a platform for action without the UN. The new African agenda is to strengthen these frameworks to try African solutions first before shouting to others for help.

Gen. Fisher: Should we set the UN aside? Or, should we say, "We've worked together since WWII, through Bosnia, why stop now?"

General Alain Faupin [France]: In answering who decides or triggers intervention, there are several responses. They should match the different types of crises and the different degrees of intensity of crisis, as well as the forecasted aftereffects of crisis. Rotberg put his finger on the lacking element: the UN. The UN represents the international community in its entirety. If there is no money, no political will, who triggers? The members of the UN Security Council, who add their veto? Kosovo was in the interest of Europeans. Europeans were interested enough to intervene. I am absolutely in line with Fisher regarding the need to reinforce and give the OAU stronger international weight.

What can be the chain of political decision? Ideally, it might be from states to sub-regional organizations, from the latter to the OAU, and from the OAU to the UN. But that does not always exist. Or if it does, it does so with lots of discrepancies among actors.

Scott Fisher: In response to Faupin, regarding the role and primacy of the UN. Consider two modalities: One, associating a hoped-for condition that the UN is concerned and the sub-regionals take over activities: should there be a direct link between a situation room in the UN and sub-regionals? Two, on the subject of an African peacekeeping support group: there was an unofficial opportunity for exchange of information convened by a French diplomat. There have been three meetings, giving opportunity for a transparent, communicating approach to peacekeeping on the continent. The UN hasn't been given permission by its African members to act on the ground. But it is a potential place for donors and leaders to meet. Right now it is not fully functional for lack of authority. Should that process move forward?

Ambassador Knut Toraasen [Norway]: Why is Norway here? It is a strong supporter of Africa. And it is among seven traditional countries supporting peacekeeping operations around the world. Norway is a strong believer in the work of the UN in representing unity. We still believe in seeking a mandate from the UN for any intervention, which will also help an intervenor to get money for its operations. The UN is the basic partner and starter of the process for peacekeeping. It takes time.

I also strongly support the OAU. It has good proposals on the table, and it has good vision. It works closely with all the sub-regions in Africa.

Faupin: In regard to the question of whether a hegemon should take charge, I would say that a hegemon can be an acceptable force. I can't imagine a "Europe" taking the lead in the UN. But resolutions *can* be taken quickly in the UN. We shouldn't confuse decision and enforcement. The resolution in the case of the Gulf War was taken very quickly, as was that in Kosovo. A mandate can be given to a major regional power or a hegemon. In the Gulf War, the U.S. was mandated by the UN. Intervention in Kosovo was mandated by NATO. What exists in Europe can exist in Africa. I don't disagree with Williams regarding the role of a hegemon in crisis resolution, but it has to have the *opportunity* to provide leadership; for that it needs a UN or an OAU mandate.

Scott Fisher: I would request, as we look at the various potential sources for mandates to bridge the process, that we distinguish between comments of practical and desired solutions. Let's move forward on all these fronts. Even if some are more operational than others, each one has particular modalities that can be moved on to improve the process.

Williams: First, I hope we do not leave with the impression that every conflict in Africa that requires intervention will be supported by the UN. Second, it appears we assume that any time the UN goes in, they are going to stay there. We need to ask ourselves, "What is the scenario for a UN commitment and need for action?" When the UN in the end withdraws, what will the OAU do then? What happens next?

Major Duke Ellington [USA]: In an ideal world, we would be working with OAU and UN mechanisms. But as the French learned in the Central African Republic (CAR), MISAB (Inter-African Mission to Monitor the Bangui Agreements) preceded the United Nations Mission in the CAR (MINURCA). The French saw something, reacted, and then the UN came on board. I suggest that the model we use for Africa be the model of Lesotho—how Botswana and South Africa reacted. Or the model of ECOMOG (Economic Community Monitoring Observer Group). There are lots of lessons. I commend those countries for their action instead of waiting for a cumbersome process. The OAU and the UN will rarely provide quick leadership. And you won't see consistency in U.S. policy.

My hope is in sub-regional levels and "coalitions of the willing." There are dangers in acting more on your own rather than under the umbrella of an organization. But these are crises, where time is of the essence. The world will join efforts based on the motivations of the actor. If there is a good motivation, the world will get involved. Africa needs to be seen as doing something for itself.

Nyambuya: Who decides? The speakers have put forward bold and substantial suggestions. The nearest we've come to consensus is accepting that we have an ideal and a real world. The real world is where you have a UN Security Council concerned with security in the world, but not really concerned. Africa is at the bottom in the post–Cold War era. Ethnic conflict is erupting, border wars are re-erupting, but the Security Council doesn't act. Under those circumstances, it is only logical to help ourselves. If we sit and do nothing, there will be more and more conflagration. We'll be back to the Stone Age, as happened in Somalia. So we should start at the sub-regional level. Treat each other as equal, sovereign states. We shouldn't try and have one leader. That will promote distrust and division. Start at the sub-region, and then go up to the OAU and the UN. Don't give up asking the UN to take its responsibilities, reminding it of them. But it is we who are not empowering the OAU. We are looking at it as just another organization. It is up to us to endow it with a staff and with financial resources. We need to keep making our voices heard.

Deputy Minister of Defence Hama Thay [Mozambique]: The solution to conflict in Africa is the intervention of great powers, but they have shown little attention to African problems. Their focus is in Europe, while this continent is marginalized. Assistance is often attached to non-African agendas. It has been acknowledged that Africans should take the lead. But account should be taken that peacekeeping and international security are solely the responsibility of the UN. There should be continued consultation among states aiming at consensus to avoid dispersion of efforts and inadequate intervention. One proposal is for the establishment of three sub-regional peacekeeping forces: in the North, Center, and South. The operationalization of such forces would happen with joint exercises one or two times a year. Economic problems hinder these objectives. Western countries are called on to provide training, logistics, and transportation. My country is always available to take part.

Clapham: On the issue of leadership, Williams is right. Nothing happens unless someone takes responsibility for making it happen. The responsibility devolves on major states. Leadership requires willing followers. We have to distinguish between leadership and taking advantage of power to impose one's will on weaker powers. How should the distinction be made? First, by structure. There should be a regional organization within which the leader and others can meet together. Second, a set of principles. Kavuma's serve as a starting point. Third, a recognition by leaders of the need for constant communication with colleagues within the region and a willingness to change position.

James I. Woods [USA]: It seems to me that the discussion has got us clearly to a point where there are two fundamentally different tracks to discuss: one, the way things ought to work; and two, the way things are working and are likely to continue in the short or medium term. On one hand, if a crisis is to be dealt with, we need UN funding and authority to deal with it. The OAU ought to be on board, contributing to the UN definition of the problem. There ought to be the support of the major powers in the Security Council.

It's not working that way, though, for the foreseeable future. Who decides, who triggers? The hegemon or the local state or states who feel that their important national interests are directly involved or threatened. They no longer feel inhibited by OAU restrictions. They recognize they won't get help from the UN, the United States, France, or anywhere else. Having launched unilateral activities, they try to broaden support from the regional organization to legitimize it. That is the realistic track.

We talk about early warning, dealing with fundamental issues of poverty, etc. International communities are very active in all of these issues through NGO efforts. There are U.S. traveling teams conducting seminars, and active humanitarian assistance programs. Lots of energy is spent at the political/diplomatic level during crises. But when it comes right down to it, you're on your own. Don't expect help from the international community. Try to find help from your neighbors. We need to dwell not on the ideal, but on the realistic situation. It may change in five or ten years, after the international community overcomes its outlook in the post–Cold War era.

Herbst: There is a contradiction in our discussion. It is obvious that for conflicts in large countries like Angola, there is no hegemon to intervene. Maybe for Liberia or Sierra Leone, a hegemon can take the lead in a regional response. But when crisis is in Angola, DRC, or Sudan, it now seems that the primacy of a regional response isn't really applicable. Now we're talking about what the international community can do. And of course the biggest crises that Africa faces are crises in large countries, since they affect the most people, and they spill across borders.

III. Cooperating with Outsiders

Britain, Canada, France, the Nordic nations, and the United States all seek genuinely to assist home-grown African efforts to resolve and limit the continent's conflicts. But whether they are ready to support Chapter VII as opposed to Chapter VI actions in Africa is not fully tested. To date, their several training initiatives focus on peacekeeping capacity-building, and on boosting command and control abilities among selected armies. Yet, from their responses at all three meetings in this series, it is evident that if African sub-regions create response forces, or make their specific needs for collective military action known to the West, technical and financial assistance will be forthcoming. The West wants Africa to resolve its own problems. It wants Africa to take charge. If the price is a strong and enduring com-

mitment of Western funds and logistical backing, it will be paid with pleasure. If SADC is the first sub-regional grouping to test this premise by creating a serious peace enforcement effort, however modest initially, the West will support it through training, equipment, and direct funds.

Majogo: There have been efforts to improve Western and others' ability to help African states and their armies to be capable of dealing with troubling situations. I was whispering to the prime minister that the topic—Western contributions to peacekeeping in Africa—is normally criticized by Africans in spite of the new policy of partnership. I was wondering whether I'm the right person to speak about what the West should do. Be that as it may, it once again underscores the fact that Africa has realized that in order to solve its problems, Africa itself must be in the forefront. The rest of the world can come in as collaborators, not as initiators. The West has realized that as well and has done a number of things toward the realization of this approach.

Note as well that we aren't sitting here as recipients of beggars' assistance. We want to share with the West—intelligence information, etc.—to enable us to stand on our own. We want to increase self-reliance in development *and* in crises. As we have observed, conflicts in Africa can be difficult, but they are not impossible. If we approach the problem in that spirit, we can come to solutions. We can't despair right from the beginning. This conference has a role to play to get this idea of partnership into our minds.

I would like to note briefly that there are lots of examples where cooperation with the West has increased African forces' capacities to respond. Exercises such as "Blue Hungwe" in Zimbabwe, "Natural Fire" in Kenya, and "Blue Crane" in South Africa all show the trend of states in the region to begin to work together and understand each other's capabilities. I was encouraged as minister of defense when our officers were invited to witness a French peacekeeping exercise on the island of Madagascar. The more exercises like those that are conducted, the higher the feasibility of creating a more permanent structure or mechanism for dealing with various crises.

Training assistance has been evident in British support of military institutions in Zimbabwe and Ghana, which enhance the capabilities of a force through the sharing of knowledge and expertise. We don't believe in permanent forces, but forces that can be ready to spring to action when required. Programs like the African Crisis Response Initiative from the United States, the Reinforcement of African Military Capabilities for Peacekeeping (RECAMP) from France, the P3 initiative from Britain, and the financial support given by Nordic countries and Canada are highly appreciated.

One of the immediate objectives of ACRI is the training of rapidly deployable, inter-operable units. Training exercises have already been conducted in Uganda, Senegal, Malawi, Mali, Ghana, and Ethiopia, and are usually carried out by U.S. Special Forces trainers working with a battalion for a period of sixty days in each country. It is a cooperative and transparent approach with other nations to achieve a common purpose. This coordination has led to a focus on standardizing basic soldiering skills down to the unit level. The U.K. is focusing on senior staff-level training, and France is concentrating on major multi-national peacekeeping exercises.

Efforts made by Western countries should not be seen as separate approaches. We would like the efforts to focus on sub-regional activities and to avoid unnecessary perception of competition among individual states.

France's effort, RECAMP, has led to the creation of a peacekeeping training center in Côte d'Ivoire. France has also invested more than F 180 million in peacekeeping programs, along with $1 million contributed to the OAU Mechanism. The U.K.'s P3 initiative and overall support of peacekeeping led to peacekeeping training programs for Zimbabwean troops deployed with the United Nations Angola Verification Mission (UNAVEM 3) in Angola and for Ghanaian troops deployed with the ECOMOG in Liberia. The U.K. also sponsored the secondment of African officers to the UN Department of Peacekeeping Operations. Nordic countries have also contributed to conflict resolution in Africa. Norway, for example, has helped finance mediation efforts in Rwanda and Burundi and has also supported post-conflict peace building in Mozambique, Ethiopia, Eritrea, and Angola. Canada has also given money for rapid deployment operations.

There have been less successful operations. Failures in Western involvement have been seen in the 1994 Rwandan genocide, the Somali debacle, and in the Angolan civil war, as well as in vacillating policies toward Congo when war broke out. The UN took a long time to take steps there, and the U.S. has taken too long to make a stand in these wars. The U.S. wants to pursue what is good for the country, not what is good for the opponents. That's why there has been long delay. They thought [President Laurent] Kabila would be a dictator, and that's why they took a long time. They thought he would go very fast, but he's still there.

All of this shows a commitment to helping African countries. Individually and collectively, these countries have helped us with the capacity to build our programs. In spite of all this, we must not tire of trying for peace. There is still evidence of a commitment to work for peace. International peacekeeping exercises are beneficial.

The OAU can play a vital role in marshaling support for member states and sub-regions, to solve problems with the partnership and cooperation of the Western world. We want self-reliance in peacekeeping, but we need the mutual cooperation of the West. The ultimate responsibility of the UN Security Council is to see that there is peace in all parts of the world. The OAU can give a helping hand to some sub-regions through sub-regional summits by heads of state. This is a necessary prerequisite to making sure that we have success in this field.

Solutions in Africa may be elusive, but we have shown initiative in the security sector. We need to be honest with each other in implementation.

Normand: First, I want to discuss the origin of the conceptual renewal of peacekeeping. There are three causes for this renewal that I identify. First, in Africa itself, the number of conflicts is spreading. In these conflicts, the initiatives taken by African countries have often not been taken after discussion by the Security Council. Africans want to develop African ownership of African problems.

Second, there is new thinking within the UN. They are drawing lessons from the end of the Cold War. There had been two conflicting trends. Before the end of the Cold War, the West and the East wanted to keep out of involvement with conflict; they wanted the UN to manage it. This explains why the UN was very active at the level of Chapter VI operations. At the same time, there was a temptation to exploit certain conflicts—Congo in 1960, for example, triggered a big crisis. It was similar to Somalia. As a backlash of the Congo operation, the UN decided to be much more cautious, adopting a lower profile. Blue Helmets were only observers.

After the Cold War, however, there were many multifunctional operations, and a number were successful: Mozambique, Namibia, and Angola to a certain stage (the final failure was not due to the UN operation itself). The only big failure was Somalia, and the reasons were explainable. The reflection in the UN was that many of the complex operations were difficult to organize. There was a gap between the beginning of a conflict and the beginning of its treatment. Often the gap was filled by the multinational operations of several countries without Blue Helmets. The UN thought it helpful to have guidelines for multinational operations, as well as to have a dialogue with African countries. As for a UN mandate, it was not compulsory if the operation were initiated under Chapter VI. Should there be a resort to force—a Chapter VII operation—a mandate was normally compulsory, according to the UN.

A third reason for the conceptual renewal of peacekeeping is the Western countries themselves. In 1996–97, the United States, France, and the U.K. held lots of talks about what to do to contribute to peace in Africa. They finally achieved a consensus among the three countries [P3] to create a new kind of overseas development assistance: Overseas Peacekeeping Assistance. Like ordinary development assistance, there would be two categories of participants—recipients and donors. And also like it, the assistance should be neutral, transparent, universal, acknowledged, and not liable to criticism. It would be necessary to involve the UN at an early stage. They agreed not to form a group of Western countries (since this was unacceptable to Africa), and decided instead in 1998 to ask the UN to take over, to organize the discussion and to involve the OAU. The first meeting was held in New York. Within the UN framework, they tried to widen the number of donor countries. It was also explained to African countries that there was the possibility of having a free market in New York, where they could ask for technical training and military assistance.

France has taken the implementation of the current concept of peacekeeping very seriously. We have kept the military operation, but the new African policy of France is to: (1) widen our interest to all African countries; (2) shift to peacekeeping preparation (not quiet relationships with a few French-speaking countries); and (3) increase training (there is a new school in Côte d'Ivoire)—involving training sessions with armies and equipment and organizing exercises. We are trying to launch the process within sub-regional organizations in order to prepare for real operations.

We have had to undergo some real conflicts on the ground, and we've tested the practical aspects in at least two cases: the Central African Republic and Guinea-Bissau. In Bangui, MISAB, a small multinational African organization, turned into a Blue Helmet operation. There were no more French helmets, though we were providing assistance, financing, and equipment. In Guinea-Bissau, it was an internal domestic conflict between rebels and the elected president. Under the peace agreement, ECOMOG decided to set up a small force to observe the cease-fire. As chairs of ECOMOG, the Togolese asked France for help. So we provided equipment and training for those on ground. Logistically it was a success, though with only one battalion, it was simply too small. Ultimately, though, it was a failure, as the peace agreement was not respected and President [João Bernardo] Vieira was overthrown.

In conclusion, I have a small disagreement with Herbst. In my view, there is a certain continuity between peacekeeping in Africa by Africans and that by UN Blue Helmets. The latter isn't a bygone era. Sub-regional activities may be desirable by certain African countries, but they take time to set up. During the time lag, it is useful for African countries to take the lead, but it is also important that the UN stay involved. Witness the case of the Central African Republic. Intervention there allowed a transition from one kind of operation to another. Peace making, peace building, and peace enforcement—they may just be different lines of the same operation, with different tools to treat it.

Ambassador Aubrey Hooks [USA]: My role is to talk about the African Crisis Response Initiative program. In the context of overall U.S. policy, it represents engagement. There are considerable areas of cooperation between the Departments of State and Defense, and the National Security Council. But ACRI is unique in that it has the non-partisan endorsement of the White House. It involves military training, yet it is managed by State, not Defense. I would like to explain why it is called the African Crisis Response *Initiative* rather than the African Crisis Response *Force*. The U.S. saw conflicts in Africa, and it wanted to help fix them. We had a strong appreciation that African countries were trying to resolve them themselves, and we also wanted to be helpful. The idea was broad-based, and we put it on the table for discussion. It is an excellent example of where we consulted with our allies and listened to what we heard. We said, "Here's the idea, what do you think?" The feedback we got was that it should not be a standing force, since that didn't match the situation. From both Africa and Europe, there was agreement that the need was for enhancing capacity. The result was that the name was changed to reflect this. Instead of an emphasis on force, it would be on capacity.

There are two parts to the initiative. The first is training, and it reflects norms of Africa's militaries. It is constantly refined and growing, based on experiences. The initial training is on exercises, of which there is lots of experience in Africa. We start with battalion training, and build on the skills already there. We also have introduced the use of computers for simulations. We've found that they are not just toys, and they allow us to stay within budget too. It is peacekeeping training, and we are trying to build up command headquarters. Most of the contributions have been at the company or battalion level, and they come together in brigades. We make recommendations based on our expertise. Whether or not the forces are deployed is a national decision. The second part is training the trainer. We want a direct effect throughout the military.

The results are that we have training in six countries, soon seven, involving over 5,000 people. Several countries want to train a second battalion. Other countries have asked to be included. Some who have participated have been involved in peacekeeping operations: Guinea, Mali, and Senegal. We want to make sure the content of instruction fits in with what they need—that it reflects reality.

Gill Coglin [U.K.]: I want to talk about four issues: (1) how Britain sees Africa; (2) what the U.K. is doing in Africa; (3) how the U.S., U.K., and French training fits in the UN process; and (4) what Africa can do to support us.

Britain views Africa as important; our commitment is genuine and long term. The Queen is visiting Mozambique, Ghana, and South Africa with the Foreign Secretary. The Prime Minister will go to South Africa this year. This demonstrates Africa's importance, and there is strong support for good governance and strong economic management. British citizens may not read a lot in the press, but they do care about what happens in Africa. My office gets many letters—about Rwanda or Congo—showing that the public is interested. But Africa has an image problem. Sixty percent of the Security Council's business is concerned with *conflicts* in Africa. These hamper Africa's ability to get the support and attention it needs. But the U.K. does want to work in partnership.

In cooperation with African partners and other donors, the U.K. is doing a lot in Africa. Peacekeeping training is a high priority for the British government. It is centered on the British Military Advisory Group. There is bilateral training and regional training in Ghana and Zimbabwe. The approach is a long-term one. We see the staff colleges in Ghana and Zimbabwe as UN centers of peacekeeping. We are training trainers and encouraging sub-regional cooperation. We are increasingly emphasizing the multidisciplinary elements of training—military and civilian. We are putting greater emphasis on working with other donors—France and the U.S. particularly. This increases transparency in initiatives, and results in more effective multilateral coordination. We want to breathe new life into efforts to build capacity. The P3 initiative is based on the idea of doing more to enhance capacity. Each country has its own programs—France has RECAMP, the U.K. has the Africa Peacekeeping Training Program, the U.S. has ACRI. These have been catalysts to start a multilateral process. There is close cooperation between P3 countries. We are working together on regional exercises. Next year we are planning Gabon 2000 and making formal contacts on how to dovetail our programs. For example, in Ghana last year we held a joint initiative. It was a peacekeeping course for forty officers from twelve countries. We drew some that had taken part in various training from the U.K., the U.S., and France.

How does the U.K., U.S., and French training fit into the UN process? P3 was a catalyst. Three meetings, in December 1997, May 1998, and January 1999, were held to discuss and propose a working group where African countries and donor countries could meet to decide what would be done to build capacity. This also has established a training program—field exercises and command post exercises—emphasizing the importance of developing national institutions. Where do we go from here? It is important that we organize logistics, finance, and training. There is a UN working group set up to do just that. But there is little African support for it. None of the remarks made by people here are being said there. We can do more by agreeing to informal, simple mechanisms. We recognize that there is more we can do with political organs in assistance at the sub-regional level. For the OAU, we agreed to provide staff for their early warning situation center. The OAU has a plan for further assistance. But we need the OAU to be more forthright in what it needs. The same is true for the ECOMOG intervention mechanism of ECOWAS—we stand ready to assist it.

We see two models of cooperation—Sierra Leone and the CAR. In Sierra Leone, the U.K. and the U.S. have supported ECOMOG, providing logistics, training, equipment, and intelligence. These have been key in allowing the ECOMOG troops to push back the rebels. It is a model of useful cooperation. In the CAR, a regional force was sent to Africa. After consultations, supported by France, it is now a UN mission. This is a useful paradigm for support.

What can Africa do to support us? We want to remain committed to long-term capacity building. That will continue. We welcome more feedback on what more we can do. A working group in the UN is a fundamental step forward in this respect. We want to hear the opinions that have been voiced in last few days. I talked yesterday about both supply and demand sides. The supply side is here—a working group in New York, a training program. Now we need the demand side to have a louder voice.

Toraasen: Norway, Denmark, and Sweden are among seven contributors to peacekeepers worldwide. Five thousand Norwegians have served as Blue Helmets. Each state gives a high priority to peacekeeping in foreign policy. We are not newcomers to Africa. We have a long history of development cooperation. More than 50 percent of bilateral contributions for development have been channeled to Africa, first to East, then to southern Africa. When it comes to African security matters and peacekeeping, however, we are newcomers. There has been a growing concern for conflicts that hamper peace and stability. So Nordic governments decided to adopt a common approach to Africa—a sub-regional approach. Norway has developed coherent rules under which cooperation efforts are made. We always involve our partners in framing any projects that concern them. There are systems for rapid and effective emergency relief, also involving NGOs. Norway has been active in mediation and conflict resolution efforts in the Middle East and Guatemala, which have been relatively successful.

In Africa, we have supported the OAU, the Sudan peace process, and the peace process in Somalia, Rwanda, and Burundi. We have also supported post-conflict peacebuilding approaches in Mozambique. We are open to dialogue on how to support further African efforts.

Specifically, we have been involved in a training the trainer program, called "Training for Peace." We have concentrated on SADC countries. It is managed through the Norwegian Institute of International Affairs, and the idea behind the program is to increase knowledge and competence. We invite African partners to seminars, and there have been courses in practically all SADC countries. We have had more than 300 participants in seminars and conference. Our targets are the military, civilians, police, NGOs, and media. The main themes in the courses are general information about the UN, sub-regional conflict analysis, election observers, military/civil cooperation, logistics, gender, and the humanitarian dimension. We started the "Training for Peace" program five years ago, and 1999 is its last year. We will analyze whether we should continue with the program. We want to coordinate with our friends, so we will go to the U.S., France, and the U.K. and consult too.

We are of the opinion that increasing African capabilities in regard to peace-keeping and conflict prevention, geared to the needs of specific countries, may contribute to stability. We are not leaving Africa alone, but we are encouraging ownership. It is part of our global responsibility, and we are willing to cooperate with other partners.

The UN working group is a useful arena to enhance African capacity. I am a member of that group. This will be a very important forum. I would urge my African friends to join in it.

Faupin: Thanks to others for referring to French efforts. But being there, I can bring up a few elements that are worth hearing. In the logistical field, there was supposed to be a permanent deployment of equipment to equip battalions. The status of this deployment is now clear: there is one deployment in Senegal. It was used in Guinea-Bissau, stored afterward, and then ferried to the Central African Republic to equip the force there. Now, for Gabon 2000, another battalion based in Libreville will be used for that exercise. That will be for the use of Gabonese and French forces. A third battalion will be deployed in Djibouti, and a fourth one—it has not yet been decided where—will be deployed in 2002.

Majogo: So we can now see that France is doing well on the western side of Africa and coming down. The rest of you should focus on the eastern and southern sides!

Kubwalo: Americans are doing very well. Malawi is a subscriber to ACRI. It was agreed in 1997, and it is training to provide a United Nations standard of peacekeeping. Follow-on training was also conducted in 1998. ACRI training has been very beneficial to our troops. Malawi feels it can put together a battalion that is adequately equipped to do a peacekeeping role. We want to continue with peace-keeping activities. We are tired of wars. We fought in World War I and World War II, and were dragged into a war in Malaya. We fought wars we didn't know. We were fighting them barefooted, while others had full gear. Now we would like to go into peacekeeping, because we can't be fighting these wars anymore.

Herbst: There is a question of the ability of African armies to undertake peace-keeping and sustain commitment, which relates to the question of the help Western countries provide. There is an increasing gap between the peacekeeping assistance provided by the West and the actual operations armies are carrying out. Training is done for Chapter VI operations. The West wants African countries to take the lead, but they haven't gotten a handle on what kind of aid they need to accomplish this.

Nancy Walker [USA]: We talk about putting together "ready-to-go-peace-keeping." But many of the challenges are beyond peacekeeping; they require a higher level of training. For those, you would want a full scope of training, not just training in Chapter VI peacekeeping. Does it make sense to have that for operations that are more complicated and more dangerous? The peacekeeping part in some sense is easy. We have an excellent training program for peacekeeping in ACRI, which is complemented by France, and the U.K. The question is how to ratchet up the level of expertise.

Hooks: There is a conundrum: political cooperation and integration against military cooperation and integration. The former isn't as advanced. I would welcome a discussion on that. We've talked about sub-regional organizations, national, and bilateral. Are there other mechanisms? ACRI has focused on battalion-level training; we need to do brigade level also. What kinds of new structures might we need? I would like guidance as to the appropriate focus of our efforts.

Professor Steven Metz [USA]: When we begin trying to understand U.S. policies toward Africa, we start with a central fact: the American public and most of its leaders have limited understanding of or concern with Africa. There is an Africanist community—inside and outside government—but few Americans know or care much about Africa. Americans *are* very concerned with national security strategy in the national interest. And the official analysis is that the thrust of our national interest in Africa is less than in other parts of the world. So there is limited interest.

A limitation on interest means the following: First, American concern with any African conflict or crisis depends on what else is going on in the world. The U.S. is involved everywhere. How we choose to respond to Africa is contingent on crises in other parts of the world. Second, our perspective on African problems is shaped by the symbolic meaning of African problems. In Somalia, it was the symbolic impact of the creation of a post–Cold War New World Order. The U.S. needs to feel that it is intervening on the side of something good. We approach it as a struggle of right and good against evil. Third, when the U.S. does decide to respond, it always looks for ways to keep its involvement limited. It will look for someone else to lead a response, and it is engaged for a limited time. It is unlikely that the U.S. would undertake Chapter VII peace enforcement in Africa.

So, how might someone who is interested in inspiring an American response go about it? First, since Americans like to intervene on the side of good, it would be valuable to cast a crisis as one of good against evil. Americans love crusades—against Hitler, Hussein, Milosovic. This means that it is difficult to provoke a response when we see two equally bad choices, for example in Liberia or Sierra Leone. It is difficult to mobilize support. Second, build the broadest possible coalition for involvement. Include African states and European allies. Third, work with contacts in the American Africanist community. African nations could encourage their graduates of American universities to preserve a network of contacts after they return home. This would give Africans inroads. Fourth, be realistic in terms of what the U.S. might be willing to provide in an African crisis. Remember that among most of the public, press, and leaders, the perspective is that many African states aren't very well governed. This can make it difficult to cast an intervention as good versus evil.

Realistically, it is possible to get humanitarian support and transportation assistance, but it is difficult to get ground forces. We are heavily influenced by our most recent experience. Somalia dissuaded us from getting involved in Rwanda and the Democratic Republic of Congo.

All of us know that American interest vacillates between lack of interest and enthusiastic bursts of taking charge. That can be frustrating for Africans. It is difficult to predict the American mood. But this is unlikely to change because of limited interest in Africa. All of us have to be aware of this fact, and try to take advantage where we can.

Majogo: You first said that there is a limited knowledge in America about Africa, and second noted that Americans care little about the continent. But at the same time, the U.S. is also the champion of democracy and the preservation of human rights. So I was trying to envision a situation where a nation is riddled with conflict, where human rights are trampled, and where one is trying to see what side is good. How do you arrive at what is good? What if you don't like both sides? How do you observe in such a situation?

Metz: That is an excellent point. It has to do with press or media coverage. We didn't pay much attention to Southern Sudan. But the greatest determinant is the position of the president and his top advisers. In Iraq, President Bush made the case as good versus evil. And in the issue of purely humanitarian intervention, there is something of an American approach. We go in and stop the dying. We are moved by television images. There is something of that thrust in American policy, but also a reluctance to lead those efforts. An example is the first few months of the war that overthrew Mobutu Sese Seko in Congo.

Nyambuya: Your presentation was enlightening, but it left questions unanswered. What are American national interests? Can you confirm that all decisions about national interest are public information? We're left guessing as to what you mean.

Metz: They are written as public documents. That is the best way to see how Americans officially define national interest.

Shalli: I question American foreign policy in Africa. I've seen recently that the

U.S. is the champion of human rights, but I want to question its humanitarian intervention in particular. There has been massive assistance to refugees in Kosovo: a transfer of toys, chocolates, and ice cream from Chicago to Europe. Why not to Africa? Why is it so discriminatory?

Williams: We have to understand in Africa that if the Americans are pursuing a policy somewhere in the world, it is usually because of a strong lobby by the citizens with ancestral linkages to those areas. There is a growing African-American lobby. That's why some of the activity in Africa is happening.

[to Shalli:] I've never seen a beggar complain. Find your own capacity. Stop complaining about what the U.S. is not doing. If the U.S. has an economic interest, they will do something. Stop complaining.

Mulongoti: Nancy Walker, will you help us understand how U.S. decisions are made? If there is a lack of interest, and a perception that these countries aren't properly governed, how do you reach the stage of supporting one? We have seen a U.S. policy of supporting strong men. Did those strong men represent what was good? They ended up being toppled by popular movements. But they fraternized with the American leadership. In whose perception is good or bad? We could have bullies masquerading as saviors. What about when Africans perceive a bully and Americans see a leader? There is a problem of shifting goalposts. In some countries, a system is accepted by the people there, but it is treated as bad. Whereas another place, where there is no democracy at all, is held up as the ideal model. You can't come in and not set parameters that are realistic and recognized by all. Again, there is the question of support and fragmentation of efforts. "Donor" is a popular term. We'd like a consolidation of the efforts. We are grateful for the French, Norwegians, etc. It would be good if these resources could be channeled through the OAU or sub-regional groupings. Then you couldn't be accused of channeling support to certain areas. If you give support to people who have been to university in the U.S., then you might be being biased.

Walker: As an official representative of the Pentagon and of the Secretary of Defense, I can report that we do have an official policy: *The National Security Strategy for a New Century*. Our interests are protecting citizens, promoting economic prosperity, taking international responsibilities to shape the environment, and responding to threats to the U.S.. The document is available on the Internet. The section on Africa is smaller and less comprehensive than the other sections. It is true that Africa is at the bottom of the list. But we do have interests there. First and foremost is protecting American citizens (for example, from bombings). Second is securing our economic interests. And third is humanitarian interests. We are proud of our democratic tradition. It is a responsibility that our policies represent that tradition. The Clinton administration has paid more attention to Africa than others have in a long time. That is purposeful. President Clinton believes in genuine partnership. He understands that the U.S. is a bigger country than anyone else, but he is most egalitarian. Clinton would rather change the nature of debate: instead of talking about transfers from donors to those assisted, he wants to talk about partnership and mutual interests. Yes, we have things to offer, and Africans look to us for assistance. But Clinton talks about a relationship of partnership, not of donor and recipient.

Col. Dan Henk [USA]: I would like to speculate on the degree to which the U.S. might involve itself in future peace operations in Africa.

We have already heard that American interests in Africa are modest. It has interests, but few, if any, vital ones. So it is difficult for policymakers to justify expensive military intervention in the region unless the suffering is so egregious that it provokes a popular outcry. *Any* intervention will be controversial, and humanitarian motives alone are not a firm foundation on which to construct a long-term, costly military involvement. A more solid basis for involvement in Africa is the U.S. interest in regional stability. That interest is reflected in the current *National Security Strategy*, which shows three overarching policy objectives: enhancing security, promoting prosperity, and promoting democracy.

Given these objectives, how would the U.S. decide whether or not to commit itself? The operations could include peacekeeping or peace enforcement. But most often they are evacuations of its citizens from an area of escalating violence. The process works as follows: The U.S. government keeps track of crises. The prospect of a serious crisis in some region of the world triggers a process of consultations among the various U.S. government agencies concerned with the region or issues. Through these consultations (the "interagency process"), the different agencies develop a consensus on how to react. To understand American foreign policy decisionmaking, it is important to recognize this process. The military plays a role, but it doesn't direct it.

How does this apply to Africa? Most African countries fall under the U.S.-European Command, headquartered in Germany; seven countries in East Africa and the Horn fall under the Central Command, headquartered in the U.S. Being honest with ourselves, we will understand that these Commands must concentrate their resources on the regions or issues of greatest concern to the U.S.. Thus, the European Command's greatest interest is Europe; Central Command's is the Middle East.

American willingness to commit forces is also constrained by its history. As a result of the Vietnam War, many civil and military leaders are convinced that the U.S. should take great pains to avoid a Vietnam-type involvement. The 1983 barracks bombing in Lebanon was another traumatic event. These incidents led to the "Weinberger Criteria," offered as an antidote to the mistakes that had led to Vietnam and Lebanon. General Colin Powell later offered a similar, but shorter, list of criteria that he believed should constrain U.S. use of power. More historical baggage is left over from the fairly recent U.S. intervention in Somalia (1992–94). Seven months after eighteen marines died in Mogadishu, President Clinton signed a directive that put greater constraints on when to deploy forces. The same presidential decision made even more restrictions on peace enforcement (Chapter VII) operations undertaken by the U.S. Though this directive did not stop the U.S. from sending forces into the Democratic Republic of Congo a few months later, the operation was very limited in scope and short in duration.

So we can say that how America responds to a crisis in Africa depends on circumstances elsewhere, the personalities and perspectives of leaders (how much they are influenced by Vietnam, Somalia, etc.), the degree to which the American public is energized, and the decision of the president. The Clinton administration has demonstrated a somewhat greater willingness to seek partnerships to manage regional conflict. This is seen in the African Crisis Response Initiative and the African Center for Strategic Studies (ACSS). It is also evident in U.S. willingness to work with regional and sub-regional organizations (for example, the U.S. provided over $95 million to ECOMOG participants in Liberia and Sierra Leone).

U.S. policymakers *are* seeking opportunities to cooperate on regional security issues with sub-regional organizations like SADC and the East African Community. The current administration has devoted resources to African efforts, particularly multilateral. This may show the limits of U.S. willingness to intervene in Africa, but it also reflects that U.S. policy recognizes that prevention is usually less expensive than cure.

Allow me to speculate on the circumstances under which the U.S. might commit itself to a substantial peace intervention in Africa. First, the crisis would have severely to challenge U.S. national interests or core values—for example, its core value to prevent suffering. But a crisis has to be sufficiently visible, drastic, and prolonged, and it depends on the closeness of the event (for example, suffering in the Caribbean or the Balkans would probably draw a response sooner than suffering in Africa). Second, the U.S. might act to secure or protect a valued ally or partner whose *stability* is seriously threatened.

Further, one could imagine a scenario in which the U.S. became increasingly involved in a sub-regional organization, and that sub-regional organization committed itself to a local peacekeeping or humanitarian operation, but the crisis deteriorated to the point that the sub-regional partners faced a real prospect of military disaster. In such circumstances, I could envision even a U.S. peace enforcement operation, though that role would certainly be brief, and designed only to restore the status quo ante.

So, what considerations would drive any U.S. peace operations intervention? The American preference would be to see an African crisis resolved multilaterally by Africans themselves, with external support as necessary. The next best solution would be a classic UN peace operation. Failing that, an international coalition with a UN mandate would be preferred, with the U.S. participating but not leading. If the situation were serious enough, and U.S. core values challenged critically, I could foresee the U.S. taking the lead in an international intervention. For this to happen, American policymakers would have to be convinced of five things: First, that our values or interests were clearly at stake. Second, that the intervention would succeed beyond reasonable doubt. Third, that only the U.S. was capable of organizing an effort in time. Fourth, that there was reasonable likelihood of public support. And fifth, that the military commitment would be limited with a clear definition of its mission and goals. Again, these are only hypothetical suggestions, and such U.S. intervention is not likely in the near future.

Let me conclude with a few words of advice. Americans are eager to reinforce success. There is a tendency to abandon programs that appear to be failing. So it is important to use the international media to advertise success. Further, Africans should involve and engage U.S. leaders at various levels; try to make us comfortable working with you. And let me suggest that it would be useful to make America part of *your* family of nations. Africans understand *ujamaa* in a way we in the West often do not. Teach it to us, and let us work together for peace and prosperity.

Williams: Regarding the experiences in SADC and West Africa, there is a big question. How long, knowing the way Western donors work, will the support last? For how many years? When it is finished, what next? This is true for all Western countries. Is there any way of institutionalizing this trend in training, so that when the Western world gets tired of supporting it, something will remain? Is it not better for us to look at a way of creating institutions? It should be a subregional approach in which there is no question of responsibilities. Under UN operations, if you are looking for communications, you go to Canada. This is the sort of thing we should institutionalize. If Zimbabwe should be a center of training, it should be. If South Africa can produce equipment, it should be a center of providing equipment.

The African Center for Strategic Studies training program that was mentioned, is it similar to the international peace training program that the British have? Are they similar? Where can they come together? Everybody will come up with their own training manuals; we need to have only one training manual.

On the issue of building a conflict management mechanism without a consensus by all the countries in the sub-region, there is always the alternative of starting with the "coalition of the willing." When this coalition takes appropriate steps and succeeds, others will join.

The issue of gender has been neglected. How many women are in security studies or defense? We need to look at a special training program for women in conflict.

Security is becoming quite an issue. How do we get civil society involved in any mechanism for security? I think it's necessary throughout Africa.

Coglin: I take issue with Fisher that the various peacekeeping training efforts are competing initiatives. We are working very closely, based on common doctrine. We are not in competition. Each initiative is trying to assure African countries they are not in competition. Regarding cooperation at the sub-regional level: yes, it is important. We can't always get the answers we need out of the OAU. They say they don't have permission from heads of state. Give us a mechanism to work with, and we'll work with it—sub-regional or Africa-wide. Mention has been made of designating countries with different roles…tell us what they are, and we'll help you. The working group is one way of discussing issues. It is an international forum. Unfortunately, we don't feel that Africans are supporting us. We need a clear statement from you.

Hooks: I endorse what Coglin has said. I am also curious. I've been looking for evidence of competition between donors. But I haven't found it. There is so much to be done, that I'm seeing close cooperation. For example, we went to Paris to work with the French—in a political and concrete sense. At our new training center, there are French instructors. And we're in their programs. There is a spirit of cooperation. In New York, there are structures we might work with. I'd like to be able to work closely with regional organizations. We have good relationships with some countries, initial contacts with others. We want to see more of that. Are there other types of structures we should be looking at? Cooperation between the U.K., France, and the U.S. is superb. I wish there were competition, but there is not, because we're all working on the same efforts. They are complementary efforts: the training we provide works well when troops participate in joint exercises.

Brigadier N.W. Banda [Malawi]: ACRI started off with Americans approaching various countries. Some accepted. Within SADC, the issue has been discussed. There is suspicion about what the U.S. is doing in Malawi. In the future, we'll go through SADC. All the students who participated in the course also participated in exercises.

Henk: The U.S. is involved with ACRI and ACSS. The latter is a new initiative. It is American, but our expectation is that Africans will take ownership. It is an opportunity for senior civil and military leaders on the continent to come together under a worldwide faculty and discuss issues of national security strategy. In that context, how should the military relate to the civil establishment? The program is brand new. The initiative has finally resulted in something substantial. This fall will see the initial iteration in Senegal; it will be a two-week course offered a couple of times a year.

Shalli: I think we should also consider the Western contribution to *peace* in Africa. We are focusing on peacekeeping so much, that we are encouraging people to make wars so we can build peace. Fundamentally, we have to look at peace in general.

What is the annual budget for programs?

The West is not competing, but we see that there seems to be a lack of coordination in any case. Americans are failing to understand Africans...how we think, what we like and don't like. I've worked with British and Americans. I find Americans difficult to do business with. They try to push and push and force people.

Brigadier General G. M. Waitara [Tanzania]: Shalli has been forthright. I wanted to add on to what he was trying to say. You said we should be frank. We have problems of means. We accept the contributions, but we need collective mechanisms for distributing them. We have seen donor countries channel donations through South Africa. If they go collectively through one point, we'll manage them.

On the subject of Americans and the evolution of ACRI: Initially it was proposed to us as an African Crisis Response Force. Sometimes we're afraid of accepting a name because we don't know the hidden agenda that might be involved. We need to be clear. So we questioned American "force" in Africa. Would it be Americans commanding Africa? That was the question. Then was proposed ACRC, the "C" for Capacity. Eventually, Americans said, "Not Capacity, but Initiative." We were clear again. Does it have a hidden agenda? We have to be very clear. If we're clear, then we have to be sure they are *collective* measures. A few things were not accepted by Americans that we suggested. That shouldn't be repeated.

We have to be able to tell Western countries how to help us in building peacekeeping forces. A contribution is required, but the mechanism is also important. It must be collective.

Hooks: I apologize if we were over-persistent on that particular project. Are we persistent? Yes. Aggressive sometimes. We think the problems are urgent. You didn't say we were indifferent, or passive. We are very concerned, and this reflects the point.

We have been discussing conflict; what is conflict but misunderstanding?

You asked about the amount of the project itself. Of course, it is never enough. It is about $20 million annually. It has been going on for a few years, and will continue.

Ellington: [UN Secretary-General] Dag Hammarskjöld said peacekeeping is not a soldier's job, but only a soldier can do it. This applies to peacebuilding. Any training any of your armies get from any source is a good thing. It doesn't matter where you go to get it. If China, India, and France offer you positions at staff colleges, is that competing? Or are we learning from many people? From what we learn from others, we can develop solutions for Africa.

On the proposal that if there were frameworks, that funds and training could be better channeled: *no* one disagrees. We're hoping for that. The fact is that there are nations that are willing to help. An analogy is AIDS awareness. It is a global concern—equal to conflict in Africa. People are ready to assist. But I've been in countries where assistance in HIV awareness was refused. Other countries have developed a framework to leverage these donations and contributions. They are coming from all over the world, and the Ministry of Health is determining how best to use them. The contributions will be there; it is up to Africans to develop a framework for dealing with them. If you are more comfortable dealing with Norway, that's fine. But if you refuse the contributions, there are always others ready to accept them.

Kavuma: I want to thank the organizers of the conference. I want to thank our friends from the North for curing the disease of instability. We commonly get sick with malaria. We're interested in a drug to cure it. We don't care where it is made. We should embrace all efforts to help us out of the problem. When small matters become diversionary, people suffer in the millions.

Africa could be looked at as a single human body. If one part of the body is sick, the rest of the body feels it. It is also a part of the world. If Africa is sick, repercussions are felt elsewhere. All efforts are beneficial, the challenge is to figure out how to use them. I would venture to propose that Uganda host the next conference.

IV. Criteria for Successful Interventions

Successful peacekeeping has been achieved in Africa. Clear mission statements and disciplined troops have managed to maintain cease-fire lines and to separate contending parties. Effective peace enforcement demands both more flexible and more carefully drawn statements of objectives. Only the work of decisive commanders created successful interventionist outcomes in West Africa. In Angola, by contrast, peacekeeping could not be converted into peace enforcement; the political authority and political will were lacking. Africa's officers and soldiers can fulfill whatever tasks they are given. A political mandate is essential, how-

ever, and much of the time that direction has been lacking. A quintessential require-ment for a successful peace intervention is robust guidance by national leaders individually or, better, collectively.

Herbst: Where has work been done? There has been some work done on longer-term political solutions to some of these conflicts. In some of the places where great powers care a lot, there has been creative work on the underlying sovereign status. We see one country with two armies in Bosnia; a sharing of authority in Ireland. In Kosovo, Iraq, and the West Bank, there is an understanding that if pol-itics are at the root of the problems, then fundamental questions have to be asked and innovative solutions provided. African countries have to be willing to exper-iment with new ideas as well.

There has been much more work on pre-deployment for prevention of conflict. Africa is an increasingly heterogeneous continent: some countries have been suc-cessful in consolidation, while others are facing crises of survival. Hope and con-flict live side by side. Perhaps that is inevitable. I have an optimistic vision of Africa's future...except that conflict runs the risk of infecting other countries that cannot insulate themselves from the neighborhood. Guinea and Zambia, for exam-ple, face flows of refugees, guns, and drugs.

The Balkans have been a moderate success in the pre-deployment of Western forces. There should be more attention to containing the conflict if nothing can be done by outsiders, so countries at the cusp don't find themselves overturned by their neighbors' troubles.

Tonje: We're being asked to play football from the terrace. This really is a problem that should be addressed to those who make the decisions. We are experts. When you watch football, you always wonder why he passed to someone else. The first thing that we should address is, what are we trying to achieve? I think it is to educate ourselves so we can talk to others.

Shalli: Before we continue the conference, we need to understand a few con-cepts. The topic is peacekeeping and peace enforcement in Africa: the concept of peacekeeping is different from peace enforcement. The success stories in Mozam-bique and Namibia were successful because there was peace to keep. We can't compare it with peacekeeping in Somalia. The latter was an intervention opera-tion. It was the same as Kosovo, and it was not peacekeeping. Similarly, with the intervention in the [Democratic Republic of] Congo, there was no peace to keep.

Maybe we're beginning the same way the Europeans started. Maybe we will end with a European Union. They did it, why can't we? So, we should proceed as follows: First, the mission of peace enforcement must be clear and unambigu-ous; the concept and rules must be clear. The mission in Angola failed because first there was peace to keep, and then the mission changed. But there was no one to tell the peacekeepers that the mission had changed. The rules of engagement were different, but no one told them.

I was listening to Herbst in regards to the deployment concept. This is a tricky concept. Some of the problems are poor governments. Are we getting to the point where we are telling governments that they are governing poorly? We knew that there was going to be ethnic cleansing in Kosovo; why didn't we deploy earlier? The mission wasn't clear, and it failed. There was no self-interest, and people withdrew. We just need to be clear about definitions and clear about our mission. And we can't confine ourselves to Africa only. We talk about a global village. Therefore we shouldn't divide the discussions; we should think as one people and talk about peacekeeping in other areas too.

Gen. Fisher: I would like to say something about definition and understanding: what do we understand about peacekeeping? There are constituencies represented by our governments. What do the constituents of peacekeeping forces understand about what they are to do? Are they to be neutral or to knock sense into people? They need to understand.

Regarding the conduct of the soldier in missions—we assume we know our soldiers. Yet, when we move into peacekeeping operations, the challenges are greater in that the soldier has no defined tactical enemy. He is supposed to be an ambassador of his country. Governments are watching soldiers carefully. Perceptions of favoritism are created. We have to make sure they are disciplined and that their conduct is impeccable. You can't take it for granted; you have to make sure. If their conduct is bad, it could undermine the success of the mission. If we bring our cultural baggage in, and don't give the wishes of the people priority, there is a problem. For the soldier, the challenges are immense. They can be ridiculed and shouted at, but we ask them to keep their cool. In Mozambique, there was a complaint that our soldiers were busy taking away children's schoolbags. How could they do that? Fortunately, officials from Mozambique proved the accusations wrong.

Some of the little things we do are not so small; some of things we take for granted should not be. What the soldiers did to Somalis shocked their nations. Commanders have to be sensitized and be swift, so we don't have to wait until they come home to deal with it.

Williams: We need to learn from the first experiment of Peace Support Operations—in Chad. It was designed in Africa by an alliance but executed by the OAU, with inadequate Western support. There was a peace accord, but the OAU Peacekeeping Force was not strong enough for the implementation. It demonstrated the general lesson that once there is a peace accord, if some of the adversaries are not ready to implement it, and the peacekeepers do not have the appropriate force, it cannot be enforced.

The best arrangement was seen in the Central African Republic with the role played by MISAB. Included in the process was an arrangement for France to provide a well-equipped and well-armed Rapid Reaction Force, which was used when necessary to bring back into line the adversaries who wanted to break the agreement. You do find that if you want to implement an accord, you need an enforcing instrument. That was the case in Guinea-Bissau. If there had been a force, Vieira would still be there; ECOWAS could have kept peace until the election. The only question would have been when the election would take place. ECOWAS was negotiating to get a second force. The first UN peacekeeping measure in Africa—in the Congo—did demonstrate to all observers that classical peacekeeping in Africa doesn't work without a standby implementation (rapid reaction force).

The Angola situation has demonstrated how you introduce force into a peace accord. In the African continent, what is the need for peacekeeping once an accord has been signed? You can only begin the task of ensuring the implementation of the accord if there is a rapid reaction force, as I have said earlier. You need an early reaction force to react quickly once a cease-fire is broken. Peace accord enforcement and peace building seem to be twin concepts that we need to develop in Africa. How can we self-operationalize the continuum is the key question on the African agenda.

There is some sense in what you're saying in regard to economic motivations. Look at Liberia, Sierra Leone, Angola—everybody is trying to protect their economic interest. They are looking for ways of bringing in money to buy arms. Who controls the international businessman? Who trades with economic warlords? How can they be controlled? If a group of experts can't control this mafia, how can sanctions work? If countries stop supplying arms to a particular group, who can control the other sources of arms? And how about all this money sitting in offshore accounts: who can find it? Western countries try to control money-laundering for drugs. Can't they do the same with economic warlords? These issues involved with Angola are complex issues. The outside influence that supports the economic activities of the two warlords in the country is going to be very difficult to stop.

V. Organizing African Response Forces

Whether crisis response forces will be organized by sub-regional entities, by hegemons, or as coalitions of the willing, there is a clear preference for pre-prepared and jointly exercised battalions (and companies) that can be summoned together quickly as a prevention brigade. Standing arrangements there should be, but no standing force is possible. Africans will require outside technical assistance to create standing arrangements, but Africans will need to write the standing orders and prepare joint exercises on a regular basis. Some of the smaller nations will contribute less militarily, but can still offer certain kinds of important material support. The larger ones will necessarily take the lead, but the crisis response forces that are likely to be most effective will be those where there is mutual respect between existing military contingents and frequent interactions between officers and soldiers from different backgrounds. East Africa already has achieved a high degree of mutual agreement and regard; some of the countries of SADC are also working together militarily. Once again, political guidance and will are critical since commanding officers say that their military establishments (including air forces and navies as well as armies) can accomplish more than their political masters now permit. Technically, there are few obstacles to the establishment of a workable series of sub-regional crisis response forces.

Faupin: We have just heard reference to the prerequisites for operating African response forces. One of the prerequisites is *organizing* forces, and that is my topic. Referring to the last four roundtables, it is already possible to see clearly what African response forces *should be*. The problem is now, given the assistance, partnership, and support that the West and international organizations can provide, what is the best way to organize the African forces? I want to say at the outset that it should be taken more as an African problem than an outsider's problem. There are three parts to this presentation: (1) What does organizing mean? (2) What does "African" imply? (3) What should a response force be?

First, what does organizing mean? It means to equip and train a permanent force, *or* make sure that the different elements are ready, available, trained, interoperable, and responsible to a unique military commander with a common doctrine, common intelligence, and common understanding of the political-military environment. "Organized" means a long-term plan on a regional and sub-regional basis. Control is at both national and international levels, and training is at both levels. It means regular funding, rather than huge occasional funding. It needs equipment, time, and skills. It also needs political will, especially on a continent where wars of aggression are not the most common. Armed forces are more for internal purposes, and numbers are not that important. What counts in this setting are dedication, responsiveness, and adaptability.

Second, what does "African" imply? I agree with Mulongoti: it *is* an African problem. In dealing with African emergencies, crises, problems, security, and cultures, it is an exercise in diversity. OA*D* would be a better name than OAU (organizing diversity would be more accurate than organizing unity). Does that exclude participating in other operations in the world? There is much to do on the continent before thinking about "other world theaters," such as Bosnia or Iraq. Should one think of Africa as a whole, or as a jigsaw of different nations, ethnicities, and sensibilities? Any defense force should be able to be employed anywhere, but to eschew language, cultural, or ethnic problems, it would be better to think in terms of a "coalition of the willing" (this could be a few countries, or it could expand to a sub-regional grouping) or a sub-regional force. This is compatible with the French and the U.S. calling for four regions—SADC, EAC, Central Africa, and West Africa. We have the example of the CAR, which is working, and of Guinea-Bissau, which failed. The latter failed not because of a problem with the concept but mainly due to a lack of international support.

There lies a risk that the leading power in a sub-region will use its position to dominate the political-military operation. It might be necessary to have a political body (OAU or sub-regional) to monitor this point.

Does that mean that a response force should be only African? Not in my understanding. Back to the example of the CAR, the peacekeeping force was mostly African, with some Canadians, and a French logistics and support element. The absence of any European element in Guinea-Bissau was due to the weakness of the force deployed there.

Third, what should a response force be? Should it be an equipped standing force? No. It should be only a provisional force to meet a given or occasional objective: restoring or maintaining peace. The permanent goal of any given country should be to provide the sub-region with a trained and well-staffed *unit*, commensurate with its financial capabilities, political interest, and democratic development. It is like building up a European defense. A force could be quickly assembled as a first element of intervention in the case of continental or regional problems. In the medium term at least, it should be not larger than brigade size, made of several battalions and staff elements belonging to constituent nations. Common training, at the company, battalion, and brigade levels, is essential to ensure a common standard of performance. Exercises, seminars, and conferences are indispensable tools. But they are not sufficient. That is what the French, U.S., and British programs are all about. It would certainly be wrong to *integrate* all these concepts and programs together into a big, single one. The UN and OAU already exist. It is better to think of diversity. What needs to be done is to help the African nations take over their security problems, each country with its own specific issues and needs. There are different molds, cultures, and sensitivities in Africa. Even where that generates problems, there is a heritage to preserve.

What comes out of this is that the ideal response should be quick to be effective; be powerful to deter, strike, protect, if necessary; be well equipped and well trained; be in line with international bodies, with communications and political/military officers attached; be legal and respecting of international laws; have a unique command and control with unique staff and logistics; have good and shared intelligence; and be well planned and well executed.

This is an ambitious program. To organize an African response force will require strong political will, not only for one given deployment, but for a long-term period. It can be the sum of sub-regional efforts, which needs—but is not totally dependent on—the support of the international community for funding, education, training, and equipment. The African diversity is a cultural heritage that needs to be preserved, but not at the expense of security.

Shalli: Should an African force be permanent, or should it be available, trained and ready to be sent anywhere in Africa? A permanent force is not something that I will back. A force available, on standby and ready to go—that is something I think we should try to do. It can't be achieved at the continental level. Only at the sub-regional level. We need to restructure the headquarters of the OAU to include an effective peacekeeping department that channels things like doctrine, rather than dealing with individual states. In Harare, in 1997, some of these types of proposals were made [at a SADC meeting]. We need to think along those lines.

Rotberg: Last year we decided that there can't be a permanent standing force, but there *can* be permanent arrangements—either entire armies trained for all purposes or dedicated battalions trained to be brought together under a developed common command and control.

Henk: Is there a preference for a "coalition of the willing" as opposed to a genuine collective defense alliance? The latter (like NATO) can over time work on standardization. Is there a strong preference for one over another?

Rotberg: This question links with the importance of standardizing and commonizing made by Williams. Another trend is that it is too difficult with new kinds of political will.

Kubwalo: Regarding whether a force should be permanent or otherwise, I found the conclusions reached last time to be most ideal. We aren't in a position on the continent to support a pan-African army. But I think the idea of getting units—a battalion from each army trained for that purpose—would be most ideal. This is especially true if the training is done jointly. In the end, we would find that we would have a viable solution to the problem of peacekeeping in Africa.

Lieutenant General A. M. Mosakeng [Lesotho]: Most of the unsolved problems are a result of the intervention of people. These intervention forces would appear to be noneffective. What about outside forces? I'm not trying to accuse anyone, but what do we do about the kind of crises that are coming into Africa?

Williams: Sometimes, we tend to exaggerate too much the role of outsiders, especially the businessmen who deal with the warlords. The problem is allocation of resources and sharing of power. African governments also tend to make the mistake of believing that those parts of the country that have resources are ready, through the central government, to share these resources with other parts of the country that have none. The rich places are saying, "No. Let us have our own riches for our own development." There has to be a beginning for communal capitalism to thrive in Africa.

We've refused to be creative. We see crises and immediately start looking elsewhere for solutions to the problems. In all this discussion about training problems, we have forgotten that if you don't have a well-organized sub-regional body with proper back-stop headquarters, you're wasting time and effort. You need coordination. If ECOWAS doesn't have a good back-stop organization, you have a problem. Setting up a proper back-stop coordinating headquarters is critical. Then you can operationalize. Before ACRI came, armies were trained. What were they training on? What systems? What are the missing gaps in former training and peacekeeping operations? What *really* is needed in terms of tactics and training to respond to these and other crises? Whatever you want to introduce in terms of equipment for any type of operations, you need to remember that peacetime conditions are different from those under fire. Equipment works differently. Finally, there needs to be a joint approach, involving army, navy, and air force.

Dlamini: Looking at organizing African response forces, we know that SADC countries have come together. We should go back and see what our economies could do in order to help ourselves, in addition to the help we get from foreigners. For instance, in a small country like Swaziland, we should discover what it can produce well, maybe better than Tanzania. Maybe it can help logistically, by providing lots of rice or sugar, even if it isn't providing a big army. We need logistically to look at our countries. It has been said that politicians are the ones that cause problems. Once they're "up there," they tend to look at us, their people, as the enemy. They lose touch with society. If you keep in touch with your country, you will try to develop it. Once it is strong, you can help with these operations in many ways. We aren't so poor that we can't help our forces, given a chance. Take Lesotho: it can produce lots of wheat in winter, peas in summer. Small as it might be, it shouldn't be ashamed of improving itself economically. If we aren't strong economically, our ideas won't mean anything, because we'll go on being beggars.

Nyambuya: There are two parts of organizing. One is organizing forces for peacekeeping. That is fairly simple and not so controversial. It involves earmarking units within a region. It doesn't imply that you don't train the rest of the army. It just means forces can be deployed at short notice if necessary. But it doesn't end there. You need a leader that will be able to command and control the units.

So you need command post exercises. And then to go further, it is an exercise in political authority. We've paid lip service to that, but have not dealt with it. It is a political, not a military action, and it should be seen as a political action. Going further, it involves the OAU, which needs to be properly staffed.

The second aspect is organizing African response forces for peace enforcement. There is more to that. You need to look at air and navy aspects.

VI. Operating African Response Forces: Command, Control, Transportation

Hegemons with organized defense establishments will have no command and control issues if they intervene alone or at the head of ad hoc coalitions. Likewise, coalitions of the willing will devise answers to command and control questions as the ad hoc coalitions are arranged. But a standing sub-regional crisis response force cannot be organized effectively without close attention to these issues. Commanders can rotate for fixed periods or they can be chosen by the states within a sub-region that are given the primary responsibility for leading a continuing sub-regional interventionist effort. That is a political decision, but it may also be based on an assessment of the critical capacities within a sub-region's collective military structure. The commander must have effective command both in training and in combat. The sub-regional crisis response force will function best if the various national components of the force report (when they have come together as a force) only to the commander, not to their national defense chiefs or to their political advisers. Likewise, once the political mandate is secured, the overall commander should be free to organize training exercises with military objectives in mind. In the field, during an intervention exercise, that operational requirement becomes even more important. Critical, too, for the creation of successful crisis response forces will be prior agreements on common languages, common doctrines, common equipment, and common use of Western assistance. Despite common backgrounds in several regions, the existing diversities must be reconciled well before a force goes into action. Interoperability and the ability to respond appropriately and rapidly to threats to peace will otherwise be compromised severely.

Tonje: My comments will be made in effort to provoke discussion. We are talking about the practical side of command, control, and communication. In Liberia, Somalia, and Sierra Leone, it came out clearly that one must be certain of what one is trying to achieve. What is the desired "end-state" at the conclusion of the operation? Then one must think through the whole project from the beginning to the desired end-state, taking into account all facets of life within the crisis. As military men, we're concerned with the military side and other logistical issues. But the NGOs and the political side are required to be brought into the picture as well.

We have talked about how best to organize African forces. Four ways have been mentioned: the UN, the OAU, sub-regional organizations, and ad-hocism. If the UN still works, let's use it; if the OAU can raise enough money, let's use it. As for sub-regional organizations—I give a spirited defense of SADC. In Lesotho and Congo, we need to look into whether it did a good job. If it were planned beforehand, did we look at all contingencies? Why weren't police employed in Lesotho, for example? We've got to analyze and then provide for every eventuality. In my view there was a lot of ad-hocism—that only two of ten countries intervened undermined the role of consensus. Ad-hocism faces problems such as lack of transportation, communications, and intelligence.

Maybe we should accept the fact that each situation will develop its own requirements, and we should therefore organize ourselves to be able to meet such an unpredictable solution. We should have a general plan to deal with quite varying responses.

How can it be done? When it is a hegemon leading, there is no problem with command, control, and communication. What about sub-regional groupings? Are we prepared, even if the idea of uniting is outlandish, to set up a standing force? We need to get away from the idea of training one battalion. We need to train *all* our forces to be deployed or employed in any situation, for all eventualities. All African armies should stand by, particularly for crises that are likely to face us. We've seen that there is a question of Angola that is staring us in the face. If all SADC countries could agree to place all their forces with giant South Africa, that fact would keep Angola from acting; it would provide deterrence to Angola. That collection of forces is big enough to establish and enforce peace. Whether they can do that and also go into Angola at the same time, I don't know. Going into the DRC raises similar problems. SADC may be biting off more than it can chew.

What is a legitimate government? To what extent can a regional ad hoc or sub-regional force decide? What are the conditions acceptable to the international community to go into a country like Congo, when the government head is himself a rebel? We need to be truthful to ourselves and really analyze this and be able to sell it to others.

What about outsiders? How much consensus should you try to develop from those not in the sub-region? The spanner thrown into the works by Uganda and Rwanda poses a problem. And there is the process of choosing a crisis force commander. Should the forces be loyal to him? This may contradict the fact that heads of state and governments are the keys to any enterprise. In solving problems with ad hoc arrangements, with sub-regional or OAU operations, you can't escape from the unique positions of heads of state and governments and the resources that come with that position. How can we in any grouping ensure that heads of states are committed to solutions to the problems?

Look at the example of NATO. The member countries are still sovereign states, but NATO has been able to keep peace in Europe and the rest of world for the last fifty years. What lessons are in that for us? There is the possibility of establishing standing forces with a command and control structure in place. If it is not possible, we can at least provide for initial, common training, using equipment that is compatible. We can integrate our schools—our training and staff. People can be prepared for a future state of integration. This gets back to determining the end-state desired.

We in East Africa, with help from the U.S., launched an exercise called Hydrofire '98. We examined some of these issues. When you go into a problem like this, you need the consent of all interested parties—those involved and those interested. The unique positions of heads of states are important—they have to be committed. The decisions taken are theirs, not an invention of ours. They do address issues from time to time. At summits, for example, they come to conclusions.

Let us use summit meetings for solving our problems. In between, there should be some mechanism—we decided on a special representative of the heads of state who would carry out their positions and report back to them. There also needs to be other staff to ensure that such an enterprise succeeds. The cooperating forces come from those countries or sub-regions that can ensure that forces are provided depending on the plan the special representative and the force commander work out. We should have all Africans training. In that case, the problem of cooperation remains, but it is mostly administrative. That was the structure we came up with [in East Africa]. We exercised it. We hope to exercise it again next year, and we intend to develop it further.

Woods: My assumption in addressing the command and control task is that the focus shouldn't be on the technical aspects and formalities. I assume that half the people in this room are capable of that. Rather, I believe the aspects that need to be addressed are those that fall outside of, or are concealed behind, the script of formal order. These aspects are inherent in the complex and peculiarly political nature of what I call here "coalition intervention."

There are two sets of considerations that establish the context in which command and control are exercised. The first is that murky area where the military receives its policy direction from political authorities which have overall policy responsibility for an operation. Political authority may operate at multiple levels, through different channels—possibly the UN Security Council, the OAU, or

African sub-regional organizations, such as SADC, and in all cases, the various national authorities of coalition partners. For a force commander to attain his objectives, a number of critical elements must be in place. These must be arrived at through careful political and military planning and consultation, considering all aspects of a crisis. These components of operations seem obvious, but it often doesn't occur. Among the matters to be accomplished at the level of the political-military interface are the following:

First, selection of a force commander. He should be of recognized stature, whose training is technically appropriate and whose nationality is not itself a potential complication in achieving mission success. Second, allocation of key staff billets among national components. Political representation should be satisfied without jeopardizing the ability of planning, battle, and support staffs to function effectively in their duties. Third, a crystal clear statement of interface, within the chain of command, where the force commander receives policy guidance and political approval. To whom does the force commander report? Who gives him orders? And other aspects of informing and advising—through what channels do they go? Fourth, an agreed statement of the mission and objectives of operations. These have to be clear and complete to ensure no misunderstandings. Fifth, exact clarity on the approved rules of engagement, particularly with respect to the circumstances that would apply to the use of lethal force. Sixth, agreement on the general "concept of operations," which is the command's planning document on the operational measures and their sequence. The document should include a proposed exit strategy, specific criteria for success of the operation, and a tentative time line if appropriate. Seventh, as practical, political authorities should provide planning factors to the commander with respect to his requirements for force constitution and support—troop contributions, equipment, and logistical and financial support. The projections should be consistent with the "concept of operations."

There is a second set of critical factors, in exercising command and control, which concerns the application of a commander's authority—the execution of guidance and orders within his command. This is the "downward aspect" of command and control. A number of the factors already mentioned are important here as well. But several other aspects are critical to the actual ability of a commander to command and control his assigned forces. In a coalition operation, the clear authority of the commander might be limited, so it is essential to understand those limitations and the procedures to be followed to deal with them. I suggest three areas of concern.

First, does the commander have true command authority over the various components, or only operational control? Second, do component unit commanders themselves have authority to respond immediately to an order from the force commander, or do they need to consult with their own national political leaders? Third, within their assigned areas of responsibility, do the component units follow similar patterns of operation, or will they routinely operate in different ways? How do you go about day to day accomplishing the task? (For example, in Somalia, the British, Americans, and French had different ways of doing things.)

The ideal is clear authority by the force commander and common doctrine, tactics, and procedures. But that may not apply. Instead, a commander's authority is limited. When he gives an order, some units may respond with, "Well, that sounds like a reasonable instruction; we'll think about it and get back to you;" others with, "We'll check with the president;" and others with, "That sounds interesting, but we see things differently." In reality, the force commander might find himself operating more as a military manager, or even as a politician, working to maintain a common approach. It is coordination, not command. Such a system is creaky and certainly difficult to steer, but it is not unmanageable if the ground rules are understood all around and in advance. You don't want to find out in the middle of a firefight that there needs to be consultation.

There are ways of overcoming differences in approach. First, development of common doctrinal literature. This involves exercises, not just field exercises but command post exercises (CPX). In the short run, whether the force is composed of African or non-African units, it will run into complexities and confusions. Success often involves mustering certain capabilities and resources. Transportation is just one element; you also need general logistical and financial support, communications, and intelligence.

Clapham: I would like to look at the list of criteria that Woods produced and pick out three critical documents: the mission statement, the rules of engagement, and the plan of operation. We ought to be aware that they're not as cut and dried as we'd like. First, there is the issue of publicity versus secrecy. On one hand, the documents should be clear and explicit, so everyone knows what the operation is trying to do. On the other hand, in peacekeeping operations as in war, there is something to be said for secrecy. You need an element of ambiguity (just like you don't want to publish your war plans).

It was a disaster that NATO committed itself publicly against ground troops in Kosovo. That gave enormous and disastrous freedom of operation to [President Slobodan] Milosovic. There were similar issues for ECOMOG forces in Liberia. So we need to agree on what is public and what is secret. Second, fixity versus variability or change. In any operation, you can't lay down in advance precisely what will happen. Circumstances change. You are left with the problem as to how to adapt to it. While bearing in mind these things, we need to see the difficulty in them as well.

General R. P. Mboma [Tanzania]: Nearly everything has already been said. The factors that affect command and control and transport are: (1) *Historical background*. We have many countries, and within countries, different tribes and cultures. Within a region, there is a historical background of rule by different nations. Most forces have had military training abroad—in the U.K., France, Portugal, the U.S., Russia, and China. This historical background has an effect on command and control at present. (2) *Language diversity*. The languages used in peacekeeping are French, Portuguese, and English. There is definite distortion in translation and interpretation. We lack standard terminologies. (3) *Adequate communication equipment*. We don't have it. There is no standard equipment. In peacekeeping operations, you need more communications equipment than in ordinary military operations. You need it in every position. (4) *Transport*. Most African countries don't have adequate and quick transportation. In SADC, we rely mostly on South Africa's big planes to fly and reach destinations quickly. Even medium transport is not adequate. We need foreign assistance. In most training exercises we're relying on foreign aid. India is aiding Tanzania. If we are to react quickly, African countries need their own transportation. If Tanzania had to participate in Congo, it could use trains; if it were to help in Angola, it would need aircraft.

So for command and control, communication and transportation are needed. We need a common doctrine, training in joint exercises, and standard operating procedures common to the region, preferably to Africa.

Now I would like to talk about how command and control works. Tactically, it begins with defense and security. Intelligence and defense personnel are working day-to-day to know the security situation so they are able to detect the possibility of conflict. Within SADC, we are working on a mechanism that will allow the exchange of intelligence information among countries and a way of briefing others of the possibility of a violation or a need for peacekeeping in neighboring countries. Operationally, it begins with the chairman of SADC ([President Robert] Mugabe) and with specific organs: an early warning system, a hot line, and a satellite. From SADC, the information should go to the OAU. Ambassadors would deliver it; they would check back home for clarifications before the Secretary-General would endorse an action. Strategically, though peacekeeping is a UN responsibility, I have heard it said here that it isn't easy for the West to identify and get information early. At the UN level, after collecting information from the OAU, it could give a mandate for a peacekeeping mission in a certain area.

The force commander is charged with the organization and integration of all the nations under his charge. If it is a multinational operation, it might be countries inside or outside his region. We don't yet have a good communication system, since we haven't trained enough together. At the mission level, we should have national contingents. If Tanzania participates, it should have its area of responsibility. At the national level, we should have areas of responsibilities in order to avoid differences. For example, in training, we had a battalion that involved many nations under the control of Tanzania. But at one point, other commands were done in Portuguese by Mozambique, so we needed an interpreter. This is a problem if there is misinterpretation. Responsibilities for certain areas would solve that problem. If we assigned areas, and something happened there, certain countries would be responsible for reacting.

Williams: We shouldn't exaggerate all these issues about command, control, and transportation. I went to defense colleges in Nigeria, France, and India. There is a basic mental doctrine in Western countries. If that is the case, then for most African armies trained in Western staff colleges, there is not much difference in basic doctrine. Yes, you have different staff colleges, but what is important is that the OAU has to create a common training center. This is very key at the middle level. We also need to think about a single operational language. In NATO it is the English language. OAU has to adopt one single language for peace-keeping. Should it be Swahili? Let every defense academy introduce Swahili. Further, most Western equipment is interoperable. There are NATO standards. There are different standards outside the West, and we're using Russian and Chinese equipment. But the Chinese are also moving toward Western standards. So sometimes we do exaggerate some of these differences, and they are not as serious as we think. In Cairo in 1994 a committee was organized to formulate such an operational doctrine. A commitment to that report would have elimi-nated these problems.

Toraasen: I would like to make two points. First, regarding language. I had the opportunity to follow a meeting on a Baltic peacekeeping battalion in Riga [Latvia]. Their first decision was to start language training. That was very impor-tant, since the countries speak three different languages, and it is important that they understand each other. Second, regarding leadership. This is important in a multifunctional peace operation. Norway has been serving with its African friends in nearly all the peace operations. Africa has provided eminent force comman-ders in all regions. We should underline the importance of getting the best people with integrity—firm but flexible—as force commanders.

Herbst: Could the military officers say something about military-to-military contact between peacekeepers and the protagonists in a conflict? If there are sep-arate units roaming without any command and control, how do they interact with the forces that are fighting?

Col. Tom Dempsey [USA]: There are three avenues of communications: (1)

direct channels of peacekeeping; (2) communication through UN observer/peace-keeping missions on the ground; (3) through local diplomatic missions.

In Liberia, there was no problem with ECOMOG talking to various factions. There were good channels of communication. In Sierra Leone, it was more problematic, since ECOMOG forces were party to the dispute. Communications with the rebels caused particular problems with ECOMOG's relationship to the government of [President Ahmed Tejan] Kabbah. When it was necessary to open chanels of communication with combatants, a key role was played by UN observers. They were perceived as being unbiased, and they were able to work without generating suspicion. Local channels are also important because of their low profile. Political factions are more willing to engage through diplomatic channels. In any case, *open* channels of communication from peacekeepers to every faction involved are absolutely essential.

Mboma: In regards to communication with factions, the peacekeeping force is often doing its job, but the factions are not aware of what is happening. If you have communication, however, they are informed and the operation won't go into more than Chapter VI. Regarding forces' headquarters: The UN, the OAU, and maybe an organization of regional chairmen should be incorporated to bring feedback to different organizations. A person in place there, watching everything, would be a very good thing for the United Nations.

Shalli: Regarding command and control, political support and direction is most critical in a peacekeeping operation. You also need to introduce a special representative for that particular operation. It should not just be the representative to the organization itself. For example, in the UN or the OAU, you need a special representative for a specific operation. You will then have the political support.

The language issue is critical, but there is no immediate solution. We have the same problem *inside* our territories: we don't have a national language. We even need an interpreter within our countries. We have a flag, currency, and anthem but no national language. But we manage to communicate very well. We allocate areas of responsibility, and that works very well. Standardization of equipment is not such a big problem. It is not a question of various equipment not being able to talk to each other. The problem is in the way of acquisition. In operating with the Libyans, for example, they won't have American equipment because Americans won't send it to them. This will be a problem until we reach a global solution.

As for the status of forces argument, we don't need to reinvent the wheel. A manual by the UN outlines standard operating procedures. It may not be as effective as we like, but it can be improved on. We can adopt it in an African environment.

Everything revolves around funding. We don't have a shortage of manpower.

We just don't have money to employ them. We need to bring all the money put outside the continent back. Nigeria has $50 billion outside the continent—plus 30,000 Ph.D.s who are outside the country. Bring them back!

On dealing with local elements: Use a joint committee and include various elements of the factions that you want to deal with. Then, if there can be a special representative that can shuttle between base A and base B and try to talk to various factions, that is also helpful. You need to create a bridge of trust between them. And you can't favor one party over another, or hell breaks lose. That would achieve the Congo of 1960s, not the Congo of 1990s.

Tonje: It is the idea of cooperation that is important. Even if it's a little problem, get everyone together. It is only in training and living together that people can fight together. We should involve all the coalition members so they can get to know each other. If they draw blood together, they are more cemented for further operations.

Woods: I want to come back to the discussion of money: if African forces don't have capabilities on hand, money can quickly buy most anything to augment capabilities. Sea lift, air lift, ancillary communications equipment, and intelligence support—there are firms out there that can provide anything to augment your own intelligence. The forces you're trying to control are probably not inhibited in the use of whatever money they have to go after these assets. They'll rent a gunship if necessary. U.S. forces rely heavily on contracting out. Africans should pay more attention to getting financial flexibility for quick-fixes, where their own units don't have capabilities. The opposition in a conflict has access to things, and they may become more technically advanced than the government.

In the command structure, there need to be two points of special coordination. One would be in public affairs, communication. This needs to be high up. This position would get the word out to the populace and disputants, clearing away any confusion. This should be built into the plan, and institutionalized. Another point would be a civil-military operations center (CMOC). Here, the NGO community and the humanitarian community could meet regularly and coordinate their activities and exchange information. These are political operations with a military and humanitarian or developmental component. They need serious planning.

Coalition efforts are complex and cumbersome. To the extent that you don't give the force commander a capability for flexibility and quick reaction, the "free actors" (the bad guys) will run rings around the operation. The force will continually find itself steps behind an evolving operation. The people on the other side aren't inhibited by political factors. There needs to be the opportunity for quick reaction and adaptation.

VII. Interventions in Africa: From ECOMOG in Liberia to SADC in Lesotho

Of the numerous peace enforcement actions in Africa, from the Tanzanian mutiny of 1963 onward, the meeting considered the recent attempts to limit and end civil war and chaos in Liberia, Sierra Leone, the Democratic Republic of Congo (DRC), Angola, Somalia, and Lesotho. Each case had peculiarities of its own; the context and confusion of each was unique. Yet there are sufficient similarities that lessons, even tentative ones, can be drawn.

—Interventions are never early enough. Potential intervenors, such as a putative crisis response force, can never anticipate the outbreak of crises sufficiently early to prevent all loss of life. The reluctance to act in a timely manner is central to the condition of civil war, everywhere. How to turn early warning and the incipient breakdown of civil order into early action by outsiders remains an extremely difficult question.

—There is a time to negotiate and a time to interpose a force for good. Negotiations often go on too long. Without military might, or exhaustion on both sides, negotiations fail.

—Intervening forces succeed best if they are powerfully led, with a determination to end hostilities in a no-nonsense manner. Tolerating continued attacks undermines the peacemaking role.

—Peacemakers or peace enforcers must themselves be militarily and ethnically uncompromised. If not, the effort unravels and the intervening force loses the support of the civilian population.

—Disarmament of contending parties, followed by enforced demobilization, is essential.

—The intervenors need more powerful communications and transport equipment than the civil warriors. They also need finance and the support of outside powers.

—UN and OAU legitimacy is essential, even if the intervention is entirely a sub-regional affair.

—Restoring order must be succeeded by keeping order and restoring stability.

—A mandate that includes rebuilding the government and refurbishing democracy is helpful. Early elections are not a requirement, but some other means of shoring up democratic rule by either a continuing regime or a new one, is critical.

—Restoring the economy is essential. It helps rebuild confidence as well as undergirding stability. The mandate of a crisis response force should be stretched to include measures such as this one.

—The end of an intervention comes only when lawless forces are imprisoned or disbanded, and when a government exists that fully controls its territory, is regarded as legitimate, and has the means to prevent civil strife.

ECOMOG

Williams: I would like to address "Weaknesses and Errors" rather than "Successes and Failures." As far as ECOWAS and ECOMOG are concerned, it was not a deliberate effort, but circumstances, that created ECOMOG. Therefore, if one is going to look at ECOMOG, we must remember that this was something that had never been tried by any economic grouping in Africa. It was an attempt at common responsibilities. And there have been many articles and analyses of its successes and failures. I would like to concentrate on its weaknesses and errors in four areas:

(1) Political Will. This is always important in Africa, especially when there are internal conflicts. This is because most African countries believe that when they authorize the OAU or sub-regional body to intervene in the internal conflict of a member-country, it may be their turn one day. So they resist any attempt at intervention in a country's internal affairs. That was the problem with ECOWAS, which because of lack of political will tried diplomatic means...also unsuccessfully. There was no way they could have stopped the factions from fighting. The standing mediation committee did succeed in getting the factions to the negotiating table, but failed to get them to arrive at political solutions. The suggestion for an international conference did not meet with international support. ECOWAS produced a mandate, which said that it needed a monitoring force to monitor the peace accord. They were hoping that [Charles] Taylor would change his mind and support ECOMOG. At the time, no one knew we were going to send troops there. The planning process was completely missing. We had to seek the assistance of the American embassy in Lagos to get maps for operational planning. The maps had to be flown in from Washington. Ghana, the Gambia, Sierra Leone, and Mali contributed officers and soldiers to ECOMOG in various numbers. ECOWAS had (and still has) no back-stop organization and resources to launch and sustain any intervention. Nigeria had no alternative but to accept the hegemonic burden. ECOMOG was there to implement the peace accord. The political will of Nigeria influenced other contributions to stay on to sustain ECOMOG. The non-support from Côte d'Ivoire and Burkina Faso made it tough. Nigeria's President, General [Ibrahim] Babangida, tried to assist in the mediation processes, and he hoped that Côte d'Ivoire's President Felix Houphouët-Boigny would agree. He had to use diplomatic skills to get him to be the chief mediator. Now, the mandate wouldn't happen without being

flexible. Earlier, it was Lt. General Arnold Quainoo of Ghana, then the First Commander of ECOMOG, who as a traditional peacekeeper wanted the consent of all adversaries before the deployment of the troops. He even suggested that the troops return to Sierra Leone. But Nigeria held firm. So you do find that the role of a hegemon, especially in protracted conflict, is very important.

(2) Resources. The performance of an intervention force also depends on the resources made available to it. Nigeria and Ghana had to do the detailed planning and execution of the details, up to the transportation of troops. It was after two years of carrying the burden that meager help came from outside the continent. ECOWAS had no resources to support the intervention. Nigeria made the larger contributions in manpower and logistics. If any sub-regional force is going to succeed in a similar operation, then there is need for a framework with an effective, efficient, and well-maintained back-stop organization and logistics. Initially, some wanted to go to ECOWAS for funds, but then they discovered that it was very weak. So they went elsewhere.

It was a terrible problem for Nigeria, which made great contributions to command and control, as well as equipment. We thought we were going to have to fight a conventional war, but then it got to the point where possibilities were limited. Nigeria needed the experience of soldiers. What did it do? It decided to create its own guerilla forces from Liberians opposed to Charles Taylor. This is how the faction came into being. It included refugees in Sierra Leone. In the short term, it was useful. In the long term, it became a problem. ECOMOG couldn't control all these forces. Of course, they didn't want to leave. Finally, they didn't want to fight Taylor anymore. That was how some of these problems were solved.

But then there was the issue of logistics. Nigeria couldn't take them all on alone. Funding was a big problem. Importantly, the operation was undertaken on the back of ECOWAS, where there were a lot of corrupt practices that made the whole exercise very costly. Now ECOMOG also had a problem getting logistical support from many sources. Sometimes the U.S. would give equipment, other times it would come from elsewhere. There was confusion in Liberia. I was commander of training and command. One of the biggest problems of the Liberian intervention was a lack of coordination. I saw that big gap. And when Nigeria was made the representative of ECOWAS, the ability there to take responsibility was gone. If anybody is going to succeed in such an operation, they need a proper framework.

(3) Outsiders' Influence: Côte d'Ivoire and Burkina Faso were the West African countries that assisted Charles Taylor in scuttling all peace accords. The international business community, especially from France, also played their part by providing commercial opportunities for Liberian warlords. Libya, as usual, played a key role.

(4) Organization of Command and Control. We worked with people who were primarily trained in Western military institutions. The Guineans, with their Soviet training, were not easy to work with. There was difficulty in bringing them into line with Western concepts. However, they have similar ethnic linkages with millions of Mandingo living in Liberia. This relationship was useful for intelligence purposes. Nigerian officers commanded ECOMOG in Liberia after Lt. Gen. Quainoo left, and until now. After some few years, we came to understand each other. But communication was a problem. The majority of forces were English speaking, except the Guinean.

On consensus, I would say that ECOMOG could have been able to deal with the situation years before it did, but sadly, the francophone countries—especially Côte d'Ivoire and Burkina Faso, with tacit support of some Western countries—were not ready to give ECOMOG all the support it needed. They pushed Taylor to ask for non-West African troops before the implementation of any of the numerous peace accords he signed. Then the UN came in through the OAU, which brought in the Tanzanians and Ugandans. They belonged to the same school of thought as Quainoo, and went back after six months because they were not ready to get involved in any deliberate firefight provoked by any of the factions.

This hopeless situation continued until there was an ECOWAS consensus that all faction leaders be brought together to run an interim government in preparation for an election. The interim period was for the factions to transform themselves into political parties, for encampment and disarmament, which were vigorously pursued in line with the Abuja Peace Accords. There were elections, and the rest is known to all of us.

It is important to emphasize the role of outsiders in complicating efforts to manage or resolve internal conflicts in African countries. Whether Nigeria got a lasting solution or not in this situation, I don't know. Let's hope.

Dempsey: I am a big fan of ECOMOG during the period of disarmament through the elections. It was one of the most successful peacekeeping and enforcement operations in the region. I have some suggestions for why it was less successful after elections. And ECOMOG in Sierra Leone was also a different animal. It was involved there in peace*making*: imposing a settlement by force of law.

The ECOMOG forces went into Sierra Leone in March 1996, followed by an April wave of fighting. Refugees threatened to become an economic burden on many areas. All of ECOWAS and the international community recognized that something needed to be done quickly. There was a major resurgence of ECOMOG. In July Major General Samuel Victor Malu was appointed to command ECOMOG. He was highly respected within the Nigerian military. He arrived with a charter from ECOWAS to transform the operation into a more aggressive one.

Disarmament began in one city. Some soldiers were taken hostage, and the rebels intended to execute them. Malu took a rebel leader into his office, and told him he would be personally punished if he did execute them. This achieved the release of soldiers, and it was a defining moment. The Abuja Peace Accords were being negotiated at the same time. These gave a mandate for an aggressive peace enforcement mission.

There was lots of assistance by the international community, especially with on-the-ground logistical support. ECOMOG was able to be robust throughout the country. It is hard to overestimate the huge change this brought about: it allowed for a military force with the logistical wherewithal to enforce its mission. In February 1997 there began the "cordon and search" operations to disarm fighters who had not voluntarily disarmed. This was another defining moment. ECOMOG found out that a warlord had an arms cache. Malu went and found the cache and forcibly took it over. This showed that all the provisions of the accords would be implemented. When I got to Liberia, no one was carrying weapons except peacekeepers and government forces, even if there were still caches hidden.

In July 1997 elections were conducted countrywide. From Liberians all across the country, as well as from observers, the consensus was that they were good, free and fair elections. In August, a new government under Taylor was inaugurated, recognized internally and by the international community. In fifteen months, Liberia went from a failed state with a vicious, costly conflict to a legitimately elected government. All parties accepted the process and were prepared to abide by it.

Why was there this success? First, the Abuja Peace Accords provided a clear mandate for peace enforcers. A broad mandate is essential in a failed state without government services. Second, parties to the conflict concluded that they could better realize their objectives by laying down their arms. The presence of a peace enforcement force was essential; all knew that no one could take on ECOMOG. And everyone was appalled at the destruction of Monrovia. Third, ECOWAS helped the actors reach political consensus on an impartial implementation of the [Abuja] agreement. Fourth, strong political leadership was provided by ECOWAS, implemented by the regional leader, Nigerian President [Sani] Abacha. Fifth, there was strong military leadership under Malu. Significantly, however, it was not a predominantly Nigerian effort. Ghana, Niger, and others participated. It was truly a multinational force. ECOWAS members backed up political commitment with material resources. Finally, the international community provided critical logistical support. It enabled ECOMOG forces to do what they needed to do. It supplied personnel, arms, and equipment, surface transportation, helicopters, communications, rations for troops—anything they needed to conduct their operations in any part of Liberia. So it was a successful peacekeeping operation.

But if you look at ECOMOG following the elections, you see a different picture. In February 1998 conflict arose between the Nigerian component of the operation and Liberia over the Sierra Leonean intervention. Efforts to renew the ECOMOG charter in Liberia were unsuccessful because of friction between the newly elected government and the ECOMOG force that had been handling government operations for awhile. In mid-1998 things were very tense. The Liberian government started incorporating many of its ex-fighters into its government. (The Liberian government said it was not a signatory to the peace accords; the accords were only signed by factions. It also said that security forces were supposed to be restructured before the elections, and that wasn't done). The result is that we had the appearance of former National Patriotic Front of Liberia (NPFL) fighters in the Taylor government. In September 1998 there was renewed fighting between factions and government forces. ECOMOG did not have a mandate to intervene.

What were the obstacles to peacekeeping after the elections? First, there was the sovereignty issue in the peace accords. Second, there was a breakdown of ECOWAS's political consensus. Third, there was an eroding of support from the international community and donors. Fourth, there was a failure of the process of disarmament, demobilization, and reintegration (DDR). Fifth, there was growing frustration of former factions, with thousands of dissatisfied soldiers. And finally, there were growing external security threats.

As a result of the deteriorating security in post-conflict Liberia, it may go back to a failed state status. Its economic assistance is currently on hold. Liberia represents a failure to sustain the effort past the point of peacekeeping to genuine conflict resolution.

What about ECOMOG in Sierra Leone? In February 1998 the Nigerian component of ECOMOG began its offensive against the Revolutionary United Front (RUF). It was an initial intervention by Guinea and Nigeria, followed by the endorsement of the sub-regional organization. In March, ECOMOG extended its control throughout most of Sierra Leone. President Kabbah was restored to power. The UN Security Council then endorsed the ECOMOG mission. In July 1998, the UN Security Council established a UN observer mission; but the rebels were more willing to engage ECOMOG than in Liberia. In December ECOMOG sustained heavy losses. From January to April 1999 ECOMOG came in with more troops, and it succeeded in retaking most of the country. On May 18, 1999, a cease-fire was agreed to by [rebel leader] Sankoh.

What were the accomplishments of ECOMOG in Sierra Leone? First, it restored a democratically elected government, thereby re-endorsing the Banjul declaration. Second, it provided the opportunity for a political resolution to the conflict by preventing any faction from imposing a settlement by force of arms (it limited the war and continues to do so). Third, it facilitated critical humanitarian assistance efforts. It is solely because of the access ECOMOG is providing that NGOs and the UN can operate in Sierra Leone. Fourth, it established the necessary conditions for RUF-government negotiations (it is unlikely they would have sat down together without it).

Gen. Fisher: In talking about how we should move forward, we shouldn't ignore the past. In all the various cases, we should be able to say what have we learned and why we have succeeded in some cases and not in others. We are talking about peacemaking, peace enforcing, and peacebuilding. In the analysis of the situation, we should come out with the design of an approach that would outline the responsibilities of the protagonists themselves. What would happen if there were cease-fire violations? If we are going to keep the peace, and there is no peace to keep, what are the chances of succeeding?

We have to look at *prevailing conditions*; each conflict has its own particularities. In Somalia, President Siad Barre's overthrow left a vacuum. None of the lords or clans could fill the vacuum. They were continually protecting themselves. There was no government, and no peace to enforce or facilitate. So even when the peacemakers came, some of the operations that were undertaken were inappropriate. We ended up glorifying warlords in the process. In Mozambique, the prevailing condition was that there was a government that was sincerely seeking to find a solution. Both sides were committed to peace. The job of the peacemakers was clear-cut. In Lesotho, the prevailing conditions were a clear-cut undermining of a democratically elected government by the military. It was an undermining of a key instrument of power. The military undermined the command of the government. They denied the police the opportunity to maintain law and order. The leaders' and other people's lives were in danger; a coup was in the making. The conditions were that the center of gravity was not on the side of the soldiers, but with the people, who were on the side of the government. So the resolution was much easier. But would you repeat the approach to Lesotho in other areas? Conditions dictate how you approach issues.

Democratic Republic of Congo (DRC)

Majogo: I wanted to remind the conference that there are so far no peacekeeping operations in the Democratic Republic of the Congo. Originally Uganda and Rwanda decided to help the rebels. This was for security reasons and because they feared genocide. [President] Kabila with his government said he needed some assistance from France. So for good reasons, France went in to help Kabila.

Namibia, Angola, and Zimbabwe also helped him. Before talking about peace-keeping, we have to have a cease-fire. So when you mentioned the example of Congo, I just want to remind you that it hasn't reached a state of peacekeeping yet. I am not a military expert, but I would like to make this clear.

Nyambuya: Regarding the allegation to the effect that addressing problems facing the region should be approved by the region as a whole. DRC wasn't a member of SADC until Kabila came to power. After he took over and started running the country, he decided to join SADC. No one forced him. In SADC, we believe in orderly change of government. When we [Zimbabwe] went into DRC, we didn't just wake up and decide to go; extensive consultations took place. We heard peoples' views. In the nonaligned summit, heads of states agreed that the intervention was legitimate. Security Council Resolution 1234 of 1999 invited our participation. I caution against choosing to have short memories or ignoring clear things.

Kavuma: I would like to make some clarifications regarding the DRC and SADC's intervention. It is true there were consultations. A team from SADC came to Uganda. What surprised us was that before the findings of the committee were made known, there was a deployment of equipment and personnel by SADC. It took us by surprise. I don't know whether anyone really strongly put forward the case. Before the findings were known [President] Museveni said, "Yes, SADC can deploy in DRC." I have my conviction that, if anything, we did not agree to deployment before the organs of states were briefed and consulted.

Second, regarding the categorization of foreign troops in DRC, and who was invited and who was not. We went in to the DRC because of strategic concerns of our countries. We couldn't sit and watch while organizations like the Interahamwe came to attack and occupy Ugandan territory for a number of days, and then ran and hid in the DRC. We couldn't watch while Interahamwes were being trained right across the border to attack us. There were real security concerns.

Uganda was the first country invited to deploy troops in the DRC. After Kabila confessed he wasn't able to control the eastern part of DRC, that it was too much for the new government, Uganda approached President Kabila and said, "There is a problem here." He knew about it. The problem had persisted from before. Kabila said, "We are willing but weak." We said we would deploy so that there would be security and stability in that area, and it would deny bandits the ability to train and be helped by the Sudan (including Idi Amin's son, who is leading some fighters). We were the first people who were invited. We are interested in coming to terms with the real issues and underlying problems in the DRC. The conflict has an internal dimension and an external one; both affect us. Once we are sure our security conditions are catered to in full, we have no business in the DRC. We will then pull out.

Angola

Dlamini: I hope that this meeting will help the relevant countries to try to find a solution to these overwhelming problems. Two weeks ago [May 1999], Swaziland tried to bring Zambia and Angola together. It seems that there is a stalemate in Angola. Two parties are content with the crisis. Perhaps they are actually benefiting from what is happening. It seems that this is the problem. I would like you to look at that. Perhaps the government and [Jonas] Savimbi are benefiting from the status quo. When we looked at the problem of Zambia, it seemed that Zambia had no problem with Angola at all. As chair of SADC, we would like to try to help Angola solve this problem.

Nyambuya: I am going to talk about my experiences with UNAVEM and UNOSOM [UN Operation in Somalia] from a personal perspective: how I felt as a peacekeeper, what we subjected our troops to. First, UNAVEM in Angola. We were there to verify and monitor the cease-fire between the two factions, the ruling government and UNITA (National Union for the Total Independence of Angola). The country got into its present position because of the Cold War. The UN was given a difficult task. Its resources were 360 unarmed military observers, 90 unarmed police observers, and election observers. The problem was that there were 200,000 army troops to be monitored and verified by these 360 unarmed observers. Further, for the elections, there were 2,000 polling stations to be monitored by 500 observers. The result was that one of the parties contested the election results, and that was the end of two years of investment.

What went wrong? The simple answer is that people spent billions waging war, but only a few million was spent on waging peace. That was not adequate. The result was a failure. The second problem was that the ceasefire agreements themselves were flawed. The chunk of documents used in UNAVEM was based on an agreement between the two parties. They wanted to be the players and the referees at the same time. The UN was relegated to the role of referee only. And the parties changed the playing ground. Further, we shouldn't use elections as a means to an end. They should be there. But we should emphasize reconciliation. Whether you are neighbors, brothers, or parents, you're bound to live where you are.

Does the UN have a chance in Africa? As for its role in peacekeeping: if you want to kill a dog, you might as well kill a big one. In other words, if you want to do peacekeeping, you must do it properly. Work with the current mandate and resources. Above all, there needs to be a proper peace before there can be peacekeeping.

Angola needs the attention of other players. Some are suggesting a regional solution; others are suggesting greater involvement for the UN. Both are debatable. One thing is certain: the international community is turning a blind eye to UNITA's activities mining and selling diamonds.

A soldier involved in peacekeeping is a frustrated man if you don't explain clearly what mission you want him to achieve and fail to give him the resources to achieve it.

Normand: I agree with the assessment of the failure of UNAVEM; it was undersized to face a big challenge. There was deep mistrust between the two sides despite the protocol that was signed. It was not interpreted in good faith, at least by UNITA. Savimbi didn't sign it personally, so there was no true commitment. That possibly bears some responsibility. And the sanctions that currently exist (regarding diamonds, oil, and the arms embargo) are not currently being implemented. The UN has decided to set up a group of experts to assess the situation and make recommendations. UNITA is not supposed to sell diamonds, but they do, and it provides huge resources to buy arms and oil. We could have more closely monitored sanctions to force the two parties to negotiate again. The only possible end for the conflict should be some kind of acquiescence by the two sides. The military solution is not solving the conflict. The war may last a long time. No one has quick solutions to provide. Maybe to better the situation, we might tighten sanctions and try to initiate some political discussions. Still, it is a very difficult situation.

Woods: I've been deeply involved in the Angola mess. Looking back on the UN operations, let me make a few comments. When it became obvious that UNITA wasn't demobilizing or turning in weapons, when it denied the UN access to large parts of the country, we all knew they were mining gold and diamonds, and we suspected rearmament. But the UN and the U.S., knowing this likelihood, went along with the charade. After the fiasco of elections, the whole charade began again. The government of Angola arrived, at the end, in saying the UN was part of the problem, because it was providing a cover for rearmament. The quest always for diplomatic solutions is not necessarily appropriate.

The start of the problem is that there is no unanimity in SADC. Some, like South Africa, say, "Neither side is going to win, let's get them back to table," while the Angolan government says, "We'll fight to the death."

I don't have a solution. Even if all the countries ganged up on Savimbi, I don't know if he would give up. There's not just the question of political will. But *is* there a political solution?

Somalia is more evidence that we officially lie about things—paper over things. . . .

Shalli: I offer some additional information (but I'm not telling you what to do). Remember that there are 20,000 ex-UNITA soldiers that have become government soldiers. UNITA's old leadership is Rwandan. Those of us who spent time in Angola knew what kind of weapons and soldiers there were (there were 40,000

UNITA regulars before 1990 and 50,000 other soldiers). Only in 1992–94 did the numbers become smaller; one wondered where the other soldiers were. They handed over less than all of their weapons. They obviously had many others. They also had tanks and artillery pieces. There wasn't a genuine peace, but we didn't discover it right away. The UN and the international community didn't understand that UNITA wasn't serious.

As for the mandate, you only need to understand what the name of the peace-keeping operation is to know what its mandate is. In Namibia, UNTAG, the UN Transition Assistance Group, was there to assist the transition. They were only there to monitor whatever was happening.

So what should be done now in Angola? UNITA has just bought 150 tanks. There are only two countries with the capability to transport 150 tanks in six months: the U.S. and Russia. There had to be an [acquiescence] of one of these two countries to get them there. UNITA also has 3,000 mercenaries, paid thousands of dollars a month. Until you freeze UNITA's assets, you can't stop these weapons and mercenaries from getting through.

Mulongoti: I've lived with Angola for a long time. This discussion makes me begin to wonder where in the history of sanctions have sanctions succeeded. All the countries that had sanctions imposed have tended to become even stronger. It seems a futile exercise. Tanks are still moving into UNITA-controlled Angola. No one is controlling the source of tanks. The other problem you can't ignore is that there is lots of money in that area. Who buys the diamonds? Powerful companies. Savimbi doesn't wear diamonds; nor do his wives. It is others and their wives. If you're given a big diamond when you are an observer, do you think you write a negative report? Savimbi was supported by the West. Are you sure that there is political will now? He has become a monster.

How about those of us who are his neighbors? Do we have the ability to stop him? The border between us is manned by UNITA. Lots of arms are peddled across. When the fighters are hungry, they exchange AK-47s for chickens and other food. While it is a concern for others, it is a nightmare to us in Zambia. I wish others knew the nightmare we are living. It poses a threat to neighbors as well as those inside Angola. We expect the West to help us have some peace.

Hooks: Angola represents a disturbing trend, where the internal conflict of one country spills over into the internal conflict of the other. We see this in both Congos. The Hutus have closely supported Savimbi. This explains Kabila's intervention. Angola is involved in Brazzaville because it feels a responsibility to protect its critical interests. The problems in the two Congos can't be resolved without looking at that in Angola, and vice versa.

Hama Thay: In Angola, there were so many agreements signed. If the world found a solution, it did not persuade Savimbi or the government. As for the tanks, how did they move from Russian territory? How were they paid for? One can have a look at sanctions. It is possible for them to work. Of course it is private citizens who are buying the diamonds and oil. Why don't the "owners" of those citizens tell them not to participate in that area? Instead, nothing is done about it. We have to control Savimbi if we are to have an agreement.

Somalia

Gen. Fisher: I have an anecdote: in Somalia, a commander was confronted by a council of elders. The council had a man that they claimed to be a rapist. They had sentenced him to death. But they'd run out of ammunition. So they asked him, "Can you help us?" The commander had a hard time. In the end, he redirected them to the UN authorities, who undoubtedly would not have agreed to that kind of solution.

Nyambuya: UNOSOM had a problem. First of all, you should never have a situation where you are trying to establish a government in a vacuum. There were many people claiming to be leaders. It was the UN peacekeeping mission that came first, undertaking its proper mandate of securing airports and being responsible for the distribution of food. UNOSOM came and was successful because it had the correct amount of resources. There was a unified command and control structure. At its peak, there were over 30,000 troops, and there was straightforward command and control. In UNOSOM2, there were clear problems of command and control, as well as a reduction in troops. UNOSOM2 failed as a result of a lack of resources.

What is the lesson? Unless the environment changes, the UN clearly cannot embark on Chapter VII operations. It is not capable. What we can have is a leading nation capacity: one nation acting on others' behalf. But there needs to be the political will: Somalia was not OK, while Bosnia was. Instead of withdrawing troops when things went wrong, as it did in the former, the U.S. reinforced troops in the latter.

Lesotho

Mosisili: To begin, let me briefly outline the historical background to the 1998 May general elections in Lesotho. These elections were only the second democratic elections after twenty-three years of non-elected, non-representative, dictatorial rule. These elections were also the first to be conducted by an Independent Electoral Commission (IEC). They were observed by over 500 observers, local and international. Without exception, all passed them as free and fair. The party that I lead, the Lesotho Congress for Democracy (LCD), was then only eight months old. That is true, but not quite true. As a new party with a new name, it was only eight months old. But we actually split from an old party that had been formed in 1952 (the Basuto [Lesotho] Congress Party—BCP). This party had won the 1993 elections—all 65 seats in Parliament. Because there was no opposition in Parliament, we created one and ended up splitting. That's how my party came into being. Therefore we went into the May elections as a separate party from the old BCP. The elections showed that the old BCP had remained only in name, but most of its support had crossed over to us in the new party. Out of eighty constituencies, the LCD won seventy-nine, and lost only one.

Almost three months after the new government assumed office, in August 1998, an alliance of three opposition parties claimed that the elections had been rigged, that we had not won fairly. They staged protest marches to the palace to demand that because elections had been rigged, the government should be disbanded, Parliament dissolved, and a government of national unity installed. When this campaign started, we were of the view that it should be stopped, because we felt that it was illegal. But the police were reluctant to stop it. Then a diplomatic initiative was started by South Africa, as chairman of SADC. [South African Deputy President Thabo] Mbeki was dispatched to Maseru to try to negotiate an agreement. We said to the deputy president and the opposition alliance that the allegations of fraud should be subjected to a verification process by a team of experts from outside Lesotho. I undertook to resign from government, to request His Majesty [Letsie III] to dissolve Parliament, and to request new elections if even *one* of the allegations of fraud were proved true. I was not prepared to be the beneficiary of a fraudulent election.

So a commission—the [Justice Pius] Langa Commission—was put together, with experts from Botswana, Zimbabwe, and South Africa. It wanted to do a ballot re-count. We had to amend the electoral code to do so. The current one allowed a re-count only in constituencies where there was a case of disputed elections. So we had to go to Parliament to allow the commission access to ballot boxes. Indeed, a re-count was made. Initially, teams from two universities in South Africa were bussed in to do the re-count. When they couldn't finish, a contingent of the South African National Defense Force was bussed in to complete it. When the report finally came out, it did not prove even one allegation to have been true. However, it did indicate that the IEC had made errors and discrepancies *after* the election results were announced in compiling and storing electoral materials. But no fraud of any type was proved.

I, however, have two criticisms to level against the Langa report: First, the findings were framed in an incongruous manner. They were not very categorical. They used double-negatives, for example. As a student of linguistics, I thought it was a terrible style of presentation. Second, it didn't give out the results of the ballot re-count. Why, I don't know. However, it did clearly indicate that the results were indeed a fair reflection of the will of the majority of electors in Lesotho. We felt that we were indeed a legitimate government. So my offer to resign automatically fell away. But there were violent demonstrations from the opposition. They began to erect illegal roadblocks, preventing traffic and normal business from proceeding. They confiscated government vehicles at gunpoint, chased civil servants out of their offices, closed the national radio station. They made access to Parliament impossible; making it inoperative. The startling aspect of all these illegal actions was why the law enforcement agencies let them happen. The police claimed that elements of the army were involved, that armed elements were cooperating with the protesters. Therefore they couldn't apprehend the protesters.

At the same time, the army was hit with a mutiny. Junior officers arrested senior ones, stripped them of their rank, and jailed them. They forced a commander to read a statement over the radio, in which he dismissed twenty-eight senior officers, and after which he announced his own resignation. Clearly, this was forced. It was not acceptable to the government. They went as far as bringing to me the names of the officers they were appointing as commanders of the army, and I refused to accept them. I told them that they had no legal power to make such appointments.

Then came the SADC summit in Mauritius, which mandated Botswana, South Africa, and Zimbabwe, together with Mozambique, to remain apprised of developments in Lesotho. The first three were already guarantors, since the 1994 "memorandum of understanding" to guarantee peace and stability. When I returned from the summit in Mauritius, I found that we were a government under siege. I immediately appealed to the four presidents who had been mandated by SADC to intervene militarily. My appeal was premised on three legal frameworks: the SADC treaty, the memorandum of understanding, and the Lesotho Defense Force Act (this says that a minister of defense can invite foreign soldiers to come to Lesotho for various activities). Much has been said of my failure to consult His Majesty, the King. My reason was simple. I saw the source of the problems that I was trying to solve as essentially emanating from the palace. It had become the center from which these people operated. I was actually trying to restrain the palace.

On September, 22, 1998, South Africa sent its forces into Maseru. They were followed by the Botswana Defense Force. When those forces came in, it was clear that a coup was in the offing—that the prime minister and cabinet ministers were to be assassinated together with members of Parliament. We have since learned that the reason for these plans was that they were aware that SADC could possibly intervene. They planned that if they did, there should be no one that could be labeled a legitimate government in place. The South Africans came in that morning, and as helicopters were flying into Maseru, someone went on the air in Lesotho to announce that the government had been toppled.

But then, as the South African forces flew in, they engaged the elements of the Lesotho Defense Force at Maweni Barracks. Because they concentrated there, those who had been at the palace dispersed to the city and began looting and torching businesses and homes.

That is how the destruction of Maseru happened. South African forces were concentrating on military tyrants. My own private home was scattered, together with everything that I'd worked on for twenty years as a university lecturer. South Africa and Botswana stopped a coup in Lesotho and saved lives. It is true that twenty-six lives of military personnel were lost—eight South African, eighteen Botswanan. But otherwise, an impending coup was stopped.

Part of the mandate of South Africa and Botswana was to disarm the Lesotho Defense Force. They carried out their mandate and restored rule of law in Lesotho. The second dimension to the intervention was that as soon as law and order had been restored, a political solution should be found. It was clear that military intervention itself would not be an answer. Indeed, as soon as law and order had been restored, an initiative sponsored by the four parliaments was mounted. Negotiations began which led to the formation of a body called the Interim Political Authority (IPA). It consists of two representatives from each party that had participated in the May general elections, or twenty-four persons. Its mandate is to level the playing field so that within a period of fifteen to eighteen months, we can have fresh general elections.

Part of the mandate of leveling the playing field was to review the Lesotho electoral system—to make it more democratically representative and inclusive and to review and restructure the independent electoral commission. They have not made much progress, I regret to report, because they've been quibbling over the definition of "consensus." The word was deliberately included in the legislation, because we thought that if it was only a simple majority required, then we would be overwhelmed by their numbers. So we insisted that decisions of the IPA be reached by consensus. They haven't agreed precisely on what that means. Where it failed to reach consensus, there were provisions to submit the problem to arbitration. So far, they have submitted the meaning of consensus to arbitration. A judge has declined to arbitrate on the meaning of consensus. But he offered his personal opinion: it doesn't mean a simple majority and is generally taken to mean a substantial majority. But how substantial? Two-thirds? That was left open. It did point out an abnormal complication in the IPA: namely, that parties represented on the IPA have been given equal status even though they do not have equal support from the electorate. Be that as it may, IPA hasn't made much progress. They have gone as far as debating the electoral model, but they haven't yet agreed on a suitable model. The opposition alliance demands a change from first-past-the-post to 100 percent proportional representation. We maintain that there is nothing wrong with the first-past-the-post model. What is wrong is that people are not democratic enough to accept defeat at the polls. But we've said we're ready to go along with any suggestion of proposed change, as long as that change can be submitted to the electorate by way of referendum. A change in an electoral model is so fundamental that it can't be the prerogative of a few people that haven't been elected. People should be given the chance to pronounce themselves on what kind of electoral model is adopted.

My friends in the opposition alliance demand 100 percent proportional representation and nothing else. We've tried proposing all sorts of compromises, such as a combination/mixed system: keep first-past-the-post for 80 constituencies and then increase the number of seats to 120 and have the extra 40 seats shared proportionally. They're not excited by it. We've come up with a dual model system: after the ballots are counted the first time, you weigh the results using both first-past-the-post and proportional representation. If one party gets more seats through first-past-the-post, you stay with that. But if another party gets more seats through proportional representation, then you say fine, you can use PR [proportional representation]. The only complication is that you wouldn't know exactly the number of seats in parliament until the whole arithmetic had been worked out. It hasn't been acceptable to my friends in the opposition alliance either. They want 100 percent PR.

On the question of the Independent Electoral Commission, the opposition alliance demands that it be disbanded and a new one be put into place. They have no confidence in the commissioners, even though all three were nominated by opposition parties. None was nominated by my party. Now they claim they no longer have confidence in these gentlemen, that they all should be disbanded. We've said they were constituted by law. The law indicates ways and means of removing them from office. But they're not prepared to do that. They want them to be thrown out overnight. We maintain we're a country that respects the rule of law.

The problem is that six months have lapsed already [June 1999]. There are only twelve months until the agreed general elections. One hopes that when this dawns, they will be more serious and agree to some system. Our proposal is to use the current system

They keep reminding us that when they undertook the campaign, they were not demanding general elections. They demanded a government of national unity and nothing else. They don't see general elections as an answer. I can't comprehend on what basis they claim that.

I would like to make a few remarks about the military. Having disarmed a coup and restored rule of law, the mandate of the intervention forces has changed. They have now been assigned a new mandate. Most of those who came in armored vehicles to forestall a coup have gone home. They have been replaced by teams of trainers mandated to restructure the Lesotho Defense Force, starting with a screening exercise in which every man and woman will be screened for suitability to remain in the force. They are also mandated to retrain the force and to produce new criteria for recruitment, criteria that can be attested to be transparent, so that they will give us a small but efficient, professional, completely apolitical Lesotho Defense Force. This exercise is just beginning. We understood that military intervention per se would not be the answer. There has to be a political solution to the Lesotho crisis.

Gen. Fisher: I would like to make a clarification about Lesotho and why other countries did not participate in the Lesotho operation. Prevailing conditions in a situation do dictate the response to that situation. Kavuma outlined some of the situations that would require immediate response—genocide, threat to life, and others. If you look at Lesotho, the decision to move in was not automatic. There were efforts made to reason with the soldiers. Meetings were held to try to convince them to allow the police to enforce law and order. It was an uphill battle. Prime Minister [Mosisili] went to the barracks to try to get them to release the commanders and allow the government to function. When he tried to go to another barracks, they refused to talk to him. The situation was moving toward a dangerous phase. One couldn't predict for sure what the next move of the soldiers would be. In Lesotho, there had been prior incidents. They had previously killed a deputy prime minister, and no soldiers were prosecuted afterwards. So there was a definite concern about the security of the prime minister and others. When it became obvious that the soldiers wouldn't budge and it was clear they couldn't find a leader, it was necessary to move swiftly to secure the lives of people.

But if you look at Lesotho's geographical situation, it is completely surrounded by South Africa. It was clear there were hostages, and if you were going to save their lives, the nearest country was South Africa. Even when there was consensus within SADC that something needed to be done, the one in the position to save the situation was South Africa. It took Botswana fourteen hours to get there. You can't save lives that way. That's why South Africa moved first: because it was in a better position than anyone else. By the time we arrived, the securing of official ministers had already been done. If you had tried to wait for other forces to come, that wouldn't have accomplished what you were trying to achieve. So again, prevailing conditions do dictate how you're going to act.

Generating consensus is really at the strategic level. The operational level is a different matter. Mistakes at that level can be dealt with. The key thing is getting consensus to legitimate an operation. In Lesotho, time was critical.

Kavuma: These questions should be taken in the context of me trying to understand, not challenging Mosisili. First, is there no limitation in a country's law about when challenges to the results of elections can be made? Are there no provisions that they should go to courts of law? Second, does the coup call into question in the eyes of your people the credibility of the party you lead, whether it has stamina to govern when the people have already spoken so loudly and clearly? Third, is there no danger that the seeds of future coups have been sown through this exercise?

Mosisili: I think these questions are well meant and articulated. First, regarding a time limit on the rejection of results: Yes, there is legislation on that. There is a provision for anyone who objects to submit his objections to a court of dispute of returns within a given period. This explains why those who raised objections by going to the palace did so only almost three months later. They waited until that legal period had lapsed. It is true enough that some had submitted objections to the court before that, but these had been dismissed without exception. The court is presided over by a judge of a high court. The few cases have been dismissed with costs. The opposition parties waited three months to cry foul, which is indicative that they didn't want to follow the legal machinery. Nowhere is there provision for an opposition party to petition His Majesty to dissolve Parliament. They can do so only if advised by the prime minister with a view to a new general election. They were demanding not fresh elections but the constitution of a government of national unity. That is not provided for anywhere in Lesotho's constitution.

On the second question, of whether my party's credibility is in question because we have abdicated the mandate to govern Lesotho for five years: Yes, it is true that we have forgone that mandate. We did so fully knowing that our election into office had been proved free and fair. It was subjected to a verification process that had absolved everyone. But we felt that no price can be too costly to buy Lesotho peace and stability. It is in the name of peace and stability that we have forgone that mandate. I know that some of my party supporters feel strongly that I have given away too much. But my response is that the peace and stability of Lesotho are paramount and are above selfish and party interests.

Third, on sowing the seeds of mutiny: On the contrary. The measures that have been taken are such that we will teach everybody that they can't engage in acts of mutiny and hope to get away with it. In the past, when some officers had mutinied or committed certain acts, they were given blanket amnesty. But since 1995, we have had new legislation—such as the Lesotho Defense Act of 1995—in which different levels within the army were themselves involved. (Botswana and South Africa were also involved.) We have felt that the days of blanket amnesties were over. In terms of law, those who engage in mutinous acts should be brought before a court of law. Hence, at present there are forty-one men facing court-martial as a result of the activities I referred to. Rather than sow seeds of mutiny, we have taken steps so that such actions would be dealt with.

Herbst: Could you say something about the prospect for the reconstruction of Maseru and its financing?

Mosisili: Thanks for asking. Yes, there is a reconstruction program. We have sought the assistance of the World Bank and cooperating partners in the EU and other friendly governments such as the U.S. So far, what reconstruction has commenced has been financed by the government of Lesotho. We are hopeful that assistance in that regard will be forthcoming.

Second, we are also aware that the restructuring of the Lesotho Defense Force will involve demobilization of some companies and that such an exercise will be costly and that people will have to be given severance packages. We are engaging other governments who have experience elsewhere to help us in this exercise. We want to make sure that the soldiers are given benefits to which they are entitled and also trained in certain skills to support themselves once they have left.

Woods: What is the current size of Lesotho's force and the proposed size after downsizing? And there is talk in South Africa about extracting reparations to cover the cost of intervention. Could you comment?

Mosisili: On the second question, no. As I speak to you, there has been no suggestion from either the Botswanan or South African governments that Lesotho take on the costs of intervention. Much has been said in Lesotho about how it is paying heavily for the presence of forces in Lesotho. But not a cent has come out of Lesotho's public purse for the cost of forces from Botswana and South Africa.

On the first question, about the size of proposed and current defense force: it is about 4,000 now, and we envisage a much smaller and much leaner force than that—about half. People engaged in the restructuring exercise are working out these questions now.

Scott Fisher: We were quite surprised at the degree of destruction; it was almost a "scorched earth" policy waged by the opposition. Is this something we should anticipate more of as we look at civil wars?

Mosisili: Yes, the extent of destruction was horrendous. They were given free hand because the police were only spectators. That's why I kept saying earlier that no government will be able to govern if its armed forces aren't performing their duty to protect life and property. The restructuring exercise also applies to police and national security services, because we are of the opinion that if those agencies had played their constitutional role, Maseru and other towns wouldn't have been destroyed.

Scott Fisher: Is there an explanation for that mentality?

Mosisili: It is believed that the people who engaged in such acts did so out of anger about the intervention of South African forces. We don't accept this conclusion. It wasn't ad hoc. It was well planned and orchestrated. When a government, particularly an elected government that respects rule of law and human rights, comes into office and does not get the loyalty of law enforcement or civil service—irrespective of the majority opinion—you have problems. We also have to engage in a civil service reform.

Shalli: I think you helped us in answering "Who decides, who triggers?" You mentioned the Mauritius summit that mandated SADC to intervene in Lesotho. Initially it was seven countries. The same thing happened in the DRC: all fourteen countries of SADC were mandated to intervene.

Does Lesotho need an army? The reason being, it is surrounded by South Africa. If defense forces are there to enforce territorial integrity against foreign aggressors, are 4,000 or even 10,000 enough to defend against South Africa? Maybe you need a police force.

What percentage of eligible voters had taken part in the elections? You mentioned that your party won seventy-nine seats out of eighty. Only one was won by the opposition. Then suddenly there were thousands of people on the streets.

Why weren't the counted results made public?

Mosisili: On your third question of why the results weren't announced: that has puzzled all of us. That's how reports came out. They didn't show the results of the re-count. We asked the minister and high commissioners who brought the report why there was that yawning gap in the report. They did not know. We'll always wonder why the report made such a significant omission. As for your second question, I'm not quite sure. I know that for the first time in the May election, we'd brought down the voting age from 21 to 18; we were giving the franchise to more people. I also know that our party got 61 percent of the popular vote and that the party that was number two had 25 percent; number three had 10 percent. All the other nine were below 2 percent.

On question number one—does Lesotho need an army?—I would say unequivocally, yes. We need an army. Lesotho is one of the few countries on the continent that have the distinction of having never been conquered by anybody. We have fought wars against the British, against the South African Boers, and against other neighbors. We were never conquered. We as a people cherish our independence and sovereignty. We maintain that we have the right to defend our sovereignty against anyone, even South Africa.

Gen. Fisher: I want to add to what the prime minister said earlier on the question of looting and burning. In a situation where a government is denied the tools, those instruments of power that will enable it to deal with such measures, it shouldn't be surprising that such activities happen. If the police are incapacitated and the army isn't there, there is no way a government is able to deal with such disturbances.

Even in Botswana, there have been instances where students have set out to demonstrate, whether against Parliament, the U.S. embassy, or whatever. On their way, sometimes they get carried away. In one instance, students left to demonstrate at Parliament. Coming back, they started to smash cars, enter shops, and take goods. The police went in, but soon we became aware that the situation was too much for police. So we brought in the armed forces, and they secured the situation. Before they got there, lots of damage occurred. I don't know the psychological and sociological reasons. But I know that in every country where there is law and order, you have violent instruments—riot police, the army—as assistance to civil authority. What happened in Lesotho shouldn't surprise you.

An intervening force also needs certain legal instruments like a curfew, or rules for intervenors against shooting looters. When a curfew was put on in Lesotho, it was easier for these troops to deal with looters. Otherwise, they would just be standing there, looking at women carrying out blankets from shops. Without the critical instrument of national power, a government is difficult to institute.

Nyambuya: I would like to make a clarification regarding Lesotho. The problems started in 1994. SADC agreed that three countries would move in. Later, Mozambique was included. SADC *did* consult very extensively about all actions in Lesotho. The intervention that finally took place happened after full consultation, and also after it was accepted that Zimbabwe couldn't participate because of [our activities in the] DRC. That it would only be two parties was agreed on.

Mosisili: Why did not all SADC member states participate? Because the sort of force you put together is determined to a large extent by exigencies of the case at hand. At any given point, the Lesotho Defence Force is around 4,000-soldiers strong. They wouldn't need all the forces of SADC member states to converge on them. On the other hand, with a big force like that in Angola, there would be need and reason for that kind of convergence. The intervention into Lesotho is undoubtedly a success story. It isn't over yet. But up to now, it has been a success. One measure is in regard to the assassination of the deputy prime minister in 1994, to which reference has already been made. For a long time, no arrests were made. A measure of the success of the SADC intervention into Lesotho is that about twenty soldiers have been arrested and committed to trial for his murder. That is something we weren't able to do before SADC intervened.

I hope that this session has thrown some light on the nature of Lesotho. Democratization in our countries is a process that is very fragile and delicate. It has to be nurtured so it can be sustained. I can't overemphasize the need for support—in terms of education even. Educating people on democratic principles, tolerance, and the rule of law is the kind of exercise which admittedly is costly but which we need if indeed we are to get to a position where we can get governments who are elected that can devote resources to improving the lives of men, women, and children in our villages. We need to secure peace, and we need stability more than anything else.

Rotberg: You taught us more than about Lesotho; you taught us about your wise qualities of leadership.

VIII. From Intervention to Sustainable Peace: Democracy, Constitutions, Elections

The goal of any military intervention to separate contending parties within a divided and conflicted state is a restoration of civil order and stability. That includes an end to violence and, if required, the reinvigoration of political authority in those situations where a state has imploded—where there has been a collapse of state institutions. An intervening force can hold the brass ring, as it did in Liberia and Sierra Leone, bringing contending parties to bargaining tables, helping to impose a cease-fire and reinvigorating governments. It can preside over elections, or at least ensure that going to the polls is a free, fair, and meaningful exercise of participatory rights. Yet whether elections should come early or late in the process is a question of some dispute; elections may destabilize situations prematurely. Or they may prove the only practical way in which to weigh the comparative appeal of contenders. Although new constitutions have been imposed on resuscitated states outside Africa, the leaders and soldiers of Africa did not favor taking an intervention to that level of decisionmaking. But they and others were desirous of improving Africa's capacity for democracy. None saw any other overarching objective of peace building; the motive for developing crisis response forces and for contemplating sub-regional military interventions for peace was the restoration of democratic practices and improving respect for human rights. The only justification for using the sword of intervention was the prevention of internecine and other forms of destructive conflict. If Africa were to sustain peace and mature politically and economically, it needs to fashion successful methods of peace enforcement.

Thay: I would like to talk about the Mozambican experience. The time has come for creating new ways to overcome crises. The different world after the Cold War is still not understood. We need to be perceptive, adaptive, and courageous, addressing both immediate and root causes of conflict (such as the absence of economic opportunities and inequalities). There needs to be a deeper commitment to true multilateralism. The Mozambican peacekeeping process showed a great deal of flexibility and good will. These were the keys to the good outcome. It is not about love affairs between the UN and parties involved. It is about successful resolution of conflict. And it needs two willing dancers to tango—perhaps three in the case of the UN. Though passion and emotion are requirements for good competition, peacekeeping shouldn't be looked on as competition over sovereignty.

In Mozambique, after the parties achieved agreement, they had the responsibility of implementing it—the responsibility to say, "Yes, we want to save our people." If they don't defend their priorities, peacekeeping can do nothing.

Clapham: My comments draw largely on the ECOMOG experience. The topic concerns developing mandates for potential intervenors. This is not classic peacekeeping, but intervention as happened in Liberia and Sierra Leone, where a basic settlement had not already been reached.

When we think of mandates, we tend to think of formal legal ones from the UN, OAU, SADC, etc. I am going to leave those aside, because I am concerned with political mandates—how to build and maintain the political support needed for an intervention to work. Using the example suggested by Henk, UNOSOM in Somalia had all the official mandates it wanted. But when eighteen U.S. marines were killed, the political mandate completely evaporated. The U.S. didn't have the political will it needed to carry on the operation. The whole thing basically folded.

There are two sorts of political mandates. First, there are mandates from the point of view of the intervenors: What keeps them there? They need to ensure that they receive essential backing, both from their own domestic constituencies and from the wider diplomatic community within which they have to operate. The new Obasanjo government in Nigeria, for example, must take account of public opinion in assessing the continued Nigerian commitment to ECOMOG forces in a way that was not necessary for its military predecessors.

Beyond that, however, there is also a need for regional political mechanisms to provide not just formal authorization but also continuing support for intervention, among the group of states whose own security is most directly affected. Where effective sub-regional organizations exist, these provide the appropriate setting. Regional security systems are then required, which are sets of conventions (like the Banjul declaration, for example), by which states within a region agree on how security is to be maintained. They include agreement on domestic political structures, agreement on political leadership, on the limitation of state sovereignty, and on circumstances where states are entitled to intervene. Within Africa, it is possible to identify two sub-regions—West Africa and southern Africa—within which a regional security system is at least partially present. Each has a sub-regional organization, ECOWAS and SADC, a broadly accepted set of principles for common regional action, and a readily identifiable leader. In other parts of the continent, and notably the Horn and Central Africa (including the DRC, despite its membership in SADC), there is no such organization, set of principles, or acceptable leader. Development of a regional security system faces massive and possibly insuperable obstacles. Where states intervene in the affairs of their neighbors, they do so simply as an expression of their own state interests and levels of power.

There is, however, a second perspective from which we can look at political mandates for intervention, and one which has been almost entirely neglected. These are the mandates for intervention among the peoples of the intervened-in states themselves. How do peacemakers gain legitimacy among the factions they're trying to bring to a condition of peace? Most basically, the function of a peacemaking mission is to make peace, and that in turn requires the creation of a viable political settlement among the peoples and major political groupings of the state within which the intervention takes place. If, when you've pulled out, you haven't enabled Somalians or Sierra Leoneans to live together peacefully, you've failed. Maybe you've made things worse. This is troubling. Because of the specifics inherent in peacemaking itself, the danger is that instead of creating a basis for political settlement, you might weaken or destroy it.

There are two common problems. The first is that the intervention changes the situation on the ground, in ways that are necessarily to the advantage of some of the local combatants, and to the disadvantage of others. When a peacemaking group moves in, who will support or oppose it? Since the faction that currently has the upper hand—Taylor in Liberia, Mohamed Farah Aidid in Somalia—will view the intervention force as thwarting its ambitions, whereas weaker groups are likely to see it as their saviors, the force may very easily become associated with the likely losers, rather than the likely winners. Unless the intervention force takes great care, it can find itself propping up a weak regime or set of factional leaders, who become further weakened by their increasing dependence on external military assistance. The opposing factions, on the other hand, will be able to present themselves as the defenders of national sovereignty against a foreign occupying force.

Second, there is a danger that the intervention will lead to a proliferation of local factions and thus obstruct the achievement of a domestic political settlement. In Liberia and Somalia, there was a strong tendency for factional divisions to take place on one side or the other. In Liberia, for example, first it was the NPFL against

President [Samuel] Doe. Then ECOMOG assisted with the formation of other groupings, such as the United Liberation Movement of Liberia for Democracy (ULIMO) or the Liberia Peace Council (LPC) which in turn split (ULIMO-K, headed by Alhaji Kromah and ULIMO-J, led by Roosevelt Johnson). This rapidly made the whole process of reaching a settlement more difficult.

What kinds of lessons can we learn? There are three negative ones. First, impartiality is a delusion. A peacekeeping force in a classic peacekeeping operation (where it is simply monitoring) can be impartial. Intervening in ongoing conflict can't be impartial. That is because it is influencing the balance of power. So recognize that intervention is deeply political. Those intervening must ask themselves what politically they are trying to achieve. It is not just a technical operation.

Second, beware the dangers of unworkable paper settlements. There is a temptation to get all the factions together around a table, sign a piece of paper, say you've done it, and let everyone go home. Unless there is a real agreement underlying it, such a signing is a waste of time—*and* a danger. Liberia saw so many paper agreements, none of which had any plausible prospect of success because they did not address the central question of how political power could be exercised in the country. Not until the Abuja Peace Accords, which rested on a détente between the two main power-holders of the country—Taylor and the Nigerian leadership of ECOMOG—was an effective settlement possible. It was similar in Somalia. The most disastrous exercise, however, was the Arusha agreement on Rwanda, which proposed a completely unworkable arrangement for sharing power between bitterly opposed groups. Any agreement that is closely followed by the slaughter of nearly a million people is a desperate failure. The external mediators should have known. There was no commitment at all.

A third danger is that of assuming that bad guys lack political support and can be defeated. In a lot of places, we have no trouble recognizing the bad guys. But they won't necessarily be rejected by the local people. [Mozambique opposition party] RENAMO, for instance, though unquestionably bad, had the support of much of the population. In Liberia, the slogan adopted for Taylor—"He killed my pa, he killed my ma, but I will vote for him"—demonstrates that you vote for who has control, who has power, because that's who can bring peace. Observers believed he wouldn't win. The same is true for the RUF in Sierra Leone. External mediators and peacekeepers readily assume that those domestic political actors who collaborate most reasonably with themselves will likewise be favored by the local electorate, but this is often far from being the case.

And now for the positive lessons: What are the local political ingredients for political success? First, you have to identify the basis for a viable political settlement in the country concerned. Be attuned to the circumstances of the particular country. There are no generalizations. It is not just about multiparty democratic elections. But you need an idea of such a settlement so the peacemaking force doesn't undermine it. There is a political center of gravity in African states, as elsewhere. You can identify centers of social power that have to be incorporated into any agreement if that settlement is to work. They may be major population groups, (controllers of) economic resources, and controllers of the human resources needed to run a government, including military resources. An intervention force needs to take account of all of these forces. Though the peacemaking force may be able to influence the distribution of power, for example by neutralizing a particularly troublesome faction, it will be able to do so only to a limited extent.

Second, you have to identify a viable political leadership. Someone has to be visibly in charge for there to be a settlement. There is a tendency for Americans to assume that it is possible to create a constitutional settlement without identifying the source of political power. That doesn't work, as far as I know, outside the U.S. It is futile to think of a settlement in the form of constitutional formulae.

Third, once these basic requirements have been satisfied, it is important to identify plausible political coalitions. Everyone who can be brought on board, who can be given some incentive, should be given the opportunity. The policy of national reconciliation implemented in 1986 by [President] Museveni in Uganda invited all factions to form a government of national unity. You need that to get started. On some occasions, it may even be necessary to buy out potentially obstructive faction leaders whose first concern is for their own personal welfare. But even having reduced the irreconcilables to a minimum, there are always "spoilers." There *is* some gain from war, some wealth created by the conflict. One of the most tragic consequences of protracted civil wars is that they bring to prominence groups and individuals who acquire a vested interest in continued conflict, and have every reason to undermine whatever settlement may be reached. So there is a group that an intervening force will have to target. The peacemaking force will need to know who that is. And because implementation is such a horrendous problem, broad mandates are acceptable

Houdek: There is no such thing as a humanitarian intervention, only political interventions. That was one of the lessons of Somalia. We moved into the height of political controversy immediately when we arrived at the port [Mogadishu] where we were going to move goods. Also, we haven't talked about the role of NGOs. If any entities have pushed intervention, it has been the NGO community. We went into Somalia to create a safe environment for them to operate; they were being robbed by various warlords. We have to think seriously about the political implications of putting forces into a country in such situations.

Herbst: Most peacekeeping operations have either failed outright or succeeded with significant limitations. Many of the operations have failed because the political and economic handoff after the intervention was incomplete or unsatisfactory. This will continue because of limited resources. It is unlikely that the intervening authority will take up sovereign power, as it did in Cambodia. There are limited political and economic means available to the intervenor.

I offer here some suggestions for intervenors to smooth the way to future peace. We aren't talking about a Marshall Plan, as resources are so limited. But each day of peace is a success in itself, since it convinces protagonists of their stable situation. The focus has to be on the short and medium term. It is incremental.

Beginning with the military angle, first the intervenor needs to understand the center of gravity and devise a solution that is appropriate. The goal is to change the military balance of power on the ground. This will involve disarmament of the combatants, at least partially. As long as men with guns can achieve their objectives, there is no way that peace is possible. Second, extraordinary violence should be used against spoilers. They will try to upset the settlement, and some kind of quick reaction force is required that remains for a time in the country. Third, start reconstruction of the national police or security apparatus so that the peace can be maintained.

On the economic side, donors and African intervenors first have to put emphasis on a program that can show immediate economic results. Haiti, for example, was a significant peace enforcement achievement. Aid was given for picking up garbage. That at least changed the tempo of events slightly, and people could associate some kind of benefit with the intervening force. Second, there need to be some military assets to rebuild the infrastructure. This infrastructure is necessary just to absorb the foreign aid that is available. Sometimes there is no alternative to using military engineers to rebuild the country's infrastructure after a conflict. Third, give immediate economic resources to people who are laying down guns. This is controversial, and not particularly equitable because there are lots of poor people in all of these countries. However, it is current and former soldiers, recently demobilized, who pose the greatest risk to a settlement. Economic resources have to be tilted toward them so they don't go back on the warpath. All of these imperatives have nothing to do with development; they are immediate steps to restore order.

Finally, politically there needs to be a strategy of encouraging as many different elements to cooperate, while at the same time discriminating against spoilers. This means first, that all meetings, when logistically possible, should be held in-country. The tradition of "de-camping" is often a mistake. In settlement talks, negotiators can't deliberate because they aren't in immediate contact with the factions that they're supposed to represent. Many use off-country sites as an excuse to enrich themselves. Having the meetings locally may strengthen people's seriousness. Second, don't focus on long-term solutions immediately. Protagonists should be given the easiest things first, while the harder things are put off. In Lesotho, putting the electoral system up for discussion was a recipe for deadlock. The rebels were not comfortable negotiating over a measure that controversial. Start with easier things. Negotiate on the composition or structure of the national police. Say that everyone who agrees, for example, gets to contribute to the national police. Reward those who agree. If you go to the most difficult issues, you'll get a crisis, or at least halt movement.

Third, and related, elections should be a last resort. They should be held late in the day, after many issues are resolved. Elections tend to fray coalitions, and they have a history of inflaming ethnic tensions by invoking an "us against them" mentality. I am a fan of competitive elections, but I am more a fan of order. "Hold the election first and the government will work it all out later" is the wrong approach. A better way is to help the protagonists to learn to trust each other. The South African process was an illuminating one. It took four years of negotiation to build up the trust before elections. Then, when an assassination occurred, elites could get on phone and discuss it. Fourth, some money should be used to buy parties out. A number of leaders might not be that interested in being in politics, and for small sums could be bought out. Mozambique is an example of a setting where some leaders could be bought out. Finally, some African countries could act as "guardians of the pack." This simply means that there would be some authority to appeal to if national political authority is deadlocked.

None of these suggestions address long-term issues. But you don't get to those issues overnight. You need to develop momentum.

Coglin: We have seen that the cause of conflict is irresponsible leaders and arms flows. To combat the latter, there are initiatives in the West: working on the supply side to try to control the transfer of money and arms. But there is scope for work on the demand side, to curb the demand for weapons. Perhaps that is something that SADC could consider doing. Africans can do it for themselves.

Houdek: First, yes, I think with the end of the Cold War that there are a number of extra-continental countries that are prepared to support and follow African leadership because they're aware of past failures. And many of the countries of the West don't want to exclude parts of the Communist world. Unfortunately, many former Republics are not prepared to play because of economic reasons. It is a double-edged sword that we face, regarding the importance of non-state actors. It isn't evil Communist Russia or a bogeyman (state actor) supporting insurgencies; they're non-state actors. We go to Russia and say, "Weapons are flowing." They say, "No, these are private actors. Individuals are allowed to trade." It is often manufacturers represented by brokers from the Western world acting in a classic money-making role.

Next, regarding our conversation about Angola: There are no easy answers, especially on the question of sanctions. I have spent a lot of time recently trying to support the sanctions committee at the UN. We are looking at economic sources of power; there has been lots of research on that subject. We can't boycott diamonds. We *can* try to put economic controls on those flows of resources. But if you can't control the delivery of 150 tanks, how can you stop the export of a bag of diamonds? Also, a major violator of sanctions is the government in Luanda. A major source of petroleum supplies is corrupt government actors in Rwanda. If you want seriously to control the sale of diamonds, there are significant corrupt elements that would produce certificates of sale. Among all the difficult spigots to try to turn off, Africa does have some capacity to try to regulate non-state actors. Savimbi doesn't have ports to receive materials. So aircraft are flying. These require overflight clearances, landing rights, and re-fueling stations. While not simple, there is an area for increased cooperation and control: that is, trying to interdict or restrict deliveries primarily by non-state actors.

During my time in the DRC, I watched non-state actors' aircraft arriving. One minute, they were heroes of the humanitarian community, delivering food. Then they were playing on the other side of the fence.

Williams: Let bygones be bygones. The basic issue is this: you need money to fight wars, and any person in Africa that can have access to money through control of resources will control power in Africa. If you look at all the big countries in the midst of wars (except the Sudan), there are resources within those countries with which rebels can support themselves. Savimbi can fight because he has money. The staying power of Kabila was that he was in the part of his country where he controlled some mineral resources.

The problems will not be resolved until we look at resources completely. We can't look at a political solution without looking at the resources question. The money question must be solved. It is difficult for you to convince an army warlord to stop fighting if he sees no way of getting to power. Without elections that he can win in the future, he won't sign a peace accord.

Why did the Europeans have a well-armed implementation force with military muscle in Bosnia? The force had to be well armed to compel the adversaries to keep the peace accord. If you are not ready to use this force or muscle, then send a police force instead of the military. Secondly, how do you convince a warlord if he has access to money to agree to negotiations? Say, "OK you can keep your access to resources." If you don't say that, there is no way to stop the conflict.

One of the issues is evident in Nigeria. What has been happening in Africa is that those in power do not want to share power and the control of resources. They want to hold the key posts—don't want to give them out. How do you convince them to? A constitution is a key concept. You need to put in all these formulas and principles when you undertake constitutional design for African crises.

Herbst: I hear Williams saying it is hopeless. I haven't heard anyone say that African armies are going to bring overwhelming military dominance in any country. Are you saying it is hopeless?

Williams: Of course I am concerned that it appears hopeless. The international community is looking to Africans to bring about African solutions. But what are the Africans bringing to the table?

Dempsey: I don't think it's hopeless. If you look at Sierra Leone, on the ECOWAS side there is a willingness to put in resources, not just troops. On the international community side, the donor countries, there is a willingness to contribute resources. As expensive as it is, it is cheaper than not doing anything. Williams is posing the real question. How do you get these regimes to share power? In regimes where there are economic resources, how do you get them to contribute to development and not to conflict?

Nyambuya: I think it goes beyond that question. It is, "What is the international community ready to absorb?" If it is the international community or a regional power that is intervening, how much are they willing to absorb in terms of expenses and political resources? International, regional, and sub-regional actors must be willing to invest in a particular area.

Rotberg: Herbst was asking what happens after a successful intervention. To manage the negotiating process, we proposed one remedy. Then there are other remedies, such as "holding the ring" for a relatively long number of years. You mentioned South Africa, but that is a different case, because there was no outside intervenor. In Namibia, the process was very well managed by UNTAG. Then there was an election, and that was conclusive. I gather from what is being said that what is needed for Liberia and Sierra Leone is enough financing from the international community.

Tonje: There are small, medium, and large countries. We can't have the same solution to them all. I think we should recognize that. Each situation will have to evolve its own solutions.

Williams: You have to differentiate between countries. In those that have resources, it is difficult and protracted. In non-resource countries, it is easier. Take Cambodia, from the point of view of non-resource countries. The issue is that what we call peacekeeping is, for those who are offshoots of the British Army, internal security, i.e., "Aid to Civil Power." When there is counterinsurgency or terrorism, you change tactics. That is the difference. If an intervention force succeeds in restoring law and order, then "military humanitarianism" immediately follows. You don't pull out because there is reconstruction to be done in a war-torn area. This is the time for soldiers that can do construction and provide logistical services to be brought in. When adversaries see these soldiers in such acts, they see their conflicts transformed in a constructive way. So you have to look at all military and humanitarian angles together and do them simultaneously whenever possible.

A weakness in Africa is leverage in negotiation. When General Colin Powell, Senator Sam Nunn and President Carter went to Haiti, they knew that the might of the U.S. was backing them. In Africa, when we send a mediator, who is backing him? There may be no regional backing. There may be no resources. As for [Herbst's] suggestion about negotiation at home—it is negotiating openly that is the problem. When you pull people out of the country, you cut them off from those who can influence them to change their positions during the negotiation process. Sometimes you have a particular problem. Each one of them says, "Do this," and you don't know what to do. We need in Africa secret negotiations and mediations.

Herbst: Look at arguably the most successful peacemaking this century—the U.S. in Germany and Japan. With overwhelming force, they came in and got the bad guys out. But ten years later, U.S. evaluations of the situations were very shaky. It was not clear things would work out well. Statebuilding processes take many decades. It is necessary to address smaller issues. Get order, peace at all costs, and push off the big questions until you have momentum. That's the way that the West has developed—not cutting the Gordian knot, but slogging along.

Rotberg: Recall that in Mozambique secret negotiations led to public negotiations, which led to a successful peace process. It involved a series of outside negotiators, and some substantial demobilization. But not everything you mentioned was taken care of. Second elections are coming. They went from a war footing to a peaceful, well-managed country in a short time. They have the strongest currency in Southern Africa.

Mosisili: The post–Cold War period presented African states in particular with an interesting scenario whereby the big powers insisted on a democratization process. I think that was good and most welcome. But the point is that it is a process. Democratization does not come to an end the day after election results are published. There is a need to nurture that young, fragile, fledgling democracy until it can be sustained. This is where I find there is a shortcoming on the part of friends who rightly make regimes democratize. Mention was made of African states not being well governed. What criteria do you put forward to judge that a particular state is well governed or not? My view is that clearly a government which has state power and uses that power to commit atrocities against its people is not a good government. One that will not respect human rights—whose governance is not transparent—can be taken to task. Is it considered legitimate for certain forces to topple illegally a democratically elected government under the pretext that it is not governing well? Isn't the right to remove such a government the prerogative of an electorate? Surely if it is not delivering services, people will throw it out at the next election. Any government, irrespective of how it gets to power, will not govern unless it has the loyalty of the law enforcement agencies. If the police, intelligence, and military are not loyal, it doesn't matter how democratic and well elected you are. The perception will be that you won't be able to govern. There is a need to strengthen democratic institutions; that will support democracies in Africa.

Gen. Fisher: For two issues—hegemons and internal constituencies—we need to give serious thought to constitutions and how they can be obstacles in some countries to participating in some of these endeavors. The constitutional requirements for Tanzania to participate in an intervention can impinge on its activities; I know this can be a problem in other countries as well. In the case of the intervention in Lesotho, South Africa had to contend with a lot of opposition in Parliament. Did Abacha have as much constraint from internal sources when he committed Nigerian forces to ECOMOG? The answer explains why countries are becoming reluctant to commit forces. President Mugabe got flack for committing forces because of internal constraints. And in Somalia, once the political mood changed, the American commitment changed.

Mulongoti: My approach, being a politician, is not from a military perspective, but from a political one. The political dimension is an important factor that can make or break a peacekeeping operation. The problems that will get in the way of successful peacekeeping and peace enforcement come from a variety of areas. One fashionable area for discussion is civil society or NGOs. Another is the press. When national leaders want to commit forces, the first hurdle is civil society. They have their own interests, while political leaders are working in the national interest. So the hands of leaders will be constrained. Donors should also consider educating civil society to accommodate the interests of society beyond the country's borders. In Zimbabwe, for example, civil society groups were opposed to the efforts of leaders to try to bring about peace in the DRC.

Tonje: Back to the topic of heads of state: Solutions and problems will begin and end with heads of state. They are the only ones who can employ the resources needed.

Williams: In Banjul [the Gambia], when the issue of Guinea-Bissau came up, Nigeria said [to Senegal and others], "This is yours." But I am afraid of what Tonje said about a regime being responsible for conflict resolution in Africa. If the solution is dependent only on heads of state, then there is a problem. I know of no society that holds its government accountable.

Houdek: We have mentioned sovereignty: if a country wants its sovereignty respected, it has to exercise it. A sovereign state must make sure that its ports, airports, and airspace are not violated by non-state actors.

Mulongoti: A problem is that the leadership of Africa is made up of people who were themselves rebels yesterday. The minute they move into the capital, they forget that they were former rebels. Internal dialogue must be encouraged. People must be helped to find common values. No matter what terms you give someone who is fighting you, remember he is a fellow citizen. There often is no difference between genuine criticism and rebellion. Africa needs to work on that. We politicians are the people responsible for most of the problems in Africa.

Another dimension has to do with problems related to sensitivity. We become sensitive because of traumatic experiences. We are sensitive to criticism from everyone, and we don't want to accept advice. So we bring back the past by saying, "That country was our oppressor before." The idea of hegemony will be resisted to the bitter end. I don't know one leader who will accept leadership from another leader. It is a non-starter. Let's not introduce conflict from beginning. We need a loose concept of leadership, not obvious leadership, like South Africa, Nigeria, or Egypt. If it is overt, we'll form new subgroups to isolate them. We need to let leadership evolve. It is not enough to have airplanes and troops; you need the respect of your people.

Another problem is the relationships that have been made: every country has its own friends. Some countries are much closer to certain powers in the world. It depends on ideology, and ideology is difficult to harmonize in relationships. Some want to follow a socialist ideology, while others want to follow capitalism. How do we harmonize? First, we have to try to influence the African mind into accepting the fact that we are all Africans. Not in terms of race, but meaning all those on the continent who identify themselves as African. How applicable are ideologies and doctrines to our situation?

Time has helped us. The older leadership is beginning to fade away. New leaders have been to school. That is an essential element. The only qualification old leaders had was that they were freedom fighters. That is now giving way to people with papers, credentials, powers of analysis. They are the new "tribes"—people who went to the same universities. Your classmates at Harvard and Cambridge—they are your brothers. This is more useful than ethnic tribes, which prey on the ignorant. The new tribes are people with equal capacities and the same opportunities in life. We want to encourage that. We need to build more universities, employ more resources in education. Look at all our countries' expenditures: military expenditures are higher than education. War is a higher priority than conciliation. Don't just talk about good governance, but look at the future of a country as dependent on how many people are educated.

Majogo: On the assertion that African countries are spending more on the military than on education: it is these crises that provoke expenditures on the side of military for protective or defensive measures. If you see someone else amassing arms, you become worried. We have to control these crises in order to enable us to deal with other social services. Crises trigger expenditure on their side.

There is also the problem of legitimacy. Leadership has come about in many ways. But as long as a group is recognized, and conferred with democratic titles, they become acceptable. We insist that if a leader comes in by the barrel of gun, he must be made legitimate through the ballot box within a certain time. But that isn't happening. As long as they fraternize with the right people, they become legitimate. The only way to go forward is to ensure that all of us who participate in the African arena ask ourselves from where our social power and legitimacy comes. Then you can stop calling others rebels just because you happen to be in the capital at the time. You only become legitimate when you've come to terms with the political arena.

Shalli: [Responding to Mulongoti] I would like to seek more explanation on the question of legitimacy and also who is a president. It all depends on what people themselves want to be called. The people in the DRC want to be rebels; there is no way we can call them otherwise. Other people call themselves freedom fighters. So they are. If they find themselves the next day in government, are they the government? Legitimacy is a tricky question. Is a government only legitimate when recognized by the international community? Yes. Several governments have come to power *not* through a ballot box. But we accept them, and deal with them on a daily basis because they are the ones we have to deal with. I know in Zambia, some people are trying to break it into two parts. What are they? Terrorists because they are preaching violence?

Walker: We haven't talked about enhancing the capacity of civilian leadership to strengthen the response to crises. Civilian leadership has to understand that soldiers must be paid, and they must have adequate training to respond effectively. So we need to ensure that the military has adequate access to intelligence and information, and has the support of the political leadership. Putting together a military operation is the easiest of challenges ahead. This group can't address this root problem, but keep it in mind. Unless there is the political will and resources to get to the root causes, our soldiers will be in place for a long time. It takes broader responses.

Majogo: We need an exhaustive list of the causes of conflict. Mulongoti said that many problems are caused by politicians squabbling. Once in power, one spends three quarters of the time trying to deal with problems of the past, excavating graves. It is a politics of revenge. Other causes are ethnic differences, which go back hundreds of years. You need to know the causes before you can come up with solutions.

Two months ago, I attended a ceremony in [President Julius] Nyerere's village. I saw Nyerere, [former President Ali Hassan] Mwinyi, and [President Benjamin William] Mkapa, all three of Tanzania's presidents sitting together in room. That is a great advantage. In other places, it is politics of vengeance, where a new government stalks former heads of state. It will take a concerted effort to learn a culture of handing over power peacefully.

Shalli: In the case of Nigeria, we have been talking about political will. But in the times it intervened in Liberia or Sierra Leone, I am not convinced its leadership was political. Malu did not need anyone else to tell him what to do. Did this make the decisionmaking process faster?

Mulongoti: When we call people rebels, it is a question of legitimacy. Whenever we get into power, it is incumbent on us to bring others into power. Otherwise, another group will be formed to fight us. Second, when we get into power, we start "eating with both hands," and that alarms others outside of power. No matter how you get into the system, you must legitimize yourself by getting popular support. Right now, it is through elections. But it doesn't matter how; you just need to demonstrate popular support.

Then there is conduct by those of us who are leaders. We never want to go away. "Once in, forever in." That's a dangerous mentality. Dignity is how you conduct yourself when put out of power. It is evident in Tanzania and Botswana. We shouldn't encourage a situation of permanency. That will help us accept the fact that leadership is not ours alone; we must share it.

Rotberg: [Responding to Herbst's earlier suggestion that elections should be a last resort] In a non-election, post-intervention period, who holds the reins? The intervenors?

Herbst: I don't think African governments are willing to do that. It needs to be some sort of coalition government, not necessarily popularly elected, but representative of most factions.

Mulongoti: When people fight and end up in the capital, and you don't give them a time-frame in which they have to conduct elections, the opposition is reluctant to come out of the bush. That's why people are supportive of elections. They are critical. But they need to be well handled.

Ellington: I'd suggest that money, while important, can do nothing if the heart of an individual is bad. In Liberia, the man who was elected is evil. All the money in the world isn't going to solve that. There are examples in southern Africa of reconciliation: in South Africa, Mozambique, and Uganda. The government of Uganda has made peace and negotiated with sixteen of the insurgent movements of its country. It boils down to political will and a *decent* will, not just money.

Mulongoti: The area of my concern is institutional weakness in those institutions that will support democracy. In a particular country, there is no proper judicial system, no policing, and no press. The army is not properly arranged. But we do nothing about it. Democracy can't survive in areas where there are no institutions to support it. The donor community has to examine structures that exist in individual countries. There are misplaced resources, with lots of money spent on things that don't contribute to peace. When you go in with an agenda, consider the long-term interests of the people within that country. Strengthen the institutional context. Then, even if there is a breakdown in law and order, you will have something to fall back on. I am not so keen on peacemaking or peace enforcement; we need to strengthen those institutions.

Herbst: Maybe Africa will do it faster, but Europe did it over many centuries. Parliaments were battling kings over control of resources. It took place incrementally, but Parliament finally wrestled control of the fisc from royal power. It isn't about democracy or development. It's about giving countries breathing space. If Savimbi continues to control the diamond mines, that may be OK if he starts paying taxes. If you try to achieve democracy first, it may be impossible.

Clapham: Elections have a role in an earlier part of conflict resolution. They aid in discovering who has support and who hasn't. In Liberia and Rwanda, for example, there were all manner of leaders making claims. Until you knew what kind of support they had, you could not put together a coalition government. Taylor is evil, but he won a large percentage of the vote. People didn't love him, but they thought he could make peace. You undercut the pretensions of would-be candidates if you hold elections. It can be seen as a "ruthless weeding out," because it is easier to reach a settlement with those who remain. But don't confuse elections with democracy.

Tonje: Why are we discarding the idea of a sword? If Nigeria and South Africa get together to intervene, there is no conflict that wouldn't stand up and take notice. In SADC, if all countries can place their resources behind intervention in a crisis, there is the possibility of a resolution.

Gen. Fisher: There is the challenge of who is going to rule in a country and how the ruler is going to be selected. The common understanding is that people must rule themselves, and no one should impose a ruler on them. We've been talking about institutions in a country—the police, courts, government, civil service—who will develop the institutions necessary to run a country? South Africans sat down and came up with a constitution themselves. Today they're following it. If there is a crisis in a country like Lesotho, where the issue was elections, an intervention is designed to solve specific problems. But we can't at same time dictate to them who should run the country. How many ways can be used to solve the problems? Some have used a winner-take-all solution. Some have been encouraged to include others, to try to ensure a lasting solution. Therefore, you'll find that many times people will resort to some type of elections to determine the equation that could be put into place so that a government and some kind of leadership could result.

You could start working on the various institutions necessary for the state to survive and succeed. Yes, we should identify the easy things first. But we will still have to come to the main questions. The big issues have to be dealt with. It may be difficult to know which are the easy ones (the composition of an army may be a big one, really). Sooner or later, the question of who is going to rule will come up. It must come from the people themselves. Whether it is through elections or some other way, I don't know. But imposing someone won't take us where we want to go.

Rotberg: Given the discussion of Lesotho, shouldn't Botswana and South Africa still be in Lesotho? Did they leave at the right moment? Could there be a period of instability ahead? Where will Lesotho be when that happens and a further intervention is required?

Gen. Fisher: History will be the judge. The timetable of when to leave and when not to is difficult. In hindsight, we can answer it. If things work out, then we left at the right time. But I don't think one can say with clarity.

Mosakeng: Recall that the problem arose out of a political situation. One is not ready just to say, "This will happen…." The unique part of it is that the head of our state is a constitutional monarch. That creates a different situation for SADC. Constitutionally, something is being worked out. I can't comment further.

Tonje: Once you obtain law and order by overwhelming force, a duty still remains for some time afterwards. That is the concept of a guarantor. You may have to ensure that what was agreed upon is carried out. The sword must remain until a time of normalcy has been introduced.

IX. Conclusions and Recommendations

Twenty-four conclusions and recommendations follow, together with comments on the conclusions and recommendations by many of the participants. The conclusions and recommendations reflect the issues raised at the meeting, some emerging consensuses and disagreements, and a continuing dialogue on peace enforcement, its uses and dangers.

1. In 1998–99, between meetings II and III, Africans proved less successful than earlier at resolving their own intrastate and interstate conflicts. Continuing troubles in the DRC, Angola, and Sierra Leone, and in Ethiopia/Eritrea, reduced the momentum for peacebuilding that emerged from the Malawi meeting.

Tonje: This implies that Africans' ability to solve their problems has receded.

Majogo: Yet, there have been some commendable strides made in the Great Lakes. The OAU, SADC, and heads of states have been meeting more than three or four times. One day I was taken from my office to fly to Zimbabwe. We went to discuss these things with President Mugabe. You're saying that there has been a proliferation of problems since we last met. But that isn't the case. Heads of state would be very discouraged if they didn't see any evidence of their efforts.

2. Africa must take charge of its own conflicts and prevent them.

Nyambuya: Whatever we do, it is by consensus. I would like to point out further, that when we say Africa must take charge, it is because we have deduced that no one will come to help us (despite the clearly laid down role for the UN in its Charter).

Mulongoti: We don't expect the UN to take charge, but we have to associate ourselves with it. It has to be in front. Intervention can't be done unilaterally. It has been said that the U.S. cares less about what is going on in Africa. If we take literally t..at we want to be on our own, then that allows you to say Africa is on its own.

3. There should be discussion at both the technical level and, more appropriately, the political—heads of state—level, of what constitutes a crisis in Africa. What is its definition, its shape? What kinds of difficulties merit intervention? What are the criteria? Kavuma listed a number of them—human rights, lack of control of the state. He had a long and very helpful list [see above]. If a benchmark could be developed at a sub-regional, heads-of-state level (or even an Africa-wide level), it might establish what constitutes an intervenable crisis. Mosisili also provided a list of his own of what would constitute a crisis [see above].

4. If the criteria could be agreed, crises could be addressed in four ways:

A. An ad hoc response;

B. A hegemonic response. The hegemon could be large or small; there could be a coup in country X responded to by country Y, or it could be, as in Liberia, that a major country would decide to intervene;

C. As an extension of A or B, there could be a large or small "coalition of the willing," put together in direct response to a particular crisis (for example, in the Comoros, or the Seychelles);

D. A fourth method flows out of a pre-planning and readiness exercise, which leads to the creation and deployment of a sub-regional crisis response force.

Gen. Fisher: I want to make a clarification regarding the concept of hegemon and that terminology. In the SADC region, that type of concept is not favored. In SADC, no state is identified as a hegemon. In the spirit of SADC, the emphasis is on consensus building, on agreed principles. I totally dissociate myself from the concept of hegemon in SADC.

Tonje: Really, only two ways of addressing a crisis have developed. The rest are *concepts* that are available. But whether to implement any of them is a sub-regional responsibility. I don't think that they are methods in themselves. "Coalitions of the willing" could be included under "ad hoc"; it is already inherent in an ad hoc response. "Pre-planning" is also included in the concept of ad hoc. Those last two are not ways in themselves, but probably means of achieving [a goal]. Therefore, I think we can separate "sub-regional" as a way. "Ad hoc" can be from different regions. The third way is the sub-regional way, and conclusions 7, 8 and 9 (below) can be subsumed under the sub-regional heading. I don't think we should strike out an OAU or a UN response. So there are five ways. Ad hoc includes action by any group with strong feelings, beginning with a consciousness on the parts of heads of state to do something about a crisis. The OAU and the UN also still have responsibility; we still expect their response.

5. African conflict prevention and peace enforcement can best be accomplished at the sub-regional level.

Herbst: I would like to underline that focus of action at the sub-regional level. At the first session, we talked about a historic movement by Africa away from the UN. There was a great deal of discussion of how this action affected peacekeeping operations. There was disaffection around the room against the UN or the OAU as guarantors of action; people were searching for different ways at the sub-regional level. African countries haven't solved the problem that arises: there are those who are disinterested and could be neutral in a peacekeeping role, while those with the most interest *do* have a motivation for intervening, but it could be more problematic. Intervention is seen as most practical at the sub-regional level rather than at the international level.

Williams: I don't know whether it is really the case that those countries that are neutral do not have incentives to contribute to peacekeeping. It is so difficult with Africa. You have to realize that most African countries that go into peacekeeping go if somebody is going to pay the bills. If no one will pay the bills, there are no incentives. Whether large or small, African countries will be interested in taking part. There have been instances where it is asked whether any countries are willing to participate. They have negotiated with, "If I participate, you must give me this or that." There are resources within Africa that if pooled together can be used in one way or the other. There is also a need for incentives on the part of the

Western world to enhance the capacity of those with resources to do what they are doing in Africa.

Metz: There is a distinction between those willing to intervene. In one category are those with a willingness to contribute to a crisis of short duration; the U.S. will fall into that category. In another are nations willing to contribute for the long time it takes to rebuild; for example, the Canadian and British commitment to Cyprus. It is a question of calming things down versus leaving troops there for years to establish stability. What determines this factor is other commitments that these countries have.

6. We can talk here and in other settings for a long time about ad hoc, hegemonic, and "coalition of the willing" interventions, but it is only the pre-planning and readiness option that merits discussion at the strategic and tactical levels. We can talk about any of the four options, but it is not useful to talk about ad hoc because that will occur in an ad hoc way. The pre-planning exercise is something that needs to be carried out in a sub-regional context.

7. If a crisis occurs, a hegemon can decide to intervene. One of the conclusions is that it is always much easier for an autocratic/authoritarian state to intervene than for a democratic state to mobilize its forces to intervene. Where there is no public opinion to take into account, it is easier to mobilize troops. A democratic state may often find it impossible to mobilize troops in a hegemonic manner.

8. Given that democracies will become more common in Africa, as they are already, only political decisions taken beforehand may help in a crisis. If the kinds of crises that merit intervention can be spelled out beforehand, then some kind of multi-state/sub-regional organization is capable of action. If one does not want to repeat the Rwandan experience, it is important to identify crises and plan for them in advance.

Tonje: For all these responses to work, there should be an encouragement for the ground rules and mechanisms to bring them about.

Metz: Maybe there are phases of re-stabilization. Phase One: calm things down. Phase Two: change the nature of the force that is there and gradually institutionalize. The end result is a return to normalcy.

Rotberg: One type of multi-state organization is a sub-regional organization, as we discussed last year in Malawi. The next set of recommendations will deal with the particulars of how a sub-regional organization might want to organize itself in order to respond. The assumption is that a sub-regional organization is a useful locus of preplanning.

9. There is no consensus on who would trigger a decision to intervene in a conflict. If we follow Kavuma's criteria, we can know what constitutes a crisis, but we haven't had a useful discussion on who decides which crisis fits the criteria.

No crisis will conform to a preexisting template. We simply can't predict how a crisis will arise. We couldn't have predicted Lesotho exactly. It has to be decided, therefore, how a sub-regional response will be triggered.

10. It is much easier to enter a crisis at the earlier stage, and harder to do so later. Yet it is extremely difficult to recognize when is the early moment. It is hard to recognize that a crisis has occurred and to deal with it when the time is early and an intervention would prove less expensive. In the Balkans, despite a long acquaintance with the situation and much pre-planning, the response was less than it needed to be. In Amin's Uganda, the response could have happened earlier. The larger the crisis, the harder it is to act in a timely manner. The smaller the state, the easier it is to recognize a crisis and to deal with it in a timely manner.

Scott Fisher: In ECOWAS, SADC, and EAC there is a security annex to what started as an economic sub-regional activity. It frames issues. If a security annex is written in such a way, you can co-opt a hegemon to act in a certain way. Once that statement is agreed to, it becomes a consensual document, and the hegemonic part of it goes away. Maybe this is true for IGAD (Inter-Governmental Authority on Development) as well. There is, in working through those details, the kind of specificity that is needed to guide necessary actions. Authenticity is built in. There is an identification of these kinds of triggers as part of the process. There will be struggles, but the details would be fairly far advanced.

Tonje: There is a difference between peacekeeping and peace enforcement. Crises don't lend themselves to peacekeeping unless the situation has already been stabilized and forces have agreed. Our problems arise much earlier. We need to begin with prevention. When that doesn't work, and a crisis occurs, there is a need to bring rival parties together. Peacekeeping is the end of the problem. Our concern is from the very beginning. It should be conflict prevention. Then we go into peace enforcement.

Who decides, who triggers? A hegemon can decide on his own. If you go to the ways of responding (whether there are five or two), you have to know the anatomy of a crisis, and decide who will react where. If it is a sub-unit, it will know what will trigger its response. If it is the UN, there are arrangements. If it is the OAU, it has mechanisms. There is a lot of fixation with sub-regions.

Scott Fisher: On the UN, SADC sees itself as operating parallel to the UN. I think it should be operating within the UN context, perhaps given a delegative role, where it doesn't see itself as a replacement for the UN.

Tonje: The problem then, is who should respond to a crisis first, second, and third.

11. It is clear that each crisis is bound to be specific and different. So the flexibility of response is always critical. It is also clear that interventions will never be neutral, even if the UN develops a framework.

12. If a sub-regional intervention response is to succeed, essential is a clear, implementable mandate, with specific criteria, a workable mission statement, and positive rules of engagement. The mandate must be designed for general problems as well as particular ones. Some flexibility must be a given. The extent to which lethal force can be used must be specified. There will be a need for an exit strategy. The criteria for success need to be determined beforehand, and not left for determination subsequently.

Herbst: We have discussed common equipment, language, and training. More difficult is the question of common doctrine. There is some disagreement as to how that would evolve, other than to say that militaries and political leaders should continue to meet. The next step—how equipment, communication, and language would begin to meld, or even be mildly complementary—was not defined.

Henk: Political decisions lead up one of two tracks: toward a coalition or toward collective defense. If the U.S. were to face a crisis in the Persian Gulf, it would try to build a coalition. Doing so is difficult because there is no common doctrine, equipment, procedures, etc. But if the U.S. were facing a crisis in the Balkans, it would use a collective defense arrangement—NATO—whose member nations do have common doctrine. Europe is unique. In Africa, either of the two tracks could be pursued, depending on the political situation.

13. Any crisis response force at a sub-regional level should be non-permanent; it would not be a standing force. It would be composed of contingents ready to be volunteered by national forces. There would be no specific earmarking of contingents beforehand. There would be readiness within national forces to contribute, without earmarking specific units to be pre-trained.

Metz: On the use of lethal force: we all know that it is important in humanitarian interventions or peacekeeping to retain public support, either within the host nation or in the home country. One of the determinants of this opinion is casualties. Recognizing this fact, one should take seriously the prospect of non-lethal weapons—a useful complementary capability. Peacekeepers with a wide array of non-lethal force at their disposal have greater capabilities than those equipped only with lethal weapons. They minimize casualties.

14. Command and control issues must be decided beforehand.

15. A sub-regional force should decide upon a common language and common methods of communication. A common military doctrine, and common training in the various national military academies, would be helpful, too.

16. As a complement, there could be standardization of equipment, and conceivably joint procurement.

17. There should be continued coordination among donors with regard to assisting sub-regional force planning operations.

18. There was discussion as to the extent to which the donors are focusing on the right level of training.

Herbst: Do African militaries perceive the peacekeeping, peace enforcement task as synonymous with the military? There seems to be a gap between what donors, tagging assistance particularly to peacekeeping, are expecting.

Dempsey: I don't see the connection between whether you designate specific units or not. We need to address training in the context of overall military readiness. Perhaps the West should do a better job of listening to what Africa's needs are.

Shalli: It is clear there is a misunderstanding about what we mean by having forces earmarked and ready. There is a UN standby arrangement system which requires member states to earmark troops for planning purposes. Namibia always has, for example, 500 men ready to go. This makes the UN's job easier for planning purposes. However, training of all our armies in peacekeeping will proceed. In planning any future peacekeeping exercises, the concrete contributions can be known.

Williams: The ACRI training and exercise in Senegal, in collaboration with France and the U.K., is more appropriate for the type of crises you find in Africa. That's the sort of training that is required. Classical peacekeeping won't work. You need to have a reaction force to compel all parties to obey the accord. If not, the warlords will test your will to keep the accord. If there is no will, it is useless. Military humanitarianism is key. The African military has to be able to undertake that. It is helping the population. You need to look at the concept of peacekeeping itself. If you have the gendarmerie concept—if they are not part of the armed forces—why don't you use them first, and then later you can use soldiers themselves as a reaction force? Put in the gendarmes first, then when there is a need for an extra reaction force, you can bring in the soldiers. Then they can do what they're trained to do—compel and enforce—while protection is done by the gendarmerie.

19. Improving the output of the African Peacekeeping Support Group (APKSG) working group in New York is essential.

Scott Fisher: There is no reason why APKSG meetings need to remain in New York. They should be held in Africa. Another issue is the tie—if there is to be one—between New York and the sub-regional organizations. I would suspect that if a sub-regional grouping were to ask for an APKSG meeting to be held in a particular African city, it could be helpful.

20. Ultimately, the peace enforcement chain of command runs from the UN to the OAU to a SADC or an ECOWAS. But can the OAU function as a forceful arbiter of quarrels within a member country? Can the UN act with speed?

Herbst: I am struck by the pessimism of the UN's operational role—at the same time that the New York operations of the Department of Peacekeeping Operations are being strengthened. There is disagreement on whether the OAU's capacity or sub-regional capacity should be built up. Given frustrations with the OAU, other organizations at the sub-regional level have been taking charge. Think about the UN's political (rather than its military) role. Sub-regional countries might provide commanders, but who would provide political leadership to talk to various factions on the ground?

Gen. Fisher: Don't confuse the limitations of the OAU with what it means to African people. It represents something to Africans. That's why it hasn't been disbanded. We still take meetings seriously. It represents a dream. It stands out as a significant achievement for African countries. It may be useful to address its limitations. Donors trying to enhance the capacity of the OAU are taking steps in the right direction. But it will remain significant in the political environment, so don't relegate it to the dustbin.

Woods: Some of the contradictions that we're hearing could be better understood and seen in a less negative way if we put things more in a longer-term historical context. We have here an attempt to describe and find improvements for a transitional situation. Our assumptions in a post–Cold War world—our naive assumptions about the relevance of Chapter VI peacekeeping—are proving to a large extent invalid. There is a certain amount of demoralization at the UN, particularly in the Security Council, with respect to having the competence and financial resources to take the lead in dealing with these types of activities. Chapter VI was an attempt to cloak ourselves; it was a fight with reality.

It is an interim period where I would say to Africa, "You're on your own." I don't know how long this will last. During this time, the most probable response to a serious crisis in Africa is no response at all. The second most likely is an ad hoc regional response. The least likely is an OAU response. Not very likely is a UN response. That isn't an acceptable long-term approach. But we need to look at this transitional period without losing sight of where Africa wants to be twenty years from now, when the international community is more sorted out, and African institutions are more capable.

It is clear that Africans want to deal with conflicts within the context of a meaningful UN/OAU presence. They don't want permanently to endorse concepts that seem to disparage the role of these organizations. We are in a messy interim period. This period works to the advantage of bad actors. We touched on the issue of capturing resources, and who is the legitimate party. A bad actor with foreign funding—Taylor, for example—comes in, sees some resources, begins to develop an organization, and challenges a legitimate government. Then the international community comes in and legitimates him with peacekeeping. That is messy. There needs to be an African response; it will be crude and ad hoc, but hopefully only for now. There is a distinction between the short run and where we want to be.

Clapham: There are different levels of crisis, with different responses. Lesotho is representative of small states, clearly nested within a sub-regional organization. But the Sudan and the DRC are states not clearly falling into sub-regional categories. Those kinds of problems can only be dealt with at the OAU level. Whether the OAU is capable is a question. But only at an all-Africa level can one look at the problem.

Williams: On the subject of the OAU: ECOWAS is ahead of the OAU in responding to crises. I think the OAU has also accepted the limitations it has, especially in dealing with member countries. It is only as strong as its members want it to be. The Central Organ is a core; if there is no consensus there, there is nothing you can do. Even with all the money in the world, it still has to face that limitation. If sub-regionals have a framework, the framework limits the excesses of hegemony.

There are two realities: One is the subcontracting response to crisis. The UN has subcontracted to the OAU, the OAU has subcontracted to sub-regional organizations. Second is the support reality on the ground. If [Secretary-General] Kofi Annan quits the UN, what will happen to Africa? All of this support you're getting from outsiders, how long will it last? Institutionalizing support is very important, so that when the support ends, we can continue. We also need to enhance our own capacity with in-continent expertise and experience.

Ellington: Regardless of the level from which a response comes, strengthening sub-regional groupings can only assist. It makes the process more efficient and timely. If you're used to working together, you have established a protocol and tripwires. This helps in having a stronger voice with the OAU and the UN. A sub-regional grouping gives outsiders a mechanism through which to operate. Sometimes doing so is more attractive than offering bilateral assistance. With ECOWAS, the U.S. had an interest in helping to solve the Liberian problem. But it had a problem working with Nigeria. ECOMOG provided a channel.

Toraasen: The UN is responsible for peace and stability in the world. It should fulfill that mandate. The process is taking a long time, but I think the UN has also been able to work out mandates for responding. As a rule, the UN should be the organ working out the mandate. It is another question, however, who should implement the mandate.

Nyambuya: The OAU accepts that it has weaknesses. The OAU charter begins, "We the heads of state," while that of the UN says, "We the people of the world." The OAU senses that its charter has to be revisited so it is more responsive to today's environment. To a certain extent it has been bold: in Cairo, for instance, when the heads of state accepted that they needed a mechanism to assist in conflict resolution. So instead of putting it in a gravesite, we should look at ways to strengthen it. Certainly in 1993, the OAU accepted the fact that there should be a mechanism for conflict prevention and resolution. Some of the efforts of P3 should be channeled through the OAU, from the U.S., France, and the U.K.. The OAU accepts that its strengths are going to come from strong sub-regional organizations.

21. A conflict prevention intervention force should disarm combatants and demobilize and pay off combatants. Violence should be used against those who would spoil the restoration of law and order. The reconstruction should begin with a retraining of police forces, the infrastructure should be rebuilt, and a democracy should be reintroduced or buttressed. But elections should not be the first order of business.

Gen Fisher: We're dealing with a set of conflicts. It is very difficult to come up with a set of prescriptions that would address all of them. If you say, "You can buy out some of the leaders in a conflict," I ask, "Can you really buy out Savimbi?" I say no. In other areas, maybe the police are still active. We need carefully to analyze a situation, and identify critical areas and centers of gravity.

Majogo: On the element of disarming the parties: it starts with cessation of hostilities. But force will start a negative approach. Most of the former combatants could be integrated within the national army, rather than using a premeditated approach to disarm them. They shouldn't get a handshake and be released into the street.

22. "Everything depends on cash." Funding issues are at the heart of all peace enforcement issues.

23. The licit and illicit flow of small arms into Africa has cascaded in this decade. There are supply questions and demand questions. Both need to be addressed. There have been successful meetings in South Africa and elsewhere on how Africans can deal with the issue. Africa, working with the West, should find ways to reduce demand. If the flow could be cut by a third, we would begin to deal with both the access of protesters to arms, and the other scourge of the continent— urban and rural crime.

24. Leadership is critical. Development of leadership in all these areas is very important. There is a need to find ways to build and strengthen leadership on the continent in order to resolve these issues as well as many others.

The Authors

Ericka Albaugh is a Ph.D. candidate in Political Science at Duke University. She is studying Comparative Politics and International Relations. Her research includes state formation, ethnic conflict, and electoral systems in Africa. She co-authored *Cyprus 2000: Divided or Federal?* WPF Report 20 (Cambridge, Mass., 1998) and *Preventing Conflict in Africa: Possibilities of Peace Enforcement*, WPF Report 24 (Cambridge, Mass., 1999).

Happyton M. Bonyongwe is a Brigadier (ret.) in the Zimbabwe Defence Force. He was Commandant, Zimbabwe Staff College, from 1997 to 1999, and has been Deputy Director of the Zimbabwe Central Intelligence Organization since 1999.

Christopher Clapham is Professor of Politics and International Relations at Lancaster University, U.K. His recent publications include *Africa and the International System: The Politics of State Survival* (Cambridge, 1996) and *African Guerrillas* (Oxford, 1998). He has also written extensively on the Horn of Africa.

Jeffrey Herbst is Professor of Politics and International Affairs at Princeton University. His primary interests are in the politics of sub-Saharan Africa, the politics of political and economic reform, and the politics of boundaries. He is the author of *States and Power in Africa: Comparative Lessons in Authority and Control* (Princeton, 2000) and several other books and articles. He has also taught at the University of Zimbabwe, the University of Ghana, the University of Cape Town, and the University of the Western Cape.

Steven Metz is Research Professor of National Security Affairs at the U.S. Army's Strategic Studies Institute (SSI). His recent publications include *Refining American Strategy in Africa* (Carlisle Barracks, Penn., 1998) and *The United States and the Transformation of Africa Security: The African Crisis Response Initiative and Beyond* (Carlisle Barracks, Penn., 1997), co-authored with Dan Henk.

Robert I. Rotberg is President, World Peace Foundation, and Director, WPF Program on Intrastate Conflict, Conflict Prevention, and Conflict Resolution in the Belfer Center of the Kennedy School of Government, Harvard University. He was Professor of Political Science and History, MIT; Academic Vice President, Tufts University; and President, Lafayette College. He is a presidential appointee to the Council of the National Endowment for the Humanities and a Trustee of Oberlin College. He is the author and editor of numerous books and articles on U.S. foreign policy, Africa, Asia, and the Caribbean, most recently *Truth v. Justice: The Morality of Truth Commissions* (Princeton, 2000), *Creating Peace in Sri Lanka: Civil War and Reconciliation* (Washington, D.C., 1999), *Burma: Prospects for a Democratic Future* (Washington, D.C., 1998), *War and Peace in Southern Africa: Crime, Drugs, Armies, and Trade* (Washington, D.C., 1998), *Haiti Renewed: Political and Economic Prospects* (Washington, D.C., 1997), *Vigilance and Vengeance: NGOs Preventing Ethnic Conflict in Divided Societies* (Washington, D.C., 1996), *From Massacres to Genocide: The Media, Public Policy, and Humanitarian Crises* (Washington, D.C., 1996), and *The Founder: Cecil Rhodes and the Pursuit of Power* (New York, 1988).

Dialogue Participants

Brigadier N. W. Banda, *Malawi*
Professor Christopher Clapham, Lancaster University, *U.K.*
Gill Coglin, Foreign and Commonwealth Office, *U.K.*
Colonel Tom Dempsey, Army War College, *United States*
Lucy M. T. Dlamini, Ministry of Defence, *Swaziland*
Brigadier Gideon Roy Fonono Dube, *Swaziland*
Major Duke Ellington, Military Attaché, *United States*
General Alain Faupin, *France*
K. Scott Fisher, Department of State, *United States*
Lt. General L. M. Fisher, *Botswana*
Lt. General J. B. Hamambo, *Namibia*
Colonel Dan Henk, Army War College, *United States*
Professor Jeffrey Herbst, Princeton University, *United States*
Ambassador Aubrey Hooks, Department of State, *United States*
Ambassador Robert Houdek, National Intelligence Council, *United States*
Minister of State for Defence Steven Kavuma, *Uganda*
Minister of Defence Joseph Kubwalo, Malawi
Brigadier P. V. Legwaila, *Botswana*
Minister of Defence Edgar Maokola-Majogo, *Tanzania*
General R. P. Mboma, *Tanzania*
Professor Steven Metz, U.S. Army War College, *United States*
Lt. General A. M. Mosakeng, *Lesotho*

Prime Minister Pakalitha Mosisili, *Lesotho*
Deputy Minister of Defence Mike Mulongoti, *Zambia*
Nicholas Normand, Foreign Office, *France*
Major General Michael R. Nyambuya, *Zimbabwe*
Colonel Ronald Roughhead, Military Attaché, *United States*
Brigadier Engelbert A. C. Rujege, Commandant, Staff College, *Zimbabwe*
Commander Geoff Scott, Military Attaché, *United States*
Major General Martin Shalli, *Namibia*
Colonel R. M. Shambana, Minister of Defence, *Zambia*
Deputy Minister of Defence Hama Thay, *Mozambique*
General David R. C. Tonje, *Kenya*
Ambassador Knut Toraasen, *Norway*
Brigadier General G. M. Waitara, *Tanzania*
Nancy Walker, Department of Defense, *United States*
Major General Ishola Williams, *Nigeria*
James L. Woods, Cohen & Woods Inc., *United States*

The World Peace Foundation

THE WORLD PEACE FOUNDATION was created in 1910 by the imagination and fortune of Edwin Ginn, the Boston publisher, to encourage international peace and cooperation. The Foundation seeks to advance the cause of world peace through study, analysis, and the advocacy of wise action. As an operating, not a grant-giving foundation, it provides financial support only for projects which it has initiated itself.

Edwin Ginn shared the hope of many of his contemporaries that permanent peace could be achieved. That dream was denied by the outbreak of World War I, but the Foundation has continued to attempt to overcome obstacles to international peace and cooperation, drawing for its funding on the endowment bequeathed by the founder. In its early years, the Foundation focused its attention on building the peacekeeping capacity of the League of Nations, and then on the development of world order through the United Nations. The Foundation established and nurtured the premier scholarly journal in its field, *International Organization*, now in its fifty-third year.

Since 1993, the Foundation has examined the causes and cures of intrastate conflict. The peace of the world in this decade has been disturbed primarily by outbreaks of vicious ethnic, religious, linguistic, and intercommunal antagonism within divided countries. The episodes of brutal ethnic cleansing that have convulsed Rwanda, Bosnia, and Kosovo are but the best known and most devastating of a rash of such attempts to oust rivals across the globe. Few places are immune from some variant of this internecine warfare, whether the immediate battles are

215

over religion, language, appearance, or color differences. Thus, the Foundation is active in and studies the problems of Cyprus and Sri Lanka, and has worked in and studied the prospects for democracy in Burma and Haiti. It has sponsored research on the role of non-governmental organizations in preventing conflict in ethnically divided societies. It has engaged in feasibility studies regarding the reduction of conflict in Africa by the creation of African crisis response forces. It has analyzed the use of preventive diplomacy in resolving ethnic and other inter-communal conflicts. Its work on truth commissions demonstrates how that method of post-conflict justice-seeking can help prevent future internal conflicts.

Intercommunal conflict often becomes civil war and, in some cases, leads to collapsed states. The Foundation is actively researching the causes of state failure, and how best to reinvigorate and manage the resuscitation of wounded states.

Contributing to widespread killings in intercommunal conflicts, civil wars, and imploding states is the easy availability of small arms and other light weapons. For this reason, the Foundation is engaged in a long-term examination of the small arms problem, and how its licit and illicit trade should be addressed.

Part of the task of the Foundation is to resolve conflicts as well as to study them. The Foundation's work in Cyprus, Burma, Sri Lanka, Haiti, and all of Africa has resolution of conflict as its goal. It has sponsored a detailed study of negotiating the end of deadly conflict within and between states. It is also engaged in a long-term examination of the successes and failures of African leadership.

Index

Abacha, Sani, 41, 101, 105, 169. *See also* Nigeria
Abuja Peace Accords, 168, 169, 189
ACRF. *See* African Crisis Response Force, 24, 72
ACSS. *See* African Center for Security Studies
Addis Ababa (Ethiopia), 22, 53
Africa: Clinton administration approach to, 71–74; colonial partitions of, 38; colonization in, 18–19; conflict in, 58–63, 98–109; crisis interventions, 10–12, 16, 17, 25–29, 106–09, 202–04; democracy in, 39, 42; economic issues, 19, 55, 60, 63, 69, 72, 154–55, 163–64, 193; failure of African states, 17–22, 31; funding for interventions, 27, 102; hegemonic intervention, 12, 16–17, 25–26, 115; history of, 98; independence of countries in, 22; interventions in, 10–12, 16, 17, 25–30, 100–01, 106–09; leadership, 55–56; nationalism in, 18; needs of, 58–59; peacebuilding in, 75–78; political systems in, 17–18, 26; nonhumanitarian interventions, 29–30,

84; regional and sub-regional security systems, 38, 40–41, 88–90; security issues, 75, 84; settlement of, 17; state size in, 21–22, 29; state weakness in, 61; sub-regional international organizations, 62, 114–15; OAU observers in, 62; threats to sovereignty, 40; UN missions in, 10, 16, 24, 115; U.S. foreign policies, 64–66; view of the UN, 23; wars in, 10, 63, 78, 100–101, 113–14. *See also* African ministers' meetings; Recommendations; individual countries
Africa—military issues: availability of arms, 19, 60–61; economic issues, 31; employment of African forces, 84–95, 98–109; organization of response forces, 151–64; training and equipment, 61–62, 76–78, 139
Africa—problem solving: ACRI and ACSS, 76–77; African solutions, 22–24, 32, 202, 208–09; Clinton administration and, 70; employment of African forces, 84–95; increasing capabilities, 75–76; initiative for, 114, 134; military readiness and response, 84–95,

217

tion by, 41; role in African peacebuilding, 75, 76; UN missions to, 3
European Union (EU), 183

Faupin, Alain, 121, 128, 129, 139
Fiji, 6
Fisher, K. Scott, 129, 184; destruction in
Lesotho, 183; location of APKSG
meetings, 207; role of the OAU,
125–26; role of the SADC, 205; role
of the UN, 128; security annexes, 205
Fisher, L. M., 176; analysis in conflicts
and peacemaking, 171, 210; assignment of country responsibilities, 122;
constitutional issues, 196; democratic
issues, 200–01; financial issues, 123;
Lesotho operation, 181–82; looting
and burning, 185; military conduct,
150; participation of hegemons, 120;
role of UN, 128; view of the OAU in
Africa, 208; view of hegemons by the
SADC countries, 203
FLINTLOCK regional program, 74
FNLA (National Front for the Liberation
of Angola), 49
Foreign aid, 19–20, 194
France: African crisis response, 11, 17,
99, 118; African Crisis Response Ini-
tiative, 73; assistance to Central
African Republic, 151; assistance to
Senegal, 28; Baltic Battalion, 88; colo-
nization in Africa, 18; peacekeeping
and interventions by, 41, 67, 131, 133,
134–35; peacekeeping exercise on
Madagascar, 132; as protector in
Africa, 40; provision of military
instructors, 76; strategic interest in
Africa, 117; support of Kabila, Lau-
rent, 171; support of OAU, 127; sup-
port of Rwanda, 49
Francis, Dana, 107
Frankel, Sally Herbert, 18
Front for the Liberation of Mozambique
(FRELIMO), 7, 48, 49–50

Gaborone (Botswana), 73

Gabon 2000, 137, 139
Genocide. See Rwanda
Georgia, 3
Ghana: African Crisis Response Initiative,
23, 73; crime in, 65; presence in
Golan Heights, 253; training in, 137; in
UN peacekeeping operations, 100
Gisselquist, Rachel M., 109
Golan Heights, 25
Gordon-Somers, Trevor, 53–54
Great Lakes region (Africa), 104, 126,
127–28, 202
Greece, 3
Grenada, 40
Guatemala, 3, 138
Guidimaka Exercise, 89
Guinea, 118
Guinea-Bissau: African Crisis Response
Initiative, 73; intervention in, 16, 28,
100, 118, 135, 151; intrastate rivalries
in, 101; mass destruction in, 20; peace-
keeping force, 153
Gulf War, 129

Haiti, 3, 191
Hammarskjöld, Dag, 67–68, 148
Harare (Zimbabwe), 30
Hegemons. See Nations and states
Helms, Jesse, 71
Henk, Dan, 143, 146–47, 154
Herbst, Jeffrey, 162, 183, 206; African
conflict and crisis, 106–07, 131;
African elections, 199; African inter-
vention, 12; African military, 139, 207;
African peacekeeping, 106–07,
116–17, 149, 190–91, 203; develop-
ment of democracy, 200; role of the
UN and the OAU, 208; role of U.S. in
Japan and Germany, 195
Herzegovina. See Bosnia and Herzegovina
Hooks, Aubrey, 135–36, 140, 146, 147
Hoon, Geoff, 9
Horn of Africa, 38, 41, 89, 104, 126, 188
Houdek, Robert, 121, 126–27, 190, 192,
197
Houphouët-Boigny, Félix, 166

Young, Crawford, 21
Yugoslavia, 3

Zaire: failure of, 20–22; foreign aid to, 20;
    interventions in, 28, 30, 70; military
    takeover, 20; overthrow of Mobutu,
    13–14, 20–21; riches of, 13–14; U.S.
    involvement in, 71. *See also* Democra-
    tic Republic of the Congo; Hutu; Tutsi
Zambia, 1, 39, 101, 173, 175
ZANU. *See* Zimbabwe African National
    Union
ZAPU. *See* Zimbabwe African People's

Union
Zimbabwe: domestic repression in, 42;
    Kabila, Laurent, and, 21, 30, 172;
    interventions in, 44, 46–47; Lesotho
    and, 178, 185; military issues, 61,
    91–92; peacekeeping and interven-
    tions by, 30, 36–37, 42, 89; in Soma-
    lia, 28; South Africa and, 41; training
    center in, 122
Zimbabwe African National Union
    (ZANU), 47
Zimbabwe African People's Union
    (ZAPU), 47

DATE DUE